Modern Bridge Conventions

Modern Bridge Conventions

**William S. Root &
Richard Pavlicek**

CROWN TRADE PAPERBACKS   New York

Copyright © 1981 by William S. Root and Richard Pavlicek

Published by Crown Publishers, Inc., 201 East 50th Street, New York, New York 10022. Member of the Crown Publishing Group.

Crown Trade Paperbacks™ and colophon are trademarks of Crown Publishers, Inc.

Manufactured in the United States of America

Library of Congress Cataloging-in-Publication Data

Root, William S.
Modern bridge conventions

1. Contract bridge.   I. Pavlicek, Richard.   II. Title.
GV1282.3.R5734   1981   795.41′52   81-9736
                                              AACR2

ISBN 0-517-58727-0

10 9 8 7 6 5 4 3

Contents

♣   ♦   ♥   ♠   ♣   ♦   ♥   ♠

Introduction

♣　　♦　　♥　　♠　　♣　　♦　　♥　　♠

This book is about many of the bidding conventions that have revolutionized the game of bridge. It would not be feasible to cover *every* convention, so we have included what we feel are the best of the lot. Although the adoption of all these conventions would closely resemble our bidding system, the book is *not* intended for this. Instead, the reader is encouraged to choose from among the proposed conventions to form his *own* bidding system.

WHAT IS A BRIDGE CONVENTION?

A bridge convention is a *call* (bid, pass, double, or redouble) that is given a specialized meaning, usually contrary to its natural interpretation. The constant improvement of bidding methods over the years is mostly due to the invention of useful conventions. All conventions, however, are not good. Some are outright poor, and others are reasonably good but hardly worth the extra memory required. In order to qualify as a *good* convention, the following three tests must be passed:

1. **Effectiveness.** Does the use of the convention greatly improve your bidding?
2. **Cost.** Can you readily dispense with the natural call taken away by the convention?
3. **Simplicity.** Is the convention simple enough to remember in the heat of battle?

If your answer is *no* to any of the above questions, then the convention is not worth adopting.

CLASSIFICATIONS

Every convention in this book has been selected because *we* feel it is good. This does *not* mean that each of these conventions is for every player. Certain conventions are too involved for casual partnerships, and some belong only in the hands of very refined partnerships. Therefore, we have implemented the following classification scheme:

    ★   Conventions—for all players. These consist only of the most popular and widely used conventions.

    ★ ★   Conventions—for experienced partnerships only.

★   ★   ★   Conventions—for tournament players with very experienced partnerships.

As is apparent, the number of "stars" indicates the category in which a convention belongs. Decide right now which categories are proper for you (and your partners), then try to stay within those bounds as much as possible. Exceeding your bounds will lower your proficiency, and is likely to result in partnership mix-ups.

SELECTING CONVENTIONS

Many players think of a bridge convention as a simple "yes or no" agreement. For example, the following conversation is typical:

Player A: "Do you play Jacoby?"
Player B: "Yes, sure."

End of subject. The truth of the matter is that *neither* player probably knows "Jacoby transfer bids!" Player B knows only that a 2 ◇ response to 1 NT shows hearts, and 2 ♡ shows spades; after that, he is lost. Player A perhaps knows a little more, but don't bet on it.

The point we are trying to make is that there is usually more than meets the eye when adopting a convention. A thorough understanding of that convention is a must; otherwise, you are just wasting your time. It is far better to play a *few* conventions well than a great many conventions erratically. Quality must come before quantity.

Thus, when selecting conventions, be realistic. Do not overburden yourself with too much, too soon. Play what you know, and know what you play.

PREREQUISITES

Occasionally, it is impractical to use a particular convention *except* in conjunction with another convention. For example, the use of a 2 ♠ response to 1 NT as "minor-suit Stayman" would be absurd unless "Jacoby transfer bids" were also adopted. Consequently, we have stated at the beginning of a convention any prerequisites required.

We have taken great care, however, to *avoid* prerequisites whenever possible, so as to allow more flexibility in selecting conventions. Therefore, the reader is given greater freedom to build his *own* bidding system, which is of course, the primary goal of this book.

POINT COUNT

Throughout this book, there will be constant references to point count. Like virtually every bridge authority, we adhere to the 4-3-2-1 count for high cards. When it comes to distributional points, however, there is much diversity of opinion as to the best method of evaluation. Observe the following two bridge hands:

	A.			B.	
	♠	A Q 10 6		♠	A Q 10 6 5
	♡	A J 9		♡	A J 9 8
	◇	5 4 3		◇	5 4 3
	♣	5 4 3		♣	5

We are sure that everyone would agree that hand **B** is better than hand **A**. As to how *much* better, that is up to your own method of evaluation, with which we will not interfere. Whatever method you use is probably adequate; and, most important, you are accustomed to it.

We make the following two references to point count:

1. **Points.** A general term, used on most occasions. This means that *all* point-count values may be counted. That is, whatever method you use to evaluate *distribution* may be considered, if and when appropriate.
2. **High-card points.** Used on rare occasions. This is to *emphasize* that only *high cards* may be counted, i.e., distribution may not be considered, even on unbalanced hands.

CHAPTER DIVISIONS

The conventions of this book are divided into six chapters according to the *area* of bidding concerned. We have made these arbitrary divisions:

Chapter 1: Balanced Notrump Openings. Conventions used in responding to an opening bid of 1 NT or 2 NT.

Chapter 2: One of a Suit Opening. Non-competitive conventions that apply after your side has opened with one of a suit.

Chapter 3: Interference After One of a Suit. Conventions to deal with enemy interference after your side has opened with one of a suit.

Chapter 4: Other Opening Bids. Conventional opening bids at the two-level or higher.

Chapter 5: Defensive Bidding. Conventions that apply after the enemy has opened the bidding.

Chapter 6: Slam Bidding. Conventions that deal with slam exploration.

The final chapter of the book is:

Chapter 7: Summary. Consists of various topics related to the proper use of conventions and duplicate bridge procedures.

In addition, there is a **Glossary**—an alphabetical listing of *all* popular bidding conventions, even those not included in this book. This is intended as a reference source as well as a useful index.

Modern Bridge Conventions

1

Balanced Notrump Openings

♣　♦　♥　♠　♣　♦　♥　♠

The conventions of this first chapter deal with responding to balanced notrump opening bids. To set the groundwork, we recommend the following point ranges for your notrump bidding:

1. **One-notrump opening** shows 15 to 17 points.
2. **Two-notrump opening** shows 20 to 22 points.
3. **Two-club opening and 2 NT rebid** shows 23 or 24 points.
4. **Two-club opening and 3 NT rebid** shows 25 to 27 points.

NOTE: It is not essential that your bidding system conform to the above recommendations. Regardless of your point ranges, any of the following conventions may be adopted, provided that appropriate point-count adjustments are made when responding.

In this chapter:

Stayman
Jacoby Transfer Bids

Texas Transfer Bids
Minor-Suit Stayman

Minor-Suit Transfer Bids
Splinter Responses
Lebensohl

Stayman ★

*Developed and popularized by Samuel Stayman of New York City, one
of America's leading players and three time World Champion*

Except perhaps for Blackwood and the takeout double, the Stayman 2 ♣ response to
1 NT is the most widely used convention in bridge. Almost every partnership uses
some form of Stayman, so a formal introduction is hardly needed.

We recommend the most popular variation, known as "nonforcing" Stayman. The
prefix "nonforcing" does not refer to the 2 ♣ bid itself (which is always forcing), but to
the two-level *rebids* by Stayman bidder, which are indeed nonforcing. The basic agreement is well known:

Two-club response (to 1 NT) is artificial and asks opener to bid a four-card major
suit. Responder typically has at least one four-card major and some ruffing potential
(not 4-3-3-3 shape), and is searching for a possible four-four trump fit. Stayman is also
used as a steppingstone to show a five-card or longer *minor* suit in a game-going hand
(usually with slam interest).

Partner	You		
		♠	9 5
		♡	A Q 7 4
1 NT	2 ♣	◇	K 7 4
		♣	7 4 3 2

The traditional use of Stayman; you wish to explore for a major suit fit.

Partner	You		
		♠	A 9 3
		♡	4 3
1 NT	2 ♣	◇	K Q J 8 5
		♣	K Q 7

*Here your 2 ♣ bid is a preliminary move. You will next bid your diamond suit
to explore for slam.*

After the 2 ♣ response, opener must make one of three possible rebids (no other
rebid is allowed). We recommend bidding "hearts first" when holding four cards in
each major. Although a departure from standard methods, this blends better with the
other conventions of this chapter, and really makes little difference. Thus, we have
these rebids:

1. **Two diamonds** denies a four-card major.
2. **Two hearts** shows a four-card heart suit and may have four spades.
3. **Two spades** shows a four-card spade suit and denies four hearts.

The reason for restricting opener to the above three rebids is to allow the use of
Stayman when responder has a weak three-suited hand short in clubs. In that event,
responder may bid 2 ♣ with little or no strength, intending to *pass* any rebid by
opener. For example:

Partner	You		
		♠	J 9 7 5
		♡	10 6 5 4
1 NT	2 ♣	◇	J 10 9 6
		♣	2

By responding 2 ♣, you have a great chance of improving the final contract.

Except for the above tactic, the use of Stayman requires a minimum of 8 points; responder must have interest in game.

REBIDS BY STAYMAN BIDDER

This is the most important aspect of Stayman, as no convention is of much value if it cannot be followed up correctly. The rebids by the 2 ♣ bidder have the following meanings:

1. **Two of a major** shows 8 or 9 points and at least a five-card suit. This is invitational, but not forcing. NOTE: If "Jacoby transfer bids" (see page 7) are used, as we recommend, this also implies four cards in the *other* major.

Partner	You		
		♠	A J 7 6 5
		♡	Q 10 7 4
1 NT	2 ♣	♦	9 2
2 ♦	2 ♠	♣	10 5

   With a minimum 1 NT opening, partner will pass your 2 ♠ bid. With a maximum, he will bid again.

2. **Two notrump** shows 8 or 9 points and is invitational to game. This sequence obviously implies an unbid four-card major.

Partner	You		
		♠	K 9 5 3
		♡	9 2
1 NT	2 ♣	♦	A 8 7 4
2 ♡	2 NT	♣	J 8 7

   With a minimum, partner will pass or correct to 3 ♠ (he may have four spades). With a maximum, he will bid 3 NT or 4 ♠.

3. **Three of a minor** shows at least 10 points (usually more) and at least a five-card suit. This is forcing to game and often a slam try. NOTE: As a corollary to this, *direct* jumps to three of a minor (over 1 NT) are weak sign-off bids.

Partner	You		
		♠	A 5
		♡	K J 3
1 NT	2 ♣	♦	4 3
2 ♠	3 ♣	♣	K J 9 7 6 3

   You show a good hand. Partner should return to 3 NT to discourage slam, or make some other rebid to encourage.

Partner	You		
		♠	6
		♡	8 6 3
1 NT	3 ♣	♦	J 7 2
		♣	J 9 8 7 6 4

   Here you show a club bust; partner must pass, or else! Similarly, a direct 3 ♦ response would show a diamond bust.

4. **Three of an unbid major** shows 10 or more points and at least a five-card suit. This is forcing to game. NOTE: Here again, if "Jacoby transfer bids" are used, this sequence implies four cards in the *other* major.

Partner	You		♠ A 9 7 5
			♡ K J 10 4 3
1 NT	2 ♣		♢ Q 7 3
2 ♢	3 ♡		♣ 2

With a doubleton heart, partner should return to 3 NT. Otherwise, he may raise to 4 ♡, or cue-bid an ace to indicate a maximum supporting hand.

5. **Raise to three of a major** shows 8 or 9 points and four-card support for opener. This is invitational to game, just as it sounds.

Partner	You		♠ J 7 5
			♡ K J 9 5
1 NT	2 ♣		♢ 8 3
2 ♡	3 ♡		♣ K 9 8 7

Partner will pass with a minimum, or bid 4 ♡ with a maximum.

6. **Three notrump** is a sign-off attempt, but promises a four-card major.

Partner	You		♠ A 9 3 2
			♡ 10 3
1 NT	2 ♣		♢ K 7 2
2 ♡	3 NT		♣ K 8 5 4

Partner should correct to 4 ♠ if, by chance, he has both majors, since you promise four spades (else, why Stayman?).

7. **Four clubs** is Gerber (see page *192*).

8. **Four of a major** is a natural signoff.

Partner	You		♠ A Q 9 7
			♡ Q 9 8 7 6 3
1 NT	2 ♣		♢ 3
2 ♢	4 ♡		♣ 10 2

You were hoping partner might have four spades, but failing that, you simply want to play 4 ♡.

9. **Four notrump** is a quantitative invitation to 6 NT. This is not Blackwood.

Partner	You		♠ A J 3
			♡ K Q 6 5
1 NT	2 ♣		♢ K 8
2 ♠	4 NT		♣ Q J 7 5

Before inviting slam in notrump, you wanted to find out if partner held four hearts; hence, Stayman.

INTERFERENCE BY THE OPPONENTS

Described here are some of the competitive situations that may be encountered and their effects on the Stayman convention:

1. **If the 1 NT opening is doubled,** Stayman is off altogether. A bid of 2 ♣ becomes a weak rescue bid showing clubs. NOTE: Responder may redouble to show at least 7 high-card points.

2. **If the 1 NT opening is overcalled,** Stayman in its normal sense is off. However,

responder may still ask for a four-card major suit by *cue-bidding* the natural enemy suit. Because this commits your side to game, responder should have at least 9 points.

Partner	Opp.	You		
			♠	K J 8 5
			♡	9 3
1 NT	2 ♡	3 ♡	◇	A J 8 2
			♣	9 8 4

Your 3 ♡ cue-bid is "Stayman," asking for spades. If partner does not have four spades, he must rebid 3 NT, which you will have to pass and hope for the best.

3. **If the Stayman 2 ♣ response is doubled,** which usually asks for a club lead, opener may (a) make his normal rebid; (b) pass with four clubs; or (c) redouble with five clubs or four good clubs.

			You	Opp.	Partner	Opp.
♠	A J 4					
♡	K 9 5					
◇	K J 8		1 NT	P	2 ♣	DBL
♣	A 9 7 5		P			

Your pass denies a four-card major and shows four clubs. With strong clubs, you would redouble. With fewer than four clubs (and therefore, a diamond suit), make your normal 2 ◇ rebid.

If opener elects to pass or redouble (after the double of 2 ♣), responder may (a) make his normal rebid; (b) redouble or pass to play in 2 ♣ redoubled; or (c) bid 2 ◇ as a rescue maneuver with the "weak three-suiter" short in clubs. For example:

Opp.	Partner	Opp.	You		
				♠	Q 10 5 3
				♡	A 6
	1 NT	P	2 ♣	◇	9 6 4 2
DBL	P	P	RDBL	♣	Q J 8

Partner has shown four clubs with his pass, so you expect to make 2 ♣ despite the indicated bad trump break.

4. **If the Stayman 2 ♣ response is overcalled,** opener may (a) bid a four-card major at the two-level; (b) double for penalty with four cards in the enemy suit; or (c) pass. In any event, responder may continue with his normal rebid, or double for penalty.

			You	Opp.	Partner	Opp.
♠	K 6					
♡	A J 8 4					
◇	K 10 7 3		1 NT	P	2 ♣	2 ♠
♣	A 9 6 2		P			

Do not bid 3 ♡. However, if partner continues with any notrump bid, he implies four hearts, and you should bid hearts. If partner's major were instead spades, he should double 2 ♠.

STAYMAN OVER TWO NOTRUMP

The Stayman convention is not limited to auctions beginning with 1 NT. Over a 2 NT opening, the following agreement applies:

Three-club response (to 2 NT) is Stayman. Opener must rebid 3 ◇, 3 ♡, or 3 ♠, according to usual practice.

Partner	You
2 NT	3 ♣

♠ K 9 8 6
♡ 4 3
♢ Q 10 5 3
♣ 7 4 2

You wish to search for a possible spade fit before raising to 3 NT.

If you use the "strong artificial 2 ♣ opening" (see page *93*), as we recommend, Stayman may also be employed after a 2 ♢ response and a 2 NT rebid by opener. For example:

Partner	You
2 ♣*	2 ♢**
2 NT	3 ♣

♠ 9 7 2
♡ Q J 8 3
♢ 5 3
♣ 10 7 6 3

*Artificial force
**Negative response

Your 3 ♣ bid is Stayman, just as if 2 NT had been the opening bid.

After using Stayman, all of responder's rebids are game-forcing and have the following meanings:

1. **Four of a minor** shows a five-card or longer suit and is a slam try. Observe that 4 ♣ is not Gerber after using Stayman.

Partner	You
2 NT	3 ♣
3 ♠	4 ♣

♠ 5
♡ K 9 3
♢ A 8 4
♣ Q 8 7 6 4 2

You show a real club suit with slam interest.

2. **Any other rebid** is identical in meaning (except for point-count adjustments) as after 1 NT. Thus, responder may (a) bid three of a major to show a five-card suit; (b) sign off in 3 NT or four of a major; or (c) bid 4 NT as a quantitative slam invitation.

STAYMAN OVER THREE NOTRUMP

The use of Stayman over 3 NT depends, of course, on the meaning of your 3 NT opening. If it shows a *balanced* hand (obsolete among experts), Stayman may be employed as follows:

Four-club response (to a balanced 3 NT) is Stayman. This promises slam interest, and opener rebids in the usual manner. If responder rebids 4 ♡, 4 ♠, or 4 NT, this is not forcing, although opener should bid again with a maximum.

Partner	You
3 NT*	4 ♣

♠ 6 4 3
♡ K 10 9 6
♢ 6 3
♣ K 9 8 3

*Balanced hand

Your 4 ♣ bid is Stayman. If partner rebids 4 ♢ or 4 ♠, you will then bid 4 NT (not forcing).

We recommend that you adopt the "Acol 3 NT opening" (see page *107*), in which case a 4 ♣ response would *not* be Stayman. To describe a game-forcing balanced hand, opener simply uses the "strong artificial 2 ♣ opening," then rebids 3 NT over a 2 ◇ response. Responder may *then* use Stayman. For example:

Partner	You		
		♠	A 9 8 5
		♡	5
2 ♣*	2 ◇**	◇	Q 10 8 7 4
3 NT	4 ♣	♣	9 8 3

       *Artificial force
      **Negative response

Your 4 ♣ bid is Stayman. Unless partner shows spades, you will continue with 5 ◇ (forcing).

Jacoby Transfer Bids

Invented by Oswald Jacoby of Dallas, Texas. An illustrious career has established "Ozzie" as one of the greatest players of all time.

Prerequisite:
STAYMAN

The "Jacoby transfer bid" is one of the most valuable contributions to the theory of responding to 1 NT opening bids. Its many advantages far outweigh the disadvantage of giving up a natural 2 ◇ response. NOTE: Another popular alternative to the natural 2 ◇ response is "two-way Stayman" (see Glossary).

    The basic idea is quite simple. When responder has a five-card or longer major suit, he bids the suit immediately below that suit at the two-level. This allows opener to become declarer in responder's suit, thus protecting the strong hand from the lead. The exact requirements are spelled out below:

Two-diamond or two-heart response (to 1 NT) shows five or more cards in the next higher major suit. Responder may have any strength, from a complete bust up to a slam-going hand; all he guarantees is a five-card major.

Partner	You		
		♠	10 7 4
		♡	J 10 7 5 4
1 NT	2 ◇	◇	4
		♣	9 8 3 2

You show at least five hearts.

Partner	You		
		♠	A K J 8 5
		♡	A 5
1 NT	2 ♡	◇	K 10 6 3
		♣	4 3

Here you promise spades.

    After this response, opener is obliged to complete the transfer by bidding two of responder's suit. This does *not* necessarily show support. For example:

♠	A Q 8	*You*	*Partner*
♡	J 2		
◇	K Q J 6	1 NT	2 ◇
♣	K 10 8 3	2 ♡	

You are simply obeying orders. Partner will not expect you to have normal heart support.

NOTE: Jacoby transfer bids are *off* altogether (two of a suit is natural) if the 1 NT opening is overcalled or doubled.

REBIDS BY TRANSFER BIDDER

Because of the wide range of the Jacoby transfer bid, responder must now tell opener more about his strength and pattern. This is done as follows:

1. **Pass** if game is out of reach, regardless of your hand pattern.

Partner	*You*		
		♠	9 8 6 4 3
		♡	2
1 NT	2 ♡	◇	K J 9 7 6
2 ♠	P	♣	10 4

Spades may not be your best trump fit, but it would be foolish indeed to keep bidding; pass before you get overboard.

2. **Two spades** shows at least five-five in the majors and is invitational to game. This is *not* forcing. NOTE: Never use Jacoby when holding a four-card major suit; use Stayman instead.

Partner	*You*		
		♠	K J 9 7 6
		♡	Q 10 7 5 4
1 NT	2 ◇	◇	8 6
2 ♡	2 ♠	♣	2

With a minimum, partner will pass or correct to 3 ♡. With a maximum, he should jump to game in his better major.

3. **Three hearts** (after a transfer to spades) shows at least five-five in the majors and is forcing to game. This could even be a slam try. NOTE: Compare with above.

Partner	*You*		
		♠	Q 10 8 7 5
		♡	A K 8 7 2
1 NT	2 ♡	◇	9 6
2 ♠	3 ♡	♣	3

By showing your majors in this order, you indicate a game-going hand.

4. **Two notrump** is invitational to game. Responder typically has a five-card major and a balanced or semi-balanced hand.

Partner	*You*		
		♠	K 3
		♡	A 9 8 6 5
1 NT	2 ◇	◇	7 4 3
2 ♡	2 NT	♣	J 9 2

With a minimum, partner will pass or correct to 3 ♡. With a maximum, he should bid 3 NT or 4 ♡.

5. **Three of a minor** shows at least a four-card suit and is forcing to game. This is very often a slam try.

Partner	You		
		♠	A K 5 4 3
		♡	3
1 NT	2 ♡	◇	K J 8 7
2 ♠	3 ◇	♣	K 10 8

Partner may indicate support for either of your suits (by bidding 3 ♠ or 4 ◇), or he may rebid 3 NT to show no fit.

6. **Raise to three** is invitational to game. Responder usually has a six-card major suit, but could have an unbalanced hand with a good five-card suit.

Partner	You		
		♠	10 6 5
		♡	Q 9 8 6 3 2
1 NT	2 ◇	◇	8
2 ♡	3 ♡	♣	A 7 2

Partner simply passes with a minimum or bids 4 ♡ with a maximum.

7. **Three notrump** offers a choice of game contracts. Responder should have a five-card major and a balanced hand.

Partner	You		
		♠	K J 7 6 5
		♡	A 3
1 NT	2 ♡	◇	Q 6 3
2 ♠	3 NT	♣	10 7 3

Partner should pass with a doubleton spade and usually correct to 4 ♠ with three or more.

8. **Raise to four** (game) shows at least a six-card major suit and is a sign-off bid. NOTE: If "Texas transfer bids" are also used, as we recommend, this sequence becomes a slam try (see page *13*).

Partner	You		
		♠	K 10 9 7 5 4
		♡	4
1 NT	2 ♡	◇	A J 9
2 ♠	4 ♠	♣	10 3 2

This is the way you would bid this hand if not using Texas transfers.

9. **Four notrump** is a quantitative invitation to slam with a balanced hand and a five-card major. This is not Blackwood.

Partner	You		
		♠	A J 8
		♡	K Q 8 7 5
1 NT	2 ◇	◇	K 5
2 ♡	4 NT	♣	Q 9 2

To reject the slam try, partner will pass or correct to 5 ♡. To accept, he may make any other rebid.

BYPASSING THE TRANSFER

Let us assume you open the bidding with 1 NT on the following hand and receive this surprising, but pleasant, response:

```
♠ Q 9 8 6                    You      Partner
♡ A 2
◇ A K 3 2                     1 NT      2 ♡
♣ A 8 6                        ?
```

If you were to complete the transfer (with 2 ♠), partner might pass when there is a good play for game. Why? Because partner could not possibly expect you to have such a tremendous supporting hand for spades. Here is what to do:

Jump to three of responder's major shows a maximum 1 NT opening, at least four-card trump support, and a ruffing value (doubleton).

With the hand previously shown, you would jump to 3 ♠, instead of bidding 2 ♠. Here is another example:

```
♠ A K 3                      You      Partner
♡ K Q 9 6
◇ 10 5                       1 NT      2 ◇
♣ A J 8 2                    3 ♡
```

You show a good heart fit and a superb hand.

After this "bypass" of the transfer, responder must disregard all of the normal rebids. Quite logically, he may (a) pass if game is still hopeless; (b) sign off in game; (c) cue-bid to try for slam; or (d) bid 4 NT as Blackwood.

INTERFERENCE BY THE OPPONENTS

We are concerned here with interference *after* the Jacoby transfer bid, since Jacoby can never be preceded by interference. This invariably occurs in the form of a penalty (lead-directing) *double* or an *overcall* of the artificial transfer bid. Here is what to do:

1. **If the Jacoby transfer bid is doubled,** opener may (a) pass as the routine action; (b) redouble (for penalty) to show a strong holding in the suit doubled; (c) complete the transfer to show at least three trumps plus the desire of having the doubled suit led; or (d) jump to three of responder's major as the "bypass."

```
♠ K Q 6 4                    You      Opp.     Partner    Opp.
♡ K 7 3
◇ A 6 2                      1 NT      P        2 ◇        DBL
♣ K J 9                      P
```

There is no advantage in becoming declarer once the diamond lead is requested (partner may have Q-X in diamonds). Had your diamonds been, say, K-J-X, then you should bid 2 ♡.

If opener elects to pass or redouble (after the Jacoby transfer is doubled), responder may (a) make his normal rebid; (b) redouble or pass to play in that contract redoubled; or (c) bid two of his major as a signoff. For example:

```
Opp.    Partner    Opp.    You              ♠ K 10 9 8 7 5
                                            ♡ K 6
        1 NT       P       2 ♡              ◇ J 6 3
DBL     P          P       3 ♠              ♣ 3 2
```

Your 3 ♠ bid is invitational to game, just as it would have been had partner bid 2 ♠. Notice that you will now be declarer, thus placing the doubler on lead!

2. **If the Jacoby transfer bid is overcalled,** opener may (a) bid three of responder's major only with a *good* supporting hand; (b) double for penalty; or (c) pass in most cases.

♠ K 9 7	*You*	*Opp.*	*Partner*	*Opp.*
♡ A 6 2				
◇ K Q J 6	1 NT	P	2 ◇	2 ♠
♣ Q J 4	<u>P</u>			

Your hand is not good enough to venture 3 ♡. Remember, partner may be completely broke.

If opener elects to pass (after the Jacoby transfer is overcalled), responder may (a) make his normal rebid; (b) double to show general strength—opener should tend to remove the double with support for responder's major; or (c) pass. For example:

Opp.	*Partner*	*Opp.*	*You*	
				♠ K Q 7 6 5
				♡ 9 8 3
	1 NT	P	2 ♡	◇ 8 5
3 ◇	P	P	<u>DBL</u>	♣ K 10 2

Your double is cooperative; partner will usually bid 3 ♠ with a fit, or pass otherwise.

JACOBY OVER TWO NOTRUMP

The Jacoby transfer bid, like Stayman, may be employed over a 2 NT opening as well. Here is the basic agreement:

Three-diamond or three-heart response (to 2 NT) is Jacoby. Opener must complete the transfer, or (rarely) bypass it by jumping to game.

Partner	*You*	
		♠ 10 6 5 4 3
		♡ 3
2 NT	<u>3 ♡</u>	◇ 9 5
		♣ 7 6 5 3 2

You intend to sign off the bidding by passing when partner bids 3 ♠.

If you use the "strong artificial 2 ♣ opening" (see page *93*), as we recommend, Jacoby may also be employed after a 2 ◇ response and a 2 NT rebid by opener. For example:

Partner	*You*	
		♠ 8 6
		♡ Q 8 7 6 3
2 ♣*	2 ◇**	◇ Q 10 3
2 NT	<u>3 ◇</u>	♣ 10 4 2

*Artificial force
**Negative response

Your 3 ◇ bid is Jacoby. Over 3 ♡, you intend to bid 3 NT, offering partner a choice of games.

After using Jacoby, all of responder's rebids are game-forcing and have the following meanings:

1. **Three spades** (after a transfer to hearts) shows at least five-five in the majors with *slam* interest.

Partner	You		
		♠	A J 9 7 5
		♡	K 10 8 7 4
2 NT	3 ◇	◇	8
3 ♡	3 ♠	♣	10 2

Your 3 ♠ bid is a slam try with five hearts and five spades. Observe that you would use Stayman with only five-four in the majors.

2. **Four hearts** (after a transfer to spades) shows at least five-five in the majors *without* slam interest.

Partner	You		
		♠	J 10 8 7 4
2 ♣*	2 ◇**	♡	Q 9 8 6 2
2 NT	3 ♡	◇	5 3
3 ♠	4 ♡	♣	7

*Artificial force
**Negative response

You wish to play either 4 ♡ or 4 ♠, i.e., whichever major partner prefers.

NOTE: The reason for the above procedure (compare rebids 1 and 2), which reverses the method used over 1 NT, is to allow *more* bidding room when the partnership is considering slam.

3. **Four of a minor** shows at least a four-card suit and promises slam interest.

Partner	You		
		♠	K 9 8 7 5
		♡	3
2 NT	3 ♡	◇	9 8 3
3 ♠	4 ♣	♣	A Q 10 7

Your 4 ♣ bid is a slam try. With a weaker hand (change your clubs to Q-10-7-5), you would have to rebid 3 NT to offer a choice of games.

4. **Any other rebid** is identical in meaning (except for point-count adjustments) as after 1 NT. Thus, responder may (a) bid 3 NT to offer a choice of games; (b) raise to game in his major; or (c) bid 4 NT as a quantitative slam invitation.

JACOBY OVER THREE NOTRUMP

As with Stayman, the use of Jacoby over 3 NT depends entirely on the meaning of your 3 NT opening. If it shows a *balanced* hand (obsolete among experts), then Jacoby may be employed as follows:

Four-diamond or four-heart response (to a balanced 3 NT) is Jacoby. Opener must complete the transfer.

Partner	You		
		♠	J 9 8 5 4 3
		♡	4
3 NT*	4 ♡	◇	8 7 3
		♣	9 4 2

*Balanced hand

Your 4 ♡ bid is Jacoby. You obviously intend to pass when partner bids 4 ♠.

Since we recommend the "Acol 3 NT opening" (see page *107*), the above use of Jacoby is *off*. If opener has a game-forcing balanced hand, he uses the "strong artificial 2 ♣ opening," then rebids 3 NT over a 2 ◇ response. Responder may *then* use Jacoby. For example:

Partner	You
2 ♣*	2 ◇**
3 NT	4 ◇

♠ 6
♡ Q J 10 5 4
◇ 8 6
♣ K 9 8 4 3

*Artificial force
**Negative response

Your 4 ◇ bid is Jacoby. Over 4 ♡, you will continue with 5 ♣ (forcing) to try for slam.

Texas Transfer Bids

Originated by David Carter of St. Louis, Missouri, a leading expert of the Midwest

The "Texas transfer bid" is another valuable device used in responding to a 1 NT opening bid. It works very much like the "Jacoby transfer bid," except at a higher level. Here is the basic agreement:

Four-diamond or four-heart response (to 1 NT) shows at least six cards in the next higher major suit. Typically, responder has no interests other than signing off in game in his major.

Partner	You
1 NT	4 ♡

♠ K Q 10 7 6 5
♡ 7 3
◇ A 5
♣ 7 6 2

You intend to make partner declarer in 4 ♠, so as to protect his hand from the opening lead.

Partner	You
1 NT	4 ◇

♠ —
♡ K 9 8 7 5 4 3
◇ 9 7 5 3
♣ 10 5

You hope to buy the contract in 4 ♡. To proceed slowly would make it much easier for the opponents to find a sacrifice (or make) in 4 ♠.

After the Texas transfer bid, opener has no choice but to complete the transfer by bidding four of responder's major. For example:

♠ 9 8
♡ A K 8 2
◇ K Q J 4
♣ K 9 5

You	Partner
1 NT	4 ♡
4 ♠	

You are not particularly fond of partner's spades, but you are obliged to bid 4 ♠, like a robot.

TEXAS IN COMPETITION

Unlike Jacoby, the Texas transfer bid may also be used when there is enemy competition over the 1 NT opening bid. This is possible because of the higher level of the bid. Note the following rule:

If the 1 NT opening is doubled or overcalled (through 3 ♣ only), the Texas transfer bid still applies.

Partner	Opp.	You
1 NT	DBL	4 ♡

♠ K J 9 8 6 5
♡ —
♢ 10 9 8 6
♣ 9 8 2

Partner is required to bid 4 ♠, just as if the double had not occurred.

Partner	Opp.	You
1 NT	2 ♠	4 ♢

♠ 9 6
♡ A Q J 7 5 4
♢ Q 6 3
♣ 10 5

Here you are transferring to 4 ♡.

Partner	Opp.	You
1 NT	3 ♢	4 ♡

♠ 9 3 2
♡ K Q J 10 7 5
♢ 3
♣ K 6 2

This is not Texas, since the overcall has exceeded the 3 ♣ limit. Observe that 4 ♢ would be a cue-bid, not a transfer to 4 ♡.

TEXAS OVER TWO NOTRUMP

The Texas transfer bid may also be employed over a 2 NT opening bid (but not in competition). The basic agreement is the same:

Four-diamond or four-heart response (to 2 NT) is Texas. Opener must complete the transfer by bidding four of responder's major.

Partner	You
2 NT	4 ♢

♠ 6
♡ Q J 9 8 6 5
♢ 6 5
♣ J 5 3 2

Your 4 ♢ bid is Texas. Partner must bid 4 ♡, which you will obviously pass.

If you use the "strong artificial 2 ♣ opening" (see page 93), as we recommend, Texas also applies after a 2 ♢ response and a 2 NT rebid by opener. For example:

Partner	You
2 ♣*	2 ♢**
2 NT	4 ♡

♠ J 10 8 7 6 4
♡ 7 3
♢ Q 8 2
♣ 8 2

*Artificial force
**Negative response

Your 4 ♡ bid is Texas, and you intend to sign off in 4 ♠.

TEXAS AND JACOBY

It has often been queried, "If you play Jacoby, why do you need Texas? Texas does not accomplish anything that could not also be accomplished by Jacoby." On the surface, this may be true, but most experts make effective use of both conventions by careful distinctions. In responding to both 1 NT and 2 NT, we recommend these understandings:

1. **Texas, then pass** is the proper way to sign off in game. Therefore:

2. **Jacoby, then raise to game** is a mild slam try. This is not forcing, but opener is invited to bid again with a maximum.

Partner	You		
		♠	A Q J 9 7 5
		♡	A 8 3
1 NT	2 ♡	♢	Q 7
2 ♠	4 ♠	♣	6 4

Your raise to 4 ♠ is a slam try! If you wished only to play 4 ♠, you would have used Texas.

Partner	You		
		♠	A 8
		♡	Q J 8 7 4 2
2 NT	3 ♢	♢	7 5
3 ♡	4 ♡	♣	Q 8 2

The same is true over 2 NT. You would use Texas to sign off, so this is a slam try.

Another rather obvious distinction is the following:

3. **Jacoby, then 4 NT** is defined as a quantitative slam invitation (see page *9*). Therefore:

4. **Texas, then 4 NT** is Blackwood.

Minor-Suit Stayman ★ ★

Prerequisite:
JACOBY TRANSFER BIDS

When "Jacoby transfer bids" are used, the response of 2 ♠ to a 1 NT opening is hardly needed as a natural bid; if responder has a real spade suit, he can always begin with a transfer bid of 2 ♡. Consequently, most experts put this idle bid to some other use. One popular agreement is that known as "minor-suit Stayman." Of the several variations played, we recommend the following:

Two-spade response (to 1 NT) shows at least five-four shape in the minor suits with interest in game or slam. Exceptionally, responder may have just four-four in the minors if he is trying for slam. In any event, this response denies a four-card major. Respond 2 ♠ with any of these hands:

♠ 8 5 3
♡ 4   *A minimum. You have mild interest in game.*
◇ K 10 7 5
♣ A 10 8 4 3

♠ 9 5
♡ —   *Your freak distribution makes game (or even slam) a*
◇ A 8 7 6 5 3   *potentiality.*
♣ J 10 8 5 4

♠ 7
♡ 10 8   *You will insist on game, but first wish to explore the*
◇ K J 7 5 3   *minor-suit possibilities.*
♣ A Q 5 4 2

♠ K 9
♡ A 7 3   *Locating a four-four minor suit fit is often the key to*
◇ Q J 10 6   *borderline slam hands.*
♣ A J 9 7

NOTE: Minor-suit Stayman (like the Jacoby transfer) is *off* altogether if the 1 NT opening is overcalled or doubled.

REBIDS BY OPENER

After the 2 ♠ response, opener should bear in mind that responder guarantees *both* minor suits and at least interest in game. Opener is thus well placed to evaluate the potential of his hand and make an informative rebid. With a *minimum* (or poor hand), opener must make one of these two rebids:

1. **Two notrump** is natural and suggests stoppers in both majors. This does not necessarily deny a four-card minor suit, but merely expresses the opinion that the hand should play in notrump.

   ♠ A J 10 7   *You*   *Partner*
   ♡ K Q 9
   ◇ K 8 3   1 NT   2 ♠
   ♣ Q 7 2   <u>2 NT</u>

   You show a minimum 1 NT opening and lack of interest in playing in a minor suit.

2. **Three of a minor** shows four cards in that suit.

   ♠ A 8 5   *You*   *Partner*
   ♡ K J 7 4
   ◇ K 10   1 NT   2 ♠
   ♣ A 9 3 2   <u>3 ♣</u>

   You again show a minimum, but with a club fit.

   With a *maximum* (or good hand), opener must make some other rebid to tell of the good news. Here are the choices:

3. **Three notrump** is natural and promises stoppers in both majors.

		You	Partner
♠	A J 9 7		
♡	K Q 8 6		
◇	A J 3	1 NT	2 ♠
♣	Q 9	<u>3 NT</u>	

You show a maximum 1 NT opening and reassure partner about the majors.

4. **Three of a major** shows a natural suit or a stopper. Opener often has a minor-suit fit, but wishes to leave the door open to 3 NT, in case responder can provide help in the other major.

		You	Partner
♠	K Q 10		
♡	J 8 3		
◇	A J 8	1 NT	2 ♠
♣	K Q J 9	<u>3 ♠</u>	

You show strength in spades. You will still be able to reach 3 NT if partner has something in hearts.

5. **Four of a minor** shows four cards in that suit, and promises no wasted values in the majors. In other words, this shows a perfect "fitting" hand that should easily produce a minor-suit game, perhaps slam.

		You	Partner
♠	A 7 3		
♡	A 9 7 4		
◇	K Q 10 5	1 NT	2 ♠
♣	K 8	<u>4 ◇</u>	

Every honor you have is gilt-edged, so jump to 4 ◇.

REBIDS BY MINOR-SUIT STAYMAN BIDDER

After using minor-suit Stayman and hearing opener's informative rebid, the following options are available to responder:

1. **Pass** (over 2 NT, three of a minor, or 3 NT) if you are satisfied with that contract.

Partner	You		
		♠	8
		♡	9 8 5
1 NT	2 ♠	◇	A J 10 4 3
3 ♣	<u>P</u>	♣	Q 10 8 4

Partner has shown a minimum, so leave well enough alone. You would also pass a 2 NT, 3 ◇, or 3 NT rebid.

2. **Three of a minor** shows at least a five-card suit and is not forcing. EXCEPTION: After opener's 3 ♣ rebid, a bid of 3 ◇ by responder would be forcing.

Partner	You		
		♠	10 9 6
		♡	—
1 NT	2 ♠	◇	A 9 8 5 3
2 NT	<u>3 ♣</u>	♣	Q J 7 6 4

You could pass 2 NT, but your distribution suggests finding a safer part-score. Partner may still correct to 3 ◇ if he chooses.

3. **Three notrump** is always a natural sign-off attempt, and implies that opener's rebid has been helpful in making this decision.

Partner	You		
		♠	10
		♡	7 4 3
1 NT	2 ♠	♢	A Q 8 5
2 NT	3 NT	♣	K J 9 6 2

You were originally unsure as to the best contract, but partner's 2 NT rebid suggests strength in the majors.

Partner	You		
		♠	Q 8 4
		♡	3
1 NT	2 ♠	♢	K J 8 5
3 ♡	3 NT	♣	Q J 7 4 2

Partner has shown a maximum with strong hearts, so you can now logically bid 3 NT.

4. **Four of a minor** shows at least a five-card suit and is forcing. EXCEPTION: A raise to four of a minor is simply a game invitation, just as it sounds.

Partner	You		
		♠	8 6 4
		♡	4
1 NT	2 ♠	♢	K J 9 7 5
3 ♠	4 ♢	♣	A 7 6 5

Your 4 ♢ rebid is forcing. Partner's 3 ♠ bid makes it clear that 3 NT is not the proper contract.

Partner	You		
		♠	7 4
		♡	K 6
1 NT	2 ♠	♢	K J 7 5
2 NT	4 ♣	♣	A K J 8 2

Your jump to 4 ♣ is not only forcing, but a definite slam try. This is not, repeat not, Gerber.

Partner	You		
		♠	3
		♡	2
1 NT	2 ♠	♢	Q 8 7 5 4 3
3 ♢	4 ♢	♣	A 7 6 4 2

Here your 4 ♢ bid is not forcing, since it is a raise; you are inviting 5 ♢.

5. **Any major-suit bid** shows a singleton or void in that suit and promises slam interest. EXCEPTION: If opener rebids three of a major, a raise of that suit shows good three-card support and suggests playing a four-three fit.

Partner	You		
		♠	3
		♡	A 5
1 NT	2 ♠	♢	K J 10 8 7
3 ♣	3 ♠	♣	A Q 9 7 5

You show slam potential and a spade splinter. Had partner rebid 2 NT or 3 ♢, you would make the same rebid.

Partner	You		
		♠	7
		♡	K J 10
1 NT	2 ♠	♢	J 10 9 3
3 ♡	4 ♡	♣	A 9 7 4 2

You are proposing a 4 ♡ contract if partner has a real heart suit. If not, partner can always correct to a minor-suit game.

6. **Four notrump** is Blackwood if a minor suit has been agreed, but natural otherwise. This follows generally accepted practice.

INTERFERENCE BY THE OPPONENTS

Minor-suit Stayman, like Jacoby, can never be preceded by interference (it is off altogether in that event). Coping with interference *after* the 2 ♠ bid is mostly a matter of applying logic and common sense:

If the 2 ♠ response is overcalled or doubled, opener may (a) pass with nothing useful to say, (b) double or redouble for penalty, or (c) make his normal rebid.

		You	*Opp.*	*Partner*	*Opp.*
♠	K J 7				
♡	A 8 3				
◇	A 9 6 5	1 NT	P	2 ♠	3 ♡
♣	K 10 2	P			

You have a minimum 1 NT opening and are unable to make your normal rebid of 3 ◇, so pass.

For the most part, enemy interference after the 2 ♠ bid does not affect the rebids by minor-suit Stayman bidder (responder). He should follow his original plan, except that a *competitive* bid of four in a minor suit is *not* forcing.

HIGHER NOTRUMP OPENINGS

The use of minor-suit Stayman over 2 NT and 3 NT is easily defined, since it is completely dependent on the use of Jacoby transfer bids. Therefore:

If Jacoby applies, so does minor-suit Stayman. That is, if a diamond or heart bid is Jacoby, then a *spade* bid is minor-suit Stayman. The use of minor-suit Stayman over 2 NT or 3 NT always shows *slam* interest.

Partner	*You*		
		♠	5
		♡	J 10 3
2 NT	3 ♠	◇	A J 9 7 5
		♣	K 10 9 4

Your 3 ♠ bid shows both minors and is a slam try, which partner can reject by rebidding 3 NT.

Partner	*You*		
		♠	7 3
		♡	4
2 ♣*	2 ◇**	◇	Q 9 7 6 5
3 NT	4 ♠	♣	K 8 7 6 2

*Artificial force
**Negative response

Since Jacoby would apply, 4 ♠ is a minor-suit slam try. Here partner can reject by rebidding 4 NT, 5 ♣, or 5 ◇.

Minor-Suit Transfer Bids ★ ★ ★

Prerequisites:
STAYMAN
JACOBY TRANSFER BIDS
MINOR-SUIT STAYMAN

Just as "Jacoby transfer bids" are used for the major suits, it is possible to employ "minor-suit transfer bids" over the 1 NT opening. Several methods have been devised for this. Two spades as a transfer to clubs, played by some, is not recommended, as it eliminates the use of "minor-suit Stayman" (see page *15*). A little ingenuity allows the use of both of these conventions.

We recommend the scheme of using 2 NT as the transfer to clubs, and 3 ♣ as the transfer to diamonds. At first, this may seem to encroach on a vital bid (2 NT), but we will later show how the normal "2 NT response" is handled. Minor-suit transfer bids apply *only* after a 1 NT opening bid, and *only* when the next player passes. Below is the basic agreement:

Two-notrump or three-club response (to 1 NT) shows at least five cards (usually six) in the next higher minor suit. Responder typically has either a "bust" or a game-going hand with slam interest.

Partner	You		
		♠	9 8 5
		♡	3
1 NT	2 NT	◇	8 6 3
		♣	J 9 8 7 6 4

You wish to sign off in clubs.

Partner	You		
		♠	8
		♡	A 8 4
1 NT	3 ♣	◇	K Q 10 8 4 2
		♣	Q J 8

Here you will always bid game, but wish to explore en route for a possible slam.

NOTE: If minor-suit transfer bids are adopted, the previously described use of 3 ♣ and 3 ◇ as natural weak responses (see page *3*) becomes obsolete.

The minor-suit transfer bid, when used in conjunction with the other methods of this chapter, must always show a *one-suited* hand. This is true because all two-suiters are conveniently handled by Stayman, Jacoby, or minor-suit Stayman. Nevertheless, do *not* use the transfer on hands like this:

Partner	You		
		♠	10 3
		♡	9 2
1 NT	?	◇	K J 8 7 5 4
		♣	A 6 3

Any attempt to describe your hand would decrease your chances of succeeding in 3 NT, the odds-on contract. A direct 3 NT response is best, giving the opponents no clues.

After the minor-suit transfer bid, opener simply bids three of responder's minor suit, which, of course, does not necessarily show support. For example:

♠	A K 9 6	*You*	*Partner*
♡	K J 8 5		
♢	A 9 3	1 NT	2 NT
♣	Q 5	<u>3 ♣</u>	

Don't forget, partner may have no points at all.

REBIDS BY TRANSFER BIDDER

After the minor-suit transfer is completed, responder continues as follows:

1. **Pass** with the "bust" hand.

Partner	*You*	♠	5
		♡	Q 5 3
1 NT	3 ♣	♢	10 8 7 6 4 2
3 ♢	<u>P</u>	♣	9 6 2

   You are signing off in diamonds, with the advantage of the strong hand being declarer.

2. **New suit** shows a singleton or void in that suit, at least six cards in your known minor, and is forcing to game. This suggests slam interest.

Partner	*You*	♠	A 8 4
		♡	3
1 NT	2 NT	♢	K 8 5
3 ♣	<u>3 ♡</u>	♣	K J 9 8 5 2

   You show a heart splinter. With a real four-card heart suit, you would employ Stayman over 1 NT.

3. **Three notrump** shows a balanced or semi-balanced hand with mild slam interest. Opener needs a maximum hand, including a fit with your minor, to bid again.

Partner	*You*	♠	K J 4
		♡	9 5 3
1 NT	3 ♣	♢	A K 9 8 5
3 ♢	<u>3 NT</u>	♣	K 9

   Slam is possible if partner has a tip-top maximum and support for diamonds. Otherwise, you will play 3 NT.

4. **Raise to four** is invitational to game. Obviously, this implies a highly distributional hand, since you are giving up on 3 NT.

Partner	*You*	♠	—
		♡	9 5 3
1 NT	3 ♣	♢	Q J 9 7 5 4 3
3 ♢	<u>4 ♢</u>	♣	K 10 8

   Partner should either pass or continue to 5 ♢.

5. **Four notrump** is a quantitative invitation to slam, similar to (but stronger than) 3 NT.

Partner	You		
		♠	A 5
		♡	K 9 3
1 NT	2 NT	◇	A 9 2
3 ♣	<u>4 NT</u>	♣	A J 7 5 2

Your bid is equivalent to a direct raise to 4 NT, but shows a five- or six-card club suit.

6. **Raise to five** is a sign-off attempt. This implies a freakish hand with few high cards.

Partner	You		
		♠	9 4
		♡	—
1 NT	2 NT	◇	J 6 4 2
3 ♣	<u>5 ♣</u>	♣	A J 10 7 5 4 2

You wish to try your luck at 5 ♣.

BYPASSING THE TRANSFER

Only on the rarest of occasions may opener take it upon himself to "bypass" the minor-suit transfer bid. Nevertheless, the following action is possible if opener has an unusually fine hand:

Three notrump indicates a strong fit with responder's minor, with the expectation of making 3 NT opposite as little as Q-X-X-X-X-X and out.

♠	A K 5	*You*	*Partner*
♡	K 9		
◇	10 9 8 5 4	1 NT	2 NT
♣	A K 7	<u>3 NT</u>	

Assuming that six club tricks are running, you can make 3 NT with a heart lead, or various other chances.

After the transfer bypass, responder is in charge. He may (a) pass in most cases, (b) sign off in four or five of his minor, (c) cue-bid a new suit (singleton or void) to try for slam, or (d) bid 4 NT to invite slam in notrump.

INTERFERENCE BY THE OPPONENTS

As with Jacoby, we are concerned only with interference *after* the transfer bid, since minor-suit transfers do not apply at all if the 1 NT opening is overcalled or doubled. We suggest this understanding:

If the minor-suit transfer bid is overcalled or doubled, opener may (a) bid *only* with a good fit for responder's minor, (b) double for penalty, or (c) pass. In any event, responder's rebids have their usual meaning.

	♠ A 8 7	*You*	*Opp.*	*Partner*	*Opp.*
	♡ K J 7 3				
	◇ K J 8	1 NT	P	3 ♣	DBL
	♣ A 10 2	3 ◇			

You show good diamond support. Without it, you should pass, then partner can rescue himself to 3 ◇ or make his normal rebid.

INVITING GAME IN NOTRUMP

As we alluded to earlier, responder must find another means of inviting game in notrump when a 2 NT response to 1 NT is used as a transfer to clubs. This is accomplished via the Stayman 2 ♣ response, as explained below:

1. **Two-notrump rebid** (by Stayman bidder) is invitational to game, but does *not* imply a four-card major suit. In other words, this sequence must be used to invite 3 NT regardless of responder's major-suit holdings.

Partner	*You*		♠ A 5
			♡ 9 7 3
1 NT	2 ♣		◇ K 9 8 2
2 ◇	2 NT		♣ J 10 7 4

You are making a "point-count" invitation to 3 NT, and may or may not have a four-card major.

One other modification is required to avoid an ambiguous situation when using minor-suit transfers. This occurs when opener rebids 2 ♡ in reply to Stayman. Since opener *might* have four spades in addition to his four-card heart suit (see page *2*), some sort of check-back is needed. Here is how it works:

2. **Two-spade rebid** (by Stayman bidder after a 2 ♡ reply) shows exactly four spades and at least game invitational strength. This is forcing for one round and serves as a check-back for a four-four spade fit. NOTE: This rebid has no natural use anyway, as responder would use Jacoby with *five* spades and no four-card heart suit.

Partner	*You*		♠ K 9 7 3
			♡ A 5
1 NT	2 ♣		◇ J 9 7 4
2 ♡	2 ♠		♣ 10 9 2

You show the values to bid at least 2 NT, but with a four-card spade suit. Remember, if you bid 2 NT yourself, that would not *show four spades.*

After this check-back, opener bids logically. With a four-card spade suit, he bids (a) 3 ♠ with a minimum, or (b) 4 ♠ with a maximum. Without a four-card spade suit, he bids (c) 2 NT with a minimum, or (d) 3 NT with a maximum. For example:

	♠ A 8 2	*You*	*Partner*
	♡ K Q J 3	1 NT	2 ♣
	◇ Q 10 2	2 ♡	2 ♠
	♣ A J 7	3 NT	

With a maximum, you must insure that game is reached, so jump to 3 NT lacking four spades.

Splinter Responses ★ ★ ★

When your partnership uses transfer bids to all four suits, there is really no meaning for the responses of 3 ◇, 3 ♡, and 3 ♠ to partner's 1 NT opening bid. Rather than leave these bids dead, we recommend the use of "splinter responses," as explained by the following agreement:

Three-diamond, -heart, or -spade response (to 1 NT) shows a three-suited hand with a singleton or void in the suit bid. This is forcing to game and shows slam interest. NOTE: This gadget is *off* over any interference.

Partner	You		
		♠	K J 8 7
		♡	3
1 NT	3 ♡	◇	A K 7 5
		♣	K 8 6 2

By jumping in your singleton, you pinpoint the exact three suits held. Notice that you would use Jacoby if you had a real heart suit.

NOTE: As should be apparent, responder cannot bid in the above manner with a singleton club (since 3 ♣ is a transfer to 3 ◇). In that event, just use Stayman and proceed as you normally would.

REBIDS BY OPENER

After the jump to 3 ◇, 3 ♡, or 3 ♠, opener has a very accurate picture of responder's hand. Opener may (a) bid 3 NT with wasted strength opposite responder's singleton; (b) set the trump suit by bidding that suit; or (c) bid 4 NT Blackwood. Here is one example:

		You	Partner
♠	K Q 9 7		
♡	Q 10 8		
◇	A J 8 5	1 NT	3 ♠
♣	K 9	3 NT	

Your strength in spades makes it clear to put on the brakes with a 3 NT rebid. Had partner instead responded 3 ◇ or 3 ♡, you would rebid 3 ♠ to set the trump suit.

Lebensohl ★ ★ ★

Devised by George Boehm of New York City, a prominent player and writer

To introduce this convention, let us assume your partner opens the bidding with 1 NT and right-hand opponent overcalls with 2 ♠. Decide what you would bid with each of these two hands:

A.	♠	9 2	B.	♠	10 2
	♡	K 9 7 6 5 2		♡	K J 9 8 6
	◇	J 9 2		◇	A 9 2
	♣	10 3		♣	Q 3 2

Having problems? Holding either hand, you would like to bid your heart suit. With hand **A**, you want partner to pass, but with hand **B**, you want to reach game in hearts or notrump. Obviously, if you bid 3 ♡ with hand **A**, you cannot also bid 3 ♡ with hand **B**, and vice versa. It is a perplexing situation indeed.

The "Lebensohl" convention not only solves this problem, but also takes care of a few more (to be mentioned later). As with any convention, a price must be paid for its use. Responder must give up a natural response of 2 NT after an enemy overcall, but this sacrifice is small compared to the advantages of Lebensohl. Here is the basic agreement:

1. **Two-notrump response** (when the 1 NT opening is overcalled) is an artificial transfer bid, forcing opener to bid 3 ♣ regardless of his hand. After the 3 ♣ "relay," responder may pass (with clubs), or bid three of his real suit as a signoff.

Opp.	Partner	Opp.	You			
				♠	4 3 2	
				♡	8	
	1 NT	2 ♡	2 NT	◇	9 8 7 3	
P	3 ♣	P	<u>P</u>	♣	K Q 10 9 8	

Your 2 NT bid forced partner to rebid 3 ♣, then you simply pass to sign off in clubs.

Opp.	Partner	Opp.	You			
				♠	9 2	
				♡	K 9 7 6 5 2	
	1 NT	2 ♠	2 NT	◇	J 9 2	
P	3 ♣	P	<u>3 ♡</u>	♣	10 3	

Your 3 ♡ rebid is a sign-off attempt in hearts.

As an obvious corollary, Lebensohl also includes this understanding:

2. **Three of a new suit** (after a two-level suit overcall) is natural and *forcing*. This is true whether or not it is a jump.

Partner	Opp.	You			
			♠	10 2	
			♡	K J 9 8 6	
1 NT	2 ♠	<u>3 ♡</u>	◇	A 9 2	
			♣	Q 3 2	

You would have bid 2 NT in order to sign off in hearts, so your 3 ♡ bid is forcing.

Partner	Opp.	You			
			♠	9 8 4	
			♡	A 8 3	
1 NT	2 ◇	<u>3 ♣</u>	◇	2	
			♣	K Q 8 7 4 2	

Similarly, your 3 ♣ bid is forcing.

INVITING GAME IN A SUIT

Another advantage of Lebensohl is that responder is sometimes able to *invite* game in his suit. Observe this rule:

If responder (after the Lebensohl 2 NT bid) bids a suit that is *higher-ranking* than overcaller's suit, it is invitational to game. The logic behind this is apparent. If responder had wished to sign off, he could have bid *two* of his suit immediately after the overcall, which would be weak, just as in standard bidding.

Opp.	Partner	Opp.	You	
				♠ K J 10 7 4 3
				♡ 4
	1 NT	2 ♡	2 NT	◇ Q 10 5
P	3 ♣	P	3 ♠	♣ 9 5 4

Your 3 ♠ bid is invitational to game, since . . .

Partner	Opp.	You	
			♠ K 10 8 5 4
			♡ 4
1 NT	2 ♡	2 ♠	◇ Q 7 5
			♣ 9 5 4 3

. . . you would bid this way to sign off.

WHO'S GOT THE STOPPER?

A common problem after an overcall of the 1 NT opening is determining whether a stopper is held in the enemy suit. All too often, 3 NT is reached with each partner hoping the other has a stopper, but in fact, *neither* has a stopper, and down it goes. This problem can effectively be solved through another application of the Lebensohl convention. Here is how:

1. **Two notrump, then 3 NT** promises a stopper in the enemy suit.

Opp.	Partner	Opp.	You	
				♠ Q 7 3
				♡ K 10
	1 NT	2 ♡	2 NT	◇ A J 10 7 6
P	3 ♣	P	3 NT	♣ 7 6 2

   By going through the Lebensohl structure, you confirm a heart stopper; partner must pass.

2. **Two notrump, then cue-bid** is "Stayman" and promises a stopper in the enemy suit.

Opp.	Partner	Opp.	You	
				♠ A 7
				♡ K 10 9 7
	1 NT	2 ♠	2 NT	◇ Q J 8 4
P	3 ♣	P	3 ♠	♣ 10 9 2

   Your belated cue-bid indicates a spade stopper as well as four hearts.

By logical inference, the following two agreements then apply:

3. **Direct 3 NT** denies a stopper in the enemy suit.

Partner	Opp.	You	
			♠ 7 6
			♡ A 8 2
1 NT	2 ♠	3 NT	◇ Q 9 7 6
			♣ K Q 10 8

   You deny a spade stopper; therefore, partner must have a spade stopper in order to pass.

4. **Direct cue-bid** is "Stayman" and denies a stopper in the enemy suit.

Partner	Opp.	You
1 NT	2 ♥	3 ♥

♠ K J 9 7
♡ 5 3
◇ A 8 4
♣ Q 10 5 2

You show four spades, but deny a heart stopper. Thus, partner needs a heart stopper to bid 3 NT.

HINT: The matching first letters in *"Direct Denies"* serve as a helpful memory aid.

TWO-SUITED OVERCALLS

With the proliferation of takeout devices, such as "Landy," "Astro," and "Brozel" (see Glossary), you will frequently encounter overcalls of partner's 1 NT opening that do not mean what they say. Invariably, these bids describe two-suited hands. Sometimes the overcall is artificial (e.g., Landy or Astro), but other times it is natural, showing one of the two suits held (e.g., Brozel).

It is still desirable to employ the Lebensohl convention, but with the modifications explained below:

1. **After a two-suited overcall** (of 1 NT), the principles of Lebensohl still apply, except (a) an artificial suit bid is still considered to be an *unbid* suit, and (b) the agreements under "Who's Got the Stopper?" are *off.*

Opp.	Partner	Opp.	You
	1 NT	2 ◇*	2 NT
P	3 ♣	P	3 ◇

♠ 8
♡ 9 5 3
◇ K J 9 8 7 5
♣ 10 9 8

*Astro (spades + another suit)

You are signing off in diamonds. The 2 ◇ bid was artificial, so diamonds are "unbid."

Partner	Opp.	You
1 NT	2 ♣*	3 ♣

♠ A 8
♡ 9 5
◇ J 10 8
♣ A J 10 5 3 2

*Landy (majors)

You show a real club suit, and, according to Lebensohl principles, your bid is forcing.

Partner	Opp.	You
1 NT	2 ♠*	3 ♠

♠ A 6 3
♡ K Q 9 8
◇ Q 10 8 6
♣ 5 4

*Brozel (spades + minor)

Your 3 ♠ cue-bid is "Stayman," but says nothing about your spade holding. After all, why tell your opponent which of his two suits to lead? Let him guess.

Another possibility comes to light after a two-suited overcall. The nature of the enemy system allows this agreement:

2. **Two-level cue-bid** (of a suit shown by overcaller) shows about 7 points or more, and is a takeout for the suits *not shown* by overcaller. If there is an "unshown" major, this cue-bid suggests four cards in that suit and is much like Stayman. Responder does *not* promise another bid, so opener should usually jump the bidding if he has a maximum 1 NT opening.

Partner	Opp.	You		
			♠	J 10 8 7
			♡	5 3
1 NT	2 ♣*	2 ♡	◇	A Q J 4
			♣	10 8 3

*Astro (hearts + minor)

Since 2 ♣ shows hearts, your 2 ♡ bid is a cue-bid and implies four spades.

Under the preceding agreement, responder often has *two* possible cue-bids at his disposal. In that event, it makes sense to play that (a) the *higher* cue-bid is game-forcing; and (b) the *lower* cue-bid shows less strength and may be just competitive. Witness these two examples:

Partner	Opp.	You		
			♠	5 2
			♡	3
1 NT	2 ♣*	2 ♠	◇	K J 9 8 5
			♣	A Q 10 5 3

*Landy (majors)

Your 2 ♠ cue-bid shows both minors and the values to reach game, whereas a 2 ♡ cue-bid would be weaker.

Partner	Opp.	You		
			♠	K 9 7 3
			♡	8 7 3
1 NT	2 ◇*	2 ♡	◇	7 4
			♣	K J 10 4

*Brozel (hearts + diamonds)

You suggest both black suits and limited strength, since you would cue-bid 3 ◇ with game-going values.

WARNING: The technique of cue-bidding overcaller's *implied* suit may be used at the two-level *only* (an obvious exception would be after an "unusual 2 NT" overcall, where both 3 ♣ and 3 ◇ would be cue-bids). Only a *naturally* bid suit may be cue-bid at the three-level or higher. Observe this example:

Opp.	Partner	Opp.	You		
				♠	7
				♡	Q J 9 7 6 5
	1 NT	2 ♣*	2 NT	◇	K 7 5 4
P	3 ♣	P	3 ♡	♣	7 5

*Landy (majors)

Your 3 ♡ bid is natural and, by Lebensohl principles, invitational to game. Similarly, a direct 3 ♡ bid over 2 ♣ would also be natural, but forcing.

DOUBLES OF OVERCALLS

If the Lebensohl convention is used, the following agreements are customary regarding *doubles* of enemy suit overcalls:

1. **After any two-level overcall,** a double is for penalty. If the enemy suit bid is artificial (e.g., Landy or Astro), doubler does not promise specific values in that artificial suit, but suggests *defensive* strength (about 7+ HCP), usually with length in one (or both) of the suits implied by the enemy.

Partner	Opp.	You		
			♠	A J 8 5
			♡	9 7
1 NT	2 ◇*	DBL	◇	7 3 2
			♣	K 10 8 4

*Astro (spades + another suit)

Your double shows general strength, not just diamonds. If the enemy runs to spades or clubs, you will double for penalty. If they run to hearts, perhaps partner can double.

2. **After a natural three-level suit overcall,** a double is for takeout, very much like the "negative double" (see page 68). The theory behind this is quite sound. Since overcaller obviously has a long suit, and opener has at least a doubleton, it is extremely unlikely that responder will have trump length. More likely, responder will have enough strength to compete, but no adequate means of doing so.

Partner	Opp.	You		
			♠	K 9 8 5
			♡	3 2
1 NT	3 ♡	DBL	◇	A 9 4 2
			♣	J 8 7

Your double is for takeout, especially for spades (the unbid major). Partner, of course, may exercise his judgment and pass when holding heart length or strength.

THE ONE DISADVANTAGE

It is only fair to conclude our discussion of Lebensohl with a brief mention of the one situation where you will regret using it. That occurs when responder would like to raise to 2 NT as a *natural* bid. Here is what to do:

With a normal "2 NT response" (after the 1 NT opening is overcalled), responder should (a) overbid to reach game; or (b) double for penalty. This does not offer a perfect solution, to be sure, so responder must generally choose the lesser of two evils.

Partner	Opp.	You		
			♠	9 3
			♡	A 9 2
1 NT	2 ♠	3 NT	◇	K 10 4 2
			♣	J 10 4 3

There is no ideal action. The overbid of 3 NT (which denies a spade stopper, remember) is probably best. With three or more spades, you should consider a double.

2

One of a Suit Opening

♣   ♦   ♥   ♠   ♣   ♦   ♥   ♠

In this chapter we will cover the conventions that are used after your side has opened the bidding with one of a suit. More specifically, these are conventions that may be used without enemy interference, as Chapter 3 will deal with the strictly competitive conventions. We recommend a standard approach to opening bids, with the following agreements:

1. **Major-suit openings** show at least a five-card suit. This concept of "five-card majors" is widely played, and steadily increasing in popularity. Exceptionally, a *very* strong four-card major may be opened to avoid rebidding problems, or in third or fourth position when opening "light."

2. **Minor-suit openings** show at least a three-card suit. When the choice is between three-card minors, tend to open 1 ♣ unless the diamonds are much stronger; then open 1 ◇.

NOTE: Of the conventions in this chapter, only "1 NT forcing" requires the practice of five-card majors. The remaining conventions may be adopted regardless of your opening-bid style.

In this chapter:

Limit Major Raises
with
Splinter bids
3 NT balanced forcing raise
Unlimited 2 NT response
One Notrump Forcing
Weak Jump-Shift Responses

Inverted Minor Raises
Structured Reverses
Reverse Drury
Preemptive Reraises

Fourth Suit Forcing
New Minor Forcing

Limit Major Raises ★

An important feature of the Kaplan-Sheinwold system, and others

In standard bidding, the jump raise of a major-suit opening bid is forcing to game. There is nothing wrong with that, in itself, but it compels responder to find some other way to describe an *invitational* raise. Traditionally, this is done by responding in a different suit, then raising opener on the next round. The end result of this roundabout procedure is often ambiguous, leaving opener in doubt as to the quality of responder's trump support.

The popularity, then, of "limit major raises" is not surprising. The basic understanding is quite simple:

Jump major raise shows 11 or 12 (or a very good 10) points, and is invitational to game. In other words, the jump raise begins where the single raise leaves off.

Partner	You		
		♠	7 4
		♡	J 7 5 4
1 ♡	3 ♡	◇	K Q 7
		♣	A 9 8 3

Your 3 ♡ bid is a limit raise, showing slightly better than a 2 ♡ bid.

Partner	You		
		♠	K 10 8 4
		♡	3
1 ♠	3 ♠	◇	A 9 8 4 2
		♣	5 4 3

Your excellent high card quality and distribution make this hand well worth a limit raise.

NOTE: The number of trumps required for a limit raise depends on whether the "1 NT forcing" convention (see page 33) is also played. If so, the jump raise shows at least *four* trumps. If not, three trumps to an honor will do.

IN COMPETITION: After an enemy overcall, limit major raises still apply, but only *three* trumps are required. After a takeout double, though, we recommend the "Truscott 2 NT" bid (see page 73) instead.

After the limit major raise, opener may (a) pass with a bare minimum opening; (b) sign off in game; or (c) make some other bid to explore for slam. Here is an example:

		You	Partner
♠	Q 9 8		
♡	K Q 10 8 3		
◇	A J 9	1 ♡	3 ♡
♣	7 4	P	

You have nothing extra, so pass. However, change one of your small clubs to a diamond, and you should take a chance and bid 4 ♡.

SPLINTER BIDS

When limit major raises are adopted, the question that immediately comes to mind is how to show a forcing raise. When responder has an *unbalanced* hand, i.e., a singleton or void suit, the problem is neatly solved by the "splinter bid." This extremely popular device is explained as follows:

Double jump-shift response (to a major opening) shows 13 to 16 points, at least four-card trump support, and a splinter—a singleton or void in the suit bid. This is forcing to at least four of opener's major.

Partner	You		
		♠	7
		♡	K J 8 6
1 ♡	3 ♠	♢	A K 3
		♣	J 9 8 4 2

You show a forcing heart raise with a spade splinter. With no slam interest, partner must sign off in 4 ♡.

Partner	You		
		♠	A J 8 5
		♡	Q 10 7 3
1 ♡	4 ♣	♢	A 7 6 5
		♣	3

You show a club splinter. Over a 1 ♠ opening, you would make the same response.

Partner	You		
		♠	K 10 6 5 4
		♡	—
1 ♠	4 ♡	♢	A Q 10 6
		♣	9 8 7 4

Here you show a heart splinter. This auction is sometimes mistaken as natural, so please take note.

IN COMPETITION: After an enemy takeout double, splinter bids are still on. After an overcall, however, they are *off*.

NOTE: For follow-up methods, see "Bidding After a Splinter Bid" (page *203*). Also, refer to "Extended Splinter Bids" (page *199*) for further applications of this valuable tool.

THREE-NOTRUMP BALANCED FORCING RAISE

Invented by Monroe Ingberman of White Plains, New York, a leading bridge theoretician and prominent player

Since the splinter bid takes care of unbalanced hands only, it still remains to find a way to show *balanced* forcing raises. Of the several methods available, we recommend borrowing the seldom-used 3 NT response, although a popular alternative is the "Jacoby 2 NT" bid (see Glossary). In its natural sense, the bid of 3 NT is very clumsy, so little is lost by this conversion. Here is how it works:

Three-notrump response (to a major opening) shows 13 to 16 points, at least four-card trump support, and no singleton or void suit. This is forcing to at least four of opener's major.

Partner	You		
		♠	K 9 7 5
		♡	A 6
1 ♠	3 NT	♢	K J 9 7
		♣	Q 10 3

You show a standard balanced forcing raise. Partner must either sign off in 4 ♠, or make some other bid to try for slam.

IN COMPETITION: After an enemy takeout double, the 3 NT forcing raise still applies. After an enemy overcall, however, it does *not* apply, although you may wish to adopt the "Eastern cue-bid" and the "Eastern 3 NT bid" (see page *79*) for a similar treatment.

UNLIMITED TWO-NOTRUMP RESPONSE

When a bid of 3 NT is used as a forcing major raise, it is customary to play that a 2 NT response (by an unpassed hand) is unlimited, as described below:

Two-notrump response (to a major opening) shows 13 or more points (no upper limit) and a balanced hand. This, of course, is forcing to game.

Partner	You		
		♠	K 7
		♡	A Q 8
1 ♠	2 NT	◇	K 10 7 6
		♣	A J 9 3

Your 2 NT bid is standard, except that the strength is unlimited.

After the 2 NT response, opener should always *assume* that responder holds a hand in the 13- to 16-point range and make his normal rebid. Therefore, responder must take it upon himself to indicate a stronger hand, i.e., 17 or more points. This may be done by (a) bidding 4 NT as a quantitative slam invitation; or (b) cue-bidding a new suit. A couple of examples follow:

Partner	You		
		♠	K Q 9
		♡	J 4 3
1 ♡	2 NT	◇	K Q 10 8
3 NT	4 NT	♣	A K 9

Your 4 NT bid shows 17 or 18 points and invites slam. With 13 to 16 points, you would just pass 3 NT.

Partner	You		
		♠	K J
		♡	A K 7
1 ♠	2 NT	◇	Q 9 7 5
3 ♠	4 ♣	♣	A 10 9 3

You are too strong to raise to 4 ♠, so cue-bid your ace of clubs. This agrees spades by inference and shows at least 17 points.

One Notrump Forcing ★

An important feature of the Roth-Stone and Kaplan-Sheinwold systems

In standard bidding, a 1 NT response to partner's major-suit opening bid has always been played as nonforcing, and indeed many experts still adhere to this method. Nevertheless, hands like the following keep cropping up:

♠ A 10 8 7 5	Partner	You	♠ 6
♡ Q J 5			♡ K 9 8 7 4 3
◇ 7 4	1 ♠	1 NT	◇ 9 8 2
♣ A Q 7	P		♣ K 10 8

Where did the bidding go wrong? Surely, a contract of 1 NT leaves much to be desired (probably down one or two tricks, with 3 ♡ virtually lay-down, and 4 ♡ a strong favorite). The fact is that neither you nor partner made a bad bid. Certainly, you could not respond 2 ♡ with only 6 high-card points, and partner's bidding is impeccable. This is just a pitfall of standard bidding.

Problems like the above led to the invention of the "1 NT forcing" agreement for use in conjunction with "five-card majors." Actually, an opening bidder who promises a five-card major *usually* bids again anyway, even when the 1 NT response is not forcing. Why? Because there is only *one* hand pattern with which opener would typically pass, namely 5-3-3-2. Therefore, it makes a lot of sense to agree that opener *must* bid again.

Given the assurance that he will have another chance to bid, responder is able to describe many more hands. Abandoning the ability to play 1 NT is but a small price to pay. Here is the basic agreement:

One-notrump response to a major-suit opening shows anywhere from 6 to 12 points and is *forcing* for one round. Responder denies the ability to make an immediate raise, and also denies four or more spades after a 1 ♡ opening bid. Otherwise, he may have almost any distribution.

Partner	You		
		♠	6
		♡	J 9 7 5
1 ♠	1 NT	◇	K 10 8 7 5
		♣	Q 9 4

A minimum; notice you would make the same response if 1 NT was not forcing.

Partner	You		
		♠	K 9 8
		♡	8 5
1 ♡	1 NT	◇	K J 9 7
		♣	K Q 8 6

A maximum; since your bid is forcing, you are assured of a second opportunity to bid.

Because the forcing 1 NT response is capable of handling many borderline game hands (up to 12 points, remember), most experts *increase* their requirements for a two-level response in a new suit. Indeed, many go as far as "two-over-one game forcing" (see Glossary). We recommend such a strategy. However, it is entirely optional; the forcing 1 NT response is equally desirable in conjunction with standard two-over-one responses.

NOTE: By a passed hand, the 1 NT response is still intended as forcing, but opener may pass (as he would a new-suit response) if game is out of reach.

IN COMPETITION: After an enemy takeout double or 1 ♠ overcall, a response of 1 NT becomes a standard bid, i.e., *not* forcing.

REBIDS BY OPENER

In most instances, opener makes the *same* rebid that he would have made under standard conditions, i.e., if the 1 NT response was not forcing. The principal difference occurs when opener would have *passed* the 1 NT response. Then he must bid as follows:

Two of a minor is natural, but could be just a three-card suit when opener holds 5-3-3-2 shape and insufficient strength to raise to 2 NT. With three cards in each minor, prefer to bid 2 ♣.

			You	Partner
♠	A J			
♡	K Q 7 4 3			
◇	K 4 3		1 ♡	1 NT
♣	9 8 2		2 ♣	

It may seem unappetizing to bid 2 ♣ on such a feeble holding, but partner will rarely leave you there.

NOTE: The astute reader may wonder what opener is supposed to bid with a minimum hand containing four spades, five hearts, and two of each minor. Fortunately, such a hand is uncommon, but tend to rebid the five-card heart suit.

WEAK REBIDS BY RESPONDER

We now come to the crux of the forcing 1 NT structure, i.e., the second bid by responder. We will assume that opener's rebid is at or below *two* of his original major suit, as it will be about 90% of the time. Responder's objective is then twofold; he must more narrowly define his strength, and state the nature of his hand. With a *minimum* 1 NT response (6 to a bad 10 points), responder has three options, as explained below:

1. **Two of opener's major** typically shows a doubleton trump. This is discouraging and not forcing. NOTE: Responder may also bid this way, as essentially a tactical maneuver, with *more* than two trumps and a hand that was too weak for an immediate single raise, i.e., about 4 to 6 points.

Partner	You			
		♠	9 7	
		♡	A 7 5 4	
1 ♠	1 NT	◇	9 8 6 3	
2 ♣	2 ♠	♣	K 9 7	

Even though you have three clubs and only two spades, the preference to 2 ♠ is desirable, since partner might have a three-card club suit and is known to hold five spades.

Partner	You			
		♠	9 2	
		♡	K 7 4 3	
1 ♡	1 NT!	◇	7 5 3	
2 ◇	2 ♡	♣	10 8 7 2	

You could have passed 1 ♡, but that might have allowed the opponents to get in the bidding. Your excellent heart support should compensate for the few points you are missing.

2. **New suit** shows at least a good five-card suit at the two-level, or a good six-card suit at the three-level. This too is discouraging and not forcing.

Partner	You			
		♠	2	
		♡	K J 10 5 4	
1 ♠	1 NT	◇	9 8 5 4	
2 ♣	2 ♡	♣	A 6 2	

You show five or more hearts and a hand too weak for an original 2 ♡ response.

Partner	You		
		♠	10 9 7
		♡	2
1 ♡	1 NT	◇	7 6 5
2 ◇	3 ♣	♣	A Q J 9 8 7

Here you promise at least six clubs.

3. **Pass** if you feel you have reached the best attainable final contract. Don't keep looking for "rainbows" if a potential misfit is at hand.

Partner	You		
		♠	3
		♡	K 9 8 6
1 ♠	1 NT	◇	J 9 4
2 ◇	P	♣	K 10 9 6 3

Partner's 2 ◇ may not be a great contract, but any attempt to improve matters could lead to disaster.

Partner	You		
		♠	5
		♡	Q 8 7
1 ♠	1 NT	◇	A J 9 7 4 3
2 ♠	P	♣	10 7 2

A bid of 3 ◇ just asks for trouble. Partner has at least six spades, so leave well enough alone.

CONSTRUCTIVE REBIDS BY RESPONDER

Now let's see what responder may do with a better hand, again assuming that opener has rebid at or below two of his major. With a *maximum* 1 NT response (good 10 to 12 points), the following rebids are available:

1. **Three of opener's original major** is invitational to game. This typically shows **three** trumps, but may be just a doubleton when opener has *rebid* his original major.

Partner	You		
		♠	A K 3
		♡	K 9 4
1 ♡	1 NT	◇	9 8 7 6
2 ♣	3 ♡	♣	J 8 5

Partner will pass 3 ♡ with a bare minimum, or continue to game with a little extra.

Partner	You		
		♠	9 7
		♡	A J 9 2
1 ♠	1 NT	◇	A Q 10 3
2 ♠	3 ♠	♣	5 4 3

Here you may raise with two trumps, since partner has shown six.

2. **Three of opener's second suit** is invitational to game. This shows at least four trumps, but usually five-card support for a minor suit. NOTE: If opener's second suit is *hearts*, this raise may be made on slightly weaker hands, say about 9 points or a very good 8 points.

	Partner	You	♠	A 3
			♡	4 2
	1 ♡	1 NT	◇	K 8 7 4
	2 ♣	<u>3 ♣</u>	♣	Q 9 8 7 5

Your 3 ♣ raise suggests five trumps, since partner may have just three.

	Partner	You	♠	9 4
			♡	K J 4 3
	1 ♠	1 NT	◇	A 9 8 2
	2 ♡	<u>3 ♡</u>	♣	8 7 6

Less strength is needed here due to the greater likelihood of game.

3. **Two notrump** is invitational to 3 NT. This implies stoppers in the unbid suits and a relatively balanced hand, although responder may have a singleton in opener's original major.

	Partner	You	♠	A J 6
			♡	5 3
	1 ♡	1 NT	◇	K 10 9 6
	2 ◇	<u>2 NT</u>	♣	Q J 8 7

Partner may pass your 2 NT bid with a bare minimum or continue to game with a little extra strength.

Finally, one other contingency should be mentioned:

4. **Jump to game** (or, rarely, four of a minor) indicates that opener's rebid has improved responder's hand to the extent that a normal invitational rebid is inadequate.

	Partner	You	♠	3
			♡	J 10 8 7 6
	1 ♠	1 NT	◇	A K 9 7 3
	2 ♡	<u>4 ♡</u>	♣	9 5

Obviously, raising to 3 ♡ would not do justice to your hand, so jump to game.

	Partner	You	♠	Q J 8
			♡	A 4
	1 ♠	1 NT	◇	5 4 3
	2 ♣	<u>4 ♠</u>	♣	K 10 4 3 2

You were originally planning to invite game in spades, but partner's 2 ♣ rebid has improved your hand.

Weak Jump-Shift Responses

An original concept of the Roth-Stone system

In standard bidding, the jump-shift response to partner's opening bid of one of a suit shows a strong hand. The majority of experts also adhere to this philosophy, and one of the better treatments is "Soloway jump shifts" (see Glossary). It cannot be denied that the discriminate use of the strong jump-shift response can greatly benefit slam bidding.

Nevertheless, we feel that these strong hands occur too infrequently; or perhaps we are just poor cardholders. As responder, it seems that many more weak hands are picked up, with which it is awkward to bid for fear of getting overboard. We therefore recommend "weak jump-shift responses" to accommodate the weak hands. Strong hands, in general, can be handled adequately by slower development through minimum forcing bids.

The weak jump-shift response has a dual advantage. It not only facilitates your own bidding, but also has a preemptive effect, should the opponents intend to enter the auction. All considered, we believe it is worth the price of giving up the strong jump shift. Here are the basic requirements:

1. **Two-level jump-shift response** typically shows about 2 to 5 high-card points and a six-card suit. Occasionally, a very meaty five-card suit, or a feeble seven-card suit may be held.

Partner	You		
		♠	5
		♡	Q J 8 7 6 3
1 ♣	2 ♡	♢	10 8 3
		♣	9 7 3

    A classic example; you are hesitant about responding 1 ♡, but hate to pass.

Partner	You		
		♠	K J 10 9 5
		♡	5 3
1 ♢	2 ♠	♢	8 5
		♣	9 8 7 4

    The exceptional quality of your suit allows you to bid 2 ♠ with just five cards.

2. **Three-level jump-shift response** typically shows about 2 to 7 high-card points and a seven-card suit (rarely, a meaty six-card suit).

Partner	You		
		♠	5
		♡	K J 9 7 6 4 3
1 ♠	3 ♡	♢	6 4
		♣	10 9 2

    Without the weak jump shift, you would have a difficult time describing this hand.

Partner	You		
		♠	9 5 3
		♡	4
1 ♢	3 ♣	♢	10 6 4
		♣	K Q J 9 8 6

    Here you may bid 3 ♣ with only six cards, because of the strong suit texture.

As with any preemptive maneuver, the vulnerability must not be overlooked. If vulnerable, responder should have reasonable suit texture, so as to minimize the danger of a severe penalty. Each of the preceding examples would be acceptable at any vulnerability, but witness the following:

Partner	You		
		♠	10 8 7
		♡	9 7 6 5 4 3
1 ♢	?	♢	8 6
		♣	K 6

A pass is recommended if vulnerable, since your suit is so weak. However, a 2 ♡ bid is justifiable if not vulnerable.

NOTE: It makes no difference if responder is a passed hand; weak jump-shift responses still apply.

REBIDS BY OPENER

Opener will usually pass the weak jump-shift response, as responder has advertised a weak hand. A misfit for responder's suit is *not* an excuse for opener to continue bidding. For example:

		You	Partner
♠	3		
♡	A K 7 6 3		
◇	A Q 8	1 ♡	2 ♠
♣	K J 8 5	P	

Any attempt to improve the contract is dangerous and dubious, so pass while you still have a chance to go plus.

Essentially, opener has two reasons for bidding again: legitimate interest in game, or a good fit for responder's suit. In the latter event, opener may want to raise as a defensive or competitive measure. Opener's rebids have the following meanings:

1. **Two notrump** is a *forcing* game try, and suggests at least a doubleton in responder's suit. With a minimum, responder must rebid *three* of his suit. With a maximum, responder may make any other rebid.

		You	Partner
♠	K 7		
♡	A K 8 5		
◇	A Q 10 4	1 ◇	2 ♠
♣	K 8 4	2 NT	

Your 2 NT rebid shows game interest; but if partner returns to 3 ♠ (discouraging), you should pass.

2. **Three of responder's suit** is strictly an obstructive bid, *not* a try for game. This increases the preempt, making it more difficult for the opponents to compete successfully.

		You	Partner
♠	A 10 7		
♡	Q 8 5		
◇	9 4	1 ♣	2 ♡
♣	A Q J 7 3	3 ♡	

You could pass 2 ♡, but that would make it easier for the enemy to back in; the 3 ♡ bid may shut them out.

3. **Any new suit or a rebid of opener's original suit** is natural and not forcing. This suggests a very distributional hand with no fit for responder's suit. Responder should usually pass (or give a simple preference), but he may raise with a useful dummy.

		You	Partner
♠	3		
♡	A K J 9 7 6		
◇	K Q 10 9 7	1 ♡	2 ♠
♣	2	3 ◇	

You show a pronounced two-suiter. Partner will usually pass or correct to 3 ♡.

4. **Four of responder's minor suit** is invitational to game, except if bid after interference by opener's right-hand opponent (then competitive).

5. **Any jump bid below game** is natural and very invitational.

6. **Any game bid** is a natural sign-off.

WEAK JUMP SHIFTS IN COMPETITION

Enemy interference does not prevent responder from making a weak jump shift. In fact, it is even *more* valuable now than without interference, since the auction threatens to become very competitive. We suggest this agreement:

If the opening bid is overcalled or doubled, weak jump-shift responses still apply. Also, the meanings of opener's rebids are unchanged, insofar as possible.

Partner	Opp.	You		
			♠	K 10 8 7 5 3
			♡	6
1 ♢	DBL	2 ♠	♢	9 2
			♣	9 8 7 4

You would make the same bid without the double.

Partner	Opp.	You		
			♠	8
			♡	9 3
1 ♣	1 ♠	3 ♢	♢	A J 8 6 5 4 3
			♣	10 9 2

After the 1 ♠ overcall, a bid of 2 ♢ would be a normal forcing response, so you must bid 3 ♢ if you bid at all.

Partner	Opp.	You		
			♠	—
			♡	9 7
1 ♠	2 ♡	4 ♣	♢	J 8 7 3
			♣	K Q J 9 6 5 2

A four-level jump shift is still weak, but suggests greater playing strength.

NOTE: Regarding the preceding example, it should be reaffirmed that "splinter bids" (see page *31*) do *not* apply after an enemy overcall.

DOUBLE JUMP-SHIFT RESPONSES

The double jump-shift response (one level higher than a jump shift) is also a *weak* bid. This is true in *standard* bidding, and is not based on the "weak jump shift" agreements. We recommend this understanding:

Double jump-shift response (or higher) shows a weak hand with a seven-card or longer suit. Responder should have within *four* playing tricks of his actual bid. NOTE: This also applies in competition.

Partner	You		
		♠	6
		♡	Q J 10 9 8 5 3
1 ♣	3 ♡	♢	10 9 3
		♣	8 5

You could respond 2 ♡, but the double jump to 3 ♡ is more accurate, showing five playing tricks.

Partner	You		
		♠	K Q J 10 7 6 4
		♡	—
1 ♢	4 ♠	♢	7 6 3
		♣	J 4 2

Here you have six playing tricks, so the triple jump to 4 ♠ is appropriate.

WARNING: If "splinter bids" are used (see page *31*), they receive first priority. Therefore, a double jump-shift response to a *major*-suit opening is a splinter bid (except after an enemy overcall).

Inverted Minor Raises

An important feature of the Kaplan-Sheinwold system

When was the last time you heard the bidding go:

Partner	Opp.	You	Opp.
1 ♣	P	2 ♣	P
P	P		

Not very often, you say? This is the principle behind "inverted minor raises." When responder has a *weak* minor raise, he isn't going to buy the contract at the two-level, so he may as well bid three. Conversely, when responder has a *good* minor raise, he wants to keep the bidding as low as possible to allow careful exploration for game, or even slam! The more you think about this, the more logical it becomes. Here is the basic strategy:

Single minor raise shows at least 10 points (no upper limit), at least four-card trump support, and is forcing for one round. This response denies holding a four-card or longer major suit.

Partner	You	
		♠ 7
		♡ 9 5 3
1 ♣	2 ♣	♢ A 10 7 4
		♣ K 9 8 7 2

A bare minimum.

Partner	You	
		♠ A K 3
		♡ 3 2
1 ♢	2 ♢	♢ K Q 9 5
		♣ A Q 7 2

As evidenced here, no hand is too strong for a single minor raise.

With a bare "10-point" raise, responder should prefer to bid 1 NT if his hand is balanced. For example:

Partner	You	
		♠ 10 6
		♡ Q 9 7
1 ♢	1 NT	♢ A Q J 3
		♣ 9 8 7 2

Your flat shape suggests keeping the bidding low, so bid 1 NT, which is not forcing, of course.

IN COMPETITION: The forcing single minor raise still applies after a simple suit overcall or a takeout double.

REBIDS BY OPENER

After the single minor raise, opener *must* bid again, except if responder is a passed hand, or if opener's right-hand opponent intervenes with a bid or a double. With a *minimum* hand, opener has a choice of the following two rebids:

1. **Two notrump** shows a balanced hand suitable for notrump, and is not forcing. Opener often has just a three-card minor suit.

♠ A Q 9 3   *You* *Partner*
♥ K J 6
♦ J 9 7   1 ♣ 2 ♣
♣ Q 9 8   <u>2 NT</u>

Your 2 NT rebid shows a minimum opening and suggests notrump as the final contract.

2. **Three of the agreed minor** shows at least a four-card minor suit, and is not forcing. This is just a catchall rebid to confirm a minimum.

♠ 9 2   *You* *Partner*
♥ K Q 5 3
♦ K 10 8 5   1 ♦ 2 ♦
♣ A 9 8   <u>3 ♦</u>

You do not wish to declare notrump, so simply raise the trump suit.

With *extra* values, opener must find some other rebid. The following two options are available:

3. **New suit** shows at least a *"queen"* better than a bare minimum opening, at least three cards (typically four) in the suit bid, and at least four cards in the agreed minor suit. This is forcing for one round.

♠ A K 8 2   *You* *Partner*
♥ 2
♦ A Q J 7 3   1 ♦ 2 ♦
♣ 9 6 5   <u>2 ♠</u>

Your 2 ♠ rebid describes your hand, while promising at least slightly extra strength.

4. **Three notrump** shows a balanced hand that was too strong for a 1 NT opening. Opener may have just a three-card minor suit.

♠ A 10 7   *You* *Partner*
♥ K Q 8
♦ K 9 8   1 ♣ 2 ♣
♣ A Q 6 5   <u>3 NT</u>

Here you show 18 or 19 points, assuming that your 1 NT opening shows 15 to 17 points.

REBIDS BY RESPONDER

After a single minor raise, responder is compelled to bid again only if opener rebids in a new suit. Otherwise, responder has the option of passing if he feels the proper contract has been reached. The meanings of responder's rebids are described below:

Two notrump or three of the agreed minor indicates *minimum* values for your first bid, and is not forcing.

Partner	You		
		♠	A J 9
		♡	7 5
1 ♢	2 ♢	♢	Q 10 5 4
2 ♡	<u>2 NT</u>	♣	K 8 7 3

Your 2 NT bid is natural, and shows that your 2 ♢ raise was minimum.

Partner	You		
		♠	3
		♡	7 4 2
1 ♣	2 ♣	♢	K 9 7 6
2 ♠	<u>3 ♣</u>	♣	A J 9 8 2

You have a minimum single raise, so try to put on the brakes with your 3 ♣ rebid.

Suit bids (other than the agreed minor) are forcing. New suit bids below 3 NT tend to show stoppers, so the partnership can determine whether 3 NT is playable.

Partner	You		
		♠	Q 7 2
		♡	5 2
1 ♣	2 ♣	♢	K J 9 7
3 ♣	<u>3 ♢</u>	♣	A K 8 6

You show strength in diamonds; perhaps this will enable 3 NT to be reached.

Partner	You		
		♠	6 4
		♡	K Q 8
1 ♢	2 ♢	♢	A Q 10 8 4
2 ♡	<u>3 ♡</u>	♣	7 6 3

Your raise to 3 ♡ shows three good trumps (you denied four when you bid 2 ♢) and is forcing. Partner may now elect to play 4 ♡.

Three notrump is a natural sign-off attempt, just as it sounds.

Partner	You		
		♠	9 7
		♡	A Q 7
1 ♣	2 ♣	♢	K 9 8
2 ♠	<u>3 NT</u>	♣	Q J 7 5 4

Partner has shown spade length and some additional values, so 3 NT is the obvious contract.

DEVELOPMENT OF THE AUCTION

After responder's rebid, any further bidding is governed by the following basic principle:

After a single minor raise, if either partner returns to three or four of the agreed minor (or 2 NT), this is *not* forcing, and indicates *minimum* values for his previous bidding. Hence, any other bid that does not complete game is forcing.

		You	Partner
♠	7 4 2	1 ♢	2 ♢
♡	K Q 10 5	2 ♡	3 ♣
♢	A K J 9 7	<u>3 ♢</u>	
♣	9		

Your 3 ♢ bid is not forcing; you told your whole story when you bid 2 ♡.

Partner	You	♠ K 4
1 ♣	2 ♣	♡ 4 3
3 ♣	3 ◇	◇ A 10 9 4
3 ♠	4 ♣	♣ K J 9 8 7

It is apparent that 3 NT is unplayable, so your 4 ♣ bid indicates you just ran out of steam.

EXCEPTION: If either partner has bid 3 NT, then a bid of four of the agreed minor is forcing (a game bid cannot be removed to play in a part-score).

JUMP MINOR RAISES

Since the single minor raise takes care of all good hands, it stands to reason that the jump minor raise is weak. Exactly! The jump minor raise is a two-edged sword. Not only does it get you immediately to your most likely final contract, but it also makes life difficult for the opponents, who frequently hold more strength than your side. Here is the basic agreement:

Jump minor raise shows about 6 to 9 points, at least five trumps (or four good trumps), and is not forcing. Responder typically has an unbalanced hand with no major-suit interest. Essentially, this is a preemptive bid.

Partner	You	♠ 5 2
		♡ 7 5
1 ♣	3 ♣	◇ 6 5 3 2
		♣ A J 9 8 4

Your 3 ♣ bid shows a weak hand.

Partner	You	♠ 9 8 2
		♡ 3
1 ◇	3 ◇	◇ K Q 10 5
		♣ J 9 5 3 2

Good four-card support is permissible.

Avoid making a jump minor raise when your hand is balanced and contains honors in the unbid suits. For example:

Partner	You	♠ J 7
		♡ Q 9 6
1 ◇	1 NT	◇ 10 9 6 5 4
		♣ K 10 3

Despite your five diamonds, 1 NT is a better response because of your scattered values.

NOTE: Higher jump minor raises, such as 1 ◇–4 ◇, or 1 ♣–5 ♣, are also weak and preemptive, but this is true in *standard* bidding, and has nothing to do with the practice of inverted minor raises. These bids obviously indicate extreme shape, often very freakish.

IN COMPETITION: After a simple overcall or a takeout double, all jump minor raises are still weak; there is no change.

Since the jump minor raise is weak, opener will usually *pass;* however, there are some hands which warrant further bidding. Opener may (a) bid 3 NT with a balanced hand too strong for a 1 NT opening; (b) bid a new suit, which is forcing one round, to try for game or slam; (c) reraise to four of the agreed minor as a further preempt ... *not* a game try; or (d) sign off in five of the agreed minor. Here is an example:

♠ A Q 10 7	*You*	*Partner*
♡ 3		
◇ A 8 2	1 ♣	3 ♣
♣ A Q 8 7 6	3 ♠	

Your 3 ♠ bid is a game try, but if partner returns to 4 ♣ (discouraging), you should pass.

Structured Reverses

The "reverse" bid by opener after a one-level suit response, and the sequences that follow, have always been a thorn in the side of many players. For example, assume you hear this bidding:

Partner	*You*
1 ♣	1 ♠
2 ♡	?

Obviously, partner is showing a good hand, but just *how* good? Is the 2 ♡ bid forcing? Also, what do your various rebids mean? Is 2 NT forward-going? What about a preference to 3 ♣? Most players could give only vague answers to these and other related questions. A well-defined structure is greatly needed. First of all, almost all modern experts would endorse this theory:

Opener's reverse bid after a one-level major-suit response is *forcing.* The minimum strength required is about 17 good points, but there is no upper limit (other than the fact that opener failed to open with 2 ♣).

Unfortunately, that's about as far as any universal agreement goes. The meanings of responder's rebids, and the bidding thereafter, are indistinct. Consequently, we recommend our own method of "structured reverses," as explained in the following pages.

THE WEAKNESS SIGNALS

After opener's reverse, if responder has a *weak* hand (less than 10 points), he is obliged to make one of the two "weakness signals." These two rebids are forcing, and simply confirm or deny the possession of a five-card major, as follows:

1. **Two of the same major** shows at least a five-card suit.

Partner	*You*		
		♠	J 9 7 5 4
		♡	A J 7
1 ◇	1 ♠	◇	9 2
2 ♡	2 ♠	♣	8 7 2

You confirm a five-card spade suit.

2. **Two notrump** denies a five-card or longer major.

Partner	You		♠ 8 7 6
			♡ A 9 7 4
1 ♣	1 ♡		◇ J 5
2 ◇	2 NT		♣ Q 7 5 3

Your 2 NT bid denies five hearts, but otherwise is completely artificial.

STOPPING BELOW GAME

After responder has made either weakness signal, opener *must* bid again. With *less* than game-forcing strength, opener must make one of the following three rebids, each of which is *not* forcing:

1. **Two notrump** shows a stopper in the fourth suit.

♠ 5		You	Partner
♡ K J 9 8		1 ◇	1 ♠
◇ A K J 10 5		2 ♡	2 ♠
♣ A J 8		2 NT	

Your 2 NT bid suggests playing there, but partner may still correct the contract or continue to game.

2. **Three of original minor** shows at least a six-card suit if responder has rebid his major, but may be a five-card suit if responder has rebid 2 NT.

♠ 9		You	Partner
♡ 3 2		1 ♣	1 ♡
◇ A K 9 6		2 ◇	2 ♡
♣ A K J 10 5 4		3 ♣	

You show a minimum reverse with six clubs.

♠ A 5		You	Partner
♡ A K 8 6		1 ♣	1 ♠
◇ 4 3		2 ♡	2 NT
♣ K Q J 7 5		3 ♣	

Here you promise only five clubs. Remember, partner's 2 NT rebid is forcing, and you are not strong enough to bid 3 NT; thus, 3 ♣ is the only logical choice.

3. **Raise to three** (after major rebid) is natural and invites game.

♠ 8 5 2		You	Partner
♡ A Q 10 8		1 ♣	1 ♠
◇ 4		2 ♡	2 ♠
♣ A K Q J 5		3 ♠	

You are simply inviting partner to bid game. With a better hand, you would jump to 4 ♠ yourself.

After any of the above three rebids, if responder bids again such a bid is natural and not forcing. Responder often may wish to correct the final contract to a more playable one. Here are a couple of examples:

Partner	You		
1 ◇	1 ♠	♠	K 9 7 6 3
2 ♡	2 ♠	♡	6 5
2 NT	<u>3 ◇</u>	◇	J 8 5 4
		♣	9 2

You wish to sign off in 3 ◇.

Partner	You		
1 ♣	1 ♠	♠	K 10 9 6 3
2 ◇	2 ♠	♡	Q J 10 8 7
3 ♣	<u>3 ♡</u>	◇	4 3
		♣	2

You are showing a weak major two-suiter.

Of course, if responder happens to be on the "top" of his weakness signal, he may continue to game, or make an obvious game invitation. Here are two possibilities:

Partner	You		
1 ♣	1 ♠	♠	K 8 7 4
2 ♡	2 NT	♡	6 5
3 ♣	<u>3 NT</u>	◇	K J 8 6
		♣	J 10 5

You wish to take a chance on game.

Partner	You		
1 ♣	1 ♡	♠	7 5
2 ◇	2 ♡	♡	A 9 6 5 4
2 NT	<u>4 ♣</u>	◇	4
		♣	9 8 7 4 3

Having already limited your hand with the weakness signal, you are now inviting game in clubs.

FORCING REBIDS AFTER A WEAKNESS SIGNAL

When opener has a *game-forcing* reverse, he must make one of the following rebids after a weakness signal:

1. **Three of responder's major** (over 2 NT) shows three-card support.

		You	Partner
♠	5	1 ♣	1 ♡
♡	A Q 9	2 ◇	2 NT
◇	A K J 7	<u>3 ♡</u>	
♣	A Q 8 7 5		

Your 3 ♡ preference is forcing. This should be apparent, as partner has denied a five-card heart suit.

2. **Rebid of second suit** shows at least five cards and, by inference, at least six cards in your original minor.

		You	Partner
♠	4	1 ◇	1 ♠
♡	A K J 9 5	2 ♡	2 ♠
◇	A K 10 9 8 5	<u>3 ♡</u>	
♣	2		

You show at least six-five shape, and partner must not pass.

3. **Three notrump** is a natural sign-off attempt.

♠ K J 9	*You*	*Partner*
♡ 3	1 ♣	1 ♡
◇ K Q J 8	2 ◇	2 ♡
♣ A K Q 10 9	3 NT	

You are slightly too strong to bid only 2 NT.

4. **Fourth-suit bid** shows a natural suit if a *minor,* but is just a convenient artificial forcing bid if a *major.* This interpretation is obvious when you consider the previous bidding.

♠ —	*You*	*Partner*
♡ A K J 6	1 ♣	1 ♠
◇ A J 9 6	2 ♡	2 NT
♣ K Q 10 9 4	3 ◇	

You show a legitimate three-suiter.

♠ A 3	*You*	*Partner*
♡ 3	1 ♣	1 ♡
◇ K Q J 9	2 ◇	2 ♡
♣ A K Q 7 6 5	2 ♠	

Here your 2 ♠ bid is non-descriptive and just forces partner to keep bidding. You would never have waited this long to show a real spade suit.

5. **Four of original minor** shows at least a six-card suit, usually seven, and implies a very distributional hand.

♠ 3 2	*You*	*Partner*
♡ A K J 8	1 ♣	1 ♠
◇ —	2 ♡	2 NT
♣ A K 10 9 8 7 4	4 ♣	

Your jump to 4 ♣ is forcing; your hand is too rich in playing strength to bid only 3 ♣ (not forcing). Notice that this is not *Gerber, as partner's 2 NT bid is not natural.*

STRONG AUCTIONS

The greatest advantage of the two weakness signals accrues when they are *not* used by responder. That is:

Failure to make a weakness signal guarantees at least 10 points and immediately creates a *game-forcing* auction.

Partner	*You*	♠ A J 8 6 5
		♡ 6 4 2
1 ♣	1 ♠	◇ 7 5
2 ◇	3 ♣	♣ K Q 7

Your preference to 3 ♣ is unlimited and forcing to game. There is no need to jump the bidding.

Partner	You	♠	A 9 7 6 5
		♡	K 10 9 4
1 ◇	1 ♠	◇	K 9
2 ♡	<u>3 ♡</u>	♣	9 5

Slam is very likely, but there is no need to panic. Your 3 ♡ raise is 100% forcing and unlimited.

Partner	You	♠	A Q 6
		♡	K 10 8 6
1 ♣	1 ♡	◇	Q 9 8
2 ◇	<u>3 NT</u>	♣	9 4 2

Your jump to 3 NT shows a maximum of about 12 or 13 points, and is not forcing, since game has been reached.

Partner	You	♠	K Q 10 8 7 6
		♡	3
1 ♣	1 ♠	◇	A J 4
2 ♡	<u>3 ♠</u>	♣	5 4 3

You show at least six spades.

If responder has game-forcing strength but no obvious rebid, he should bid the *fourth* suit, which is essentially a waiting bid. For example:

Partner	You	♠	A K 7 5 4
		♡	9 6 3
1 ◇	1 ♠	◇	A 5
2 ♡	<u>3 ♣</u>	♣	8 4 3

No descriptive bid is available, so 3 ♣ bides time while creating a game force. To show a legitimate black two-suiter, you must continue with 4 ♣ at your next turn.

REVERSES AFTER A ONE-NOTRUMP RESPONSE

Up until now we have been concerned only with opener's reverse bid after a major-suit response. Another possibility is the reverse bid after a response of 1 NT. For example:

Partner	You
1 ◇	1 NT
2 ♡	?

We still recommend that this type of reverse be unlimited and *forcing,* but a change is required in responder's rebidding structure. Responder's hand already is quite limited, so we suggest the following agreements:

1. **Two notrump or a simple preference** is natural and not forcing. These are the only two discouraging rebids available to responder.

Partner	You	♠	J 5
		♡	8 3 2
1 ◇	1 NT	◇	K 7 4
2 ♡	<u>3 ◇</u>	♣	Q 9 6 5 4

You are trying to sign off in 3 ◇. Partner should pass unless he has a game-forcing reverse.

	Partner	*You*	♠	9 4 3
			♡	9
	1 ♡	1 NT	◇	Q J 8 6
	2 ♠	<u>2 NT</u>	♣	K 10 9 7 5

Your 2 NT rebid is nonforcing and discouraging.

NOTE: The use of the "1 NT forcing" response to a major (see page *33*) does not affect any of these agreements regarding opener's reverse.

2. **Any other rebid** is natural and game-forcing.

	Partner	*You*	♠	9 5
			♡	K 10 3
	1 ◇	1 NT	◇	J 7 4
	2 ♠	<u>3 NT</u>	♣	A J 5 4 3

You have a maximum, so jump to 3 NT since you have the unbid suits protected.

	Partner	*You*	♠	Q 9 7
			♡	9 8 3
	1 ♣	1 NT	◇	A 8 6 5
	2 ♠	<u>3 ♠</u>	♣	K 8 2

Your 3 ♠ raise is forcing and obviously shows only three good trumps, since your 1 NT response denied holding a four-card major.

	Partner	*You*	♠	9 6 3
			♡	8
	1 ♡	1 NT	◇	A K J 5 4
	2 ♠	<u>3 ◇</u>	♣	6 5 4 3

You show a real diamond suit.

	Partner	*You*	♠	K Q 8
			♡	9 5 3
	1 ◇	1 NT	◇	A 10 7
	2 ♡	<u>2 ♠</u>	♣	9 7 6 5

Here you cannot be showing a real spade suit, so you show a spade stopper.

JUMP REVERSES

Once it is agreed that all of opener's reverse bids are *forcing* for at least one round, there is really no need for a "jump reverse." For example, look at this auction:

	You	*Partner*
	1 ◇	1 ♠
	<u>3 ♡</u>	

What could this possibly mean? You would always bid 2 ♡ (forcing) any time you held a heart suit, so the jump to 3 ♡ is useless as a natural bid. Consequently, many experts assign a special meaning to such a bid. One of the more popular treatments is explained below:

1. **Jump reverse after a major-suit response** shows a *singleton* in the suit bid, at least four-card support for responder's major, and game-forcing strength.

		You	Partner
♠	K 9 8 7		
♡	A K 3		
◇	4	1 ♣	1 ♠
♣	A K 9 8 5	3 ◇	

You show a hand strong enough to bid 4 ♠, but with a singleton diamond. Similarly, 3 ♡ would show a singleton heart.

NOTE: When the above treatment is used in conjunction with "splinter bids" (see "Extended Splinter Bids," page *199*), a pleasing bonus is obtained. Since the jump reverse shows a singleton, a double jump reverse (4 ◇ or 4 ♡ in the above auction) would specifically promise a *void.*

What about a jump reverse after a 1 NT response? Obviously, this cannot be a "raise" of partner's suit, since partner bid no suit. Nevertheless, it can still be put to good use. There is little expert agreement in this area, so we offer our own recommendation here:

2. **Jump reverse after a 1 NT response to a minor opening** shows a *singleton* or void in the suit bid, at least six cards in opener's original minor suit, and **game-forcing** strength.

		You	Partner
♠	K Q 9		
♡	3		
◇	A 7 5	1 ♣	1 NT
♣	A K Q J 7 5	3 ♡	

In effect, you are showing a "forcing 3 ♣" rebid with shortness in hearts. This will enable partner to decide intelligently between 3 NT and 5 ♣, depending on his heart holding. Even 6 ♣ is possible if partner has the right maximum.

Reverse Drury ★ ★

Based on the invention by the late Douglas Drury, a prominent American bridge teacher and player

After a major-suit opening in third or fourth position, responder often has a good supporting hand and would like to explore for game *without* getting overboard in the event that partner has a "light" opening bid. Such is the function of the "Drury" convention.

Regular Drury is good, but even better is an improved version, known as "reverse Drury." The "reverse" prefix refers to opener's rebidding structure, which will be explained shortly. But first, here is the basic agreement:

Two-club response by a passed hand (to a major-suit opening) is artificial and forcing. Responder typically has at least three-card support for opener's major and at least 11 (or a good 10) points. However, this bid may also be made with a good six-card or longer club suit and at least 9 high-card points.

		You	Partner
♠	K J 5		
♡	A 6 3		
◇	Q 10 8 5 4	P	1 ♠
♣	9 7	2 ♣	

You are too strong for a single raise to 2 ♠, so start out with 2 ♣.

♠ 8 7 5   *You   Partner*
♡ 6
◇ A 9 5   P   1 ♡
♣ K Q 10 8 7 3   2 ♣

Holding a long club suit, you make the same response. Your subsequent bidding will reveal this.

NOTE: Reverse Drury does *not* apply if the major-suit opening is overcalled or doubled by an opponent.

REBIDS BY OPENER

After the 2 ♣ response, opener *must* bid again, unless his right-hand opponent bids or doubles. This is true *even* with a sub-minimum opening. Here are the permissible rebids:

1. **Two diamonds** indicates a full opening bid. This is completely artificial, and is the *only* way to show a legitimate opening.

   Partner   You   ♠ A 5 4
                                ♡ A K J 7 3
   P   1 ♡   ◇ 6
   2 ♣   2 ◇   ♣ 10 8 6 2

   You would have opened 1 ♡ in first seat, so your 2 ◇ rebid is mandatory.

   NOTE: You now see why this is called reverse Drury—in regular Drury, the 2 ◇ rebid *denies* a full opening. One advantage in reversing that procedure is to *conceal* opener's shape when he has a legitimate opening, since at least 80% of the time you are simply headed for game in opener's major. This way, the enemy has no clue as to the best lead and subsequent defense.

2. **Two of the same major** denies a full opening bid. This also is artificial, and has no bearing on the actual length of opener's major.

   Partner   You   ♠ K Q 10 7
                                ♡ A 8 6
   P   1 ♠   ◇ Q 8 7
   2 ♣   2 ♠   ♣ 10 5 3

   Even with just four spades (permissible in third or fourth seat), you must rebid 2 ♠. Partner will pass or correct to 3 ♣.

3. **Two hearts** (after a 1 ♠ opening) denies a full opening bid and shows at least four hearts. The purpose of this is to reach a superior four-four heart fit in the event that responder also has four hearts.

   Partner   You   ♠ K J 9 7 5
                                ♡ K Q 10 6
   P   1 ♠   ◇ 7 5
   2 ♣   2 ♡   ♣ J 8

   You show four hearts, but still deny a full opening. Partner may pass, or correct to 2 ♠ or 3 ♣.

   NOTE: Opener must restrict himself to one of the above rebids, regardless of his hand. This is to allow responder a chance to clarify his 2 ♣ response at a convenient level.

REBIDS BY RESPONDER

When opener *denies* a full opening bid, responder's rebids are clear-cut; he either passes or places the final contract. Thus, we need be concerned only when opener *confirms* a full opening bid (by rebidding 2 ◇). In that event, responder continues as follows:

1. **Two of opener's major** shows a supporting hand of at most 11 points. This is not forcing.

		You	Partner
♠	A 9 5	P	1 ♡
♡	K Q 4		
◇	Q 8 7 6	2 ♣	2 ◇
♣	8 7 2	2 ♡	

   You show a minimum 2 ♣ response with a heart fit. Even though partner has a full opening, game is still in doubt.

2. **Three clubs** shows a real club suit and denies support for opener's major. This is invitational to game, but not forcing.

		You	Partner
♠	7	P	1 ♠
♡	A 7 3		
◇	K 6 2	2 ♣	2 ◇
♣	Q J 10 9 5 4	3 ♣	

   You show at least six clubs, but no spade fit.

3. **Three of opener's major** shows a supporting hand of at least 12 points. This emphasizes good trumps, and is forcing to game.

		You	Partner
♠	A 4	P	1 ♡
♡	K 9 8 3		
◇	9 8 2	2 ♣	2 ◇
♣	A 7 6 4	3 ♡	

   You are too strong to bid only 2 ♡. Do not jump to 4 ♡, as partner's hand is unlimited and slam is possible.

4. **Any other rebid** is natural and guarantees support for opener's major. This is forcing if below game; but if opener immediately returns to the agreed major, that is not forcing and game may be avoided.

		You	Partner
♠	K 8 3	P	1 ♠
♡	K J 9 5		
◇	A 7 5 2	2 ♣	2 ◇
♣	9 6	2 ♡	

   Your 2 ♡ bid agrees spades by inference, and also shows four hearts in case a four-four heart fit exists.

		You	Partner
♠	Q J 7	P	1 ♡
♡	A 8 2		
◇	K 9 6	2 ♣	2 ◇
♣	Q 10 7 5	2 NT	

   You suggest notrump as the final contract, but still promise a heart fit.

Preemptive Reraises ★ ★

After a single raise by responder, the opening bidder traditionally makes a game try by raising to three of that same suit. This is the standard way, but unfortunately not the best way. Too many times, opener wants to bid three of his suit as a competitive or preemptive gesture but is afraid to, for fear that responder will continue to game.

By adopting "preemptive reraises," you can have your cake, and icing too! It is a very simple understanding, and works as follows:

Reraise to three of the agreed suit (with or without interference) is *not* an invitation to game, but merely a competitive or preemptive bid. Responder should pass.

		You	Partner
♠	7 3		
♡	K Q 9 7 6 5		
◇	A Q 8	1 ♡	2 ♡
♣	10 4	3 ♡	

Your 3 ♡ bid is preemptive. You might pass 2 ♡, but experience has shown that this allows the opponents an easy opportunity to balance.

		You	Opp.	Partner	Opp.
♠	A J 10 9 4				
♡	J 9 3				
◇	4	1 ♠	2 ◇	2 ♠	3 ◇
♣	A Q 8 5	3 ♠			

You are competing; rather than sell out to 3 ◇, you simply wish to try your luck at 3 ♠.

NOTE: If your partnership uses "inverted minor raises" (see page *41*), as we recommend, preemptive reraises do *not* apply after a forcing single minor raise.

HOW TO TRY FOR GAME

When preemptive reraises are used, opener must obviously find some other means of inviting game. One possibility is to bid 2 NT (not forcing) as a natural game try, but most of the time opener will rebid in a different suit. This method is described below:

New-suit rebid (after a single raise) is a game try, and is forcing for one round. Opener typically has *length* (at least three cards) in the suit bid, although not necessarily any strength there.

		You	Partner
♠	A K 10 6 4		
♡	A K 3		
◇	7	1 ♠	2 ♠
♣	9 8 5 2	3 ♣	

Your 3 ♣ bid is a game try in spades, but does not promise a real club suit.

		You	Opp.	Partner	Opp.
♠	A 10 7				
♡	A Q 10 9 7 3				
◇	K 2	1 ♡	2 ♣	2 ♡	3 ♣
♣	9 5	3 ◇			

The enemy bidding has restricted your options, so 3 ◇ is an all-purpose game try in hearts, but otherwise non-descriptive.

After this new-suit trial-bid, responder may (a) bid three of the agreed suit to discourage game; (b) jump to game in the agreed suit; or (c) make any other bid to encourage game. Occasionally, opener's game try will help responder evaluate his hand. For example:

Partner	You		
		♠	J 10 8 6
		♡	9 3
1 ♠	2 ♠	◇	K Q 5
3 ◇	4 ♠	♣	10 6 4 2

Once partner has shown length in diamonds, your mediocre raise has become quite good, so jump to 4 ♠.

EXTENDED APPLICATIONS

The principles of preemptive reraises and new-suit trial-bids are so logical and effective that many partnerships extend them to cover all related situations. We recommend this rule:

After a nonforcing raise to the two-level, or to three of a minor, a reraise is *not* a game try. Any other suit bid is forcing for one round and shows game interest.

Partner	You		
		♠	7
		♡	A J 9 6 3
1 ♣	1 ♡	◇	10 9 4
2 ♡	3 ♡	♣	J 7 4 3

Your 3 ♡ bid is preemptive, hoping to shut out the enemy. To try for game, you must bid 2 ♠, 2 NT, 3 ♣, or 3 ◇.

Opp.	Partner	Opp.	You		
				♠	J 10 8 5 4
				♡	A 6 2
	1 ♣	1 ◇	1 ♠	◇	9 8 3
2 ◇	2 ♠	3 ◇	3 ♠	♣	Q 10

You are competing; you must bid 3 ♡ to try for game.

The defensive side may also employ this rule:

Opp.	Partner	Opp.	You		
				♠	10 9 5
				♡	A 9 3
		1 ♡	2 ♣	◇	3
2 ◇	3 ♣	P	4 ♣	♣	A K Q 10 9 8

Your 4 ♣ bid is not a game try, but a blocking bid to deprive the enemy of bidding room. Perhaps it will give them a problem.

Opp.	Partner	Opp.	You		
				♠	A J 9 8 6 5
				♡	A 9 3
		1 ♡	1 ♠	◇	7
2 ♡	2 ♠	3 ♡	3 ♠	♣	9 8 7

Your 3 ♠ bid is competitive. A game try cannot be made here, unless you adopt the "maximal overcall double" (see page 91).

EXCEPTION: Preemptive reraises are *off* if your side has bid *three* (or more) different denominations. For example:

♠ A J 9 5	**You**	**Partner**
♡ 9 3	1 ♣	1 ♡
◇ K 2	1 ♠	2 ♠
♣ A K 5 4 3	<u>3 ♠</u>	

You are inviting game in spades, just as in standard bidding.

Fourth Suit Forcing ★ ★ ★

Before introducing this convention, let us look at a few commonplace auctions. In each of these sequences, is your jump bid forcing or invitational?

Partner	*You*	*Partner*	*You*
1 ◇	1 ♡	1 ♣	1 ♡
1 ♠	<u>2 NT</u>	1 ♠	<u>3 ♣</u>

Partner	*You*	*Partner*	*You*
1 ♣	1 ◇	1 ◇	1 ♠
1 ♡	<u>3 ♡</u>	2 ♣	<u>3 ♠</u>

Some players consider these bids forcing, others play them invitational, and yet others have individual interpretations for each. One thing is clear; whichever way you treat them, something is lacking. If they are *forcing,* how do you invite game? If they are *invitational,* how do you make a forcing bid?

That is where "fourth-suit forcing" comes in. This convention applies at responder's second bid (assuming his first bid was at the one-level), where the bid of the *fourth* suit is used as an *artificial* forcing bid. NOTE: In standard bidding, the fourth-suit bid by responder is also forcing, but denotes a real suit. Observe these two auctions:

Partner	*You*	*Partner*	*You*
1 ◇	1 ♡	1 ♣	1 ♡
1 ♠	<u>2 ♣</u>	1 ♠	<u>2 ◇</u>

Using this convention, your last bid does not show a real suit. The logic behind this is rather apparent. Once three suits have been bid naturally, the chances of finding a normal trump fit in the fourth suit are exceedingly poor. In contrast, there is often the need for a low-level forcing bid.

There are two schools of thought regarding the use of fourth suit forcing. It may be used as a prelude to making either a game *invitation* or a game *force.* The method you select must be the *opposite* of your interpretation of responder's second-round jump bids (the four sequences at the beginning of this section). We recommend the first school. That is, responder's second-round jump bids are game forcing, and fourth suit forcing is employed primarily on *game-invitational* hands. The complete agreement is explained below:

Fourth-suit bid (at responder's second turn, following a one-over-one response) shows at least *game-invitational* strength. This bid is completely artificial and is forcing for one round.

Partner	You	
		♠ 6 5
		♡ K Q 10 8 6
1 ◇	1 ♡	◇ J 8 3
1 ♠	2 ♣	♣ A J 8

Your 2 ♣ bid is merely a waiting bid. You are interested in game, but not strong enough to jump.

Partner	You	
		♠ A 3
		♡ J 8 7 4
1 ♣	1 ♡	◇ 7 5 3
1 ♠	2 ◇	♣ K Q J 9

You are too strong for 2 ♣ but not strong enough for a forcing jump to 3 ♣, so temporize with 2 ◇.

Partner	You	
		♠ A Q 10 9 8 6
		♡ A 10 3
1 ◇	1 ♠	◇ 4
2 ♣	2 ♡	♣ 10 5 3

You would like to bid "2½ ♠." By using the fourth suit, you will be able to do just that.

Partner	You	
		♠ A J 10 8 3
		♡ Q J 8
1 ♡	1 ♠	◇ Q 9 4
2 ◇	3 ♣	♣ 8 3

In order to invite game in hearts, you must proceed in this roundabout manner.

The fourth-suit-forcing mechanism also comes in handy when responder has game-forcing strength but is unsure of the final denomination. For example:

Partner	You	
		♠ A K 9 8 3
		♡ Q 3
1 ♡	1 ♠	◇ 9 8 2
2 ♣	2 ◇	♣ A J 4

You have the values to reach game, but where? Perhaps partner's next bid will help you.

There is one specific auction in which fourth suit forcing may be used with *less* than game-invitational strength. This occurs when responder holds a real spade suit, and is able to rebid 1 ♠, as follows:

Partner	You	
		♠ A J 7 3
		♡ 9
1 ♣	1 ◇	◇ Q 10 9 7 4
1 ♡	1 ♠	♣ 8 4 2

Your 1 ♠ rebid is still forcing, and might be artificial, but less strength is required when your suit is real.

IN COMPETITION: If either opponent has *bid,* the fourth-suit-forcing convention is *off.* In this event, responder's bid of the fourth suit (although still forcing by an unpassed hand) should show a real suit.

OPENER'S THIRD BID

After the artificial fourth-suit bid, opener's next bid can be very helpful in reaching the best contract. With a *minimum* hand, opener should describe his hand further at the most economical level. This third bid by opener is *not* forcing if it is at or below 2 NT. Here are the possibilities:

1. **Preference to responder's first suit** shows three trumps. This is a very desirable holding, since responder often has five cards in his first suit.

♠	A 9 8 7		*You*	*Partner*
♡	Q 7 3		1 ♣	1 ♡
◇	K 4		1 ♠	2 ◇
♣	K J 8 5		2 ♡	

   You show exactly three hearts, since you would have raised immediately with four.

2. **Rebid of one of your own suits** shows extra length or strength in that suit.

♠	A 10 7 2		*You*	*Partner*
♡	8 3		1 ◇	1 ♡
◇	A K J 6 5		1 ♠	2 ♣
♣	9 5		2 ◇	

   Your 2 ◇ rebid shows at least five diamonds.

   When responder's fourth-suit bid happens to be 3 ♣ (see auction below), a slight modification is required. With a minimum hand, opener may *not* bid beyond 3 ♠. Therefore, a rebid of 3 ◇ may be employed as a "waiting" bid, to allow responder a chance to clarify his intentions. For example:

♠	7		*You*	*Partner*
♡	K J 7 6 5		1 ♡	1 ♠
◇	A Q J 6		2 ◇	3 ♣
♣	J 4 2		3 ◇	

   Your 3 ◇ bid does not promise five-five shape, but is made to keep the bidding low, in case partner intends to invite game with 3 ♡ or 3 ♠ (either of which you will pass).

3. **Raise of the fourth suit** (rare) shows four cards in that suit. This does *not* establish a trump fit, but merely describes opener's hand. If responder next bids any other denomination, he denies interest in playing in the fourth suit.

♠	K J 8 4		*You*	*Partner*
♡	A 10 7 3		1 ♣	1 ◇
◇	3		1 ♡	1 ♠
♣	A 10 8 4		2 ♠	

   You show four spades, but this does not necessarily mean that spades will be trumps.

4. **Two notrump** (or 1 NT over 1 ♠) shows a hand unsuitable for any of the above bids. This usually shows a stopper in the fourth suit, but not necessarily so.

♠	4		*You*	*Partner*
♡	A J 7 4 3		1 ♡	1 ♠
◇	Q 8 7		2 ♣	2 ◇
♣	A Q 4 2		2 NT	

   You have nothing else to say, so bid 2 NT.

If opener has *more* than a minimum hand, the following option is available:

5. **Three notrump or any jump bid** is natural in meaning and promises additional strength. This is forcing to game. EXCEPTION: When responder's fourth-suit bid is 1 ♠, opener's jump bids are invitational to game.

		You	Partner
♠	A 9 7	1 ◇	1 ♠
♡	3	2 ♣	2 ♡
◇	A J 9 7 5	3 ♠	
♣	K Q J 7		

Your jump to 3 ♠ (forcing) shows extra values and, of course, three-card support.

		You	Partner
♠	A K J 7	1 ♣	1 ♡
♡	9	1 ♠	2 ◇
◇	K 9 8	3 NT	
♣	A 10 9 4 3		

You are too strong to rebid just 2 NT.

		You	Partner
♠	A 5	1 ♣	1 ◇
♡	A Q 8 6	1 ♡	1 ♠
◇	3	3 ♣	
♣	K Q J 9 8 7		

Here your jump to 3 ♣ is invitational, since partner's 1 ♠ rebid may be weaker than usual (with a real spade suit).

Opener must *never* jump the bidding beyond 3 NT at his third bid. Thus, it is often necessary to make a minimum rebid at the three-level, even when holding additional strength. This presents no problem, however, since responder is forced to bid again. For example:

		You	Partner
♠	4	1 ♡	1 ♠
♡	A K J 4 3	2 ♣	2 ◇
◇	5 4	3 ♣	
♣	A K J 6 5		

Despite your extra values, it is too awkward to jump the bidding. Your 3 ♣ bid is ambiguous in strength and partner must not pass.

RESPONDER'S THIRD BID

After using the fourth-suit-forcing convention, responder is *not* required to bid again when opener's third bid is at or below 2 NT. The following options are available to responder at his third turn:

1. **Pass** if opener's third bid is the logical final contract.

Partner	You		
1 ◇	1 ♠	♠	A Q 8 5 2
2 ♣	2 ♡	♡	A 4 3
2 NT	P	◇	5 3
		♣	J 5 2

Partner has confirmed a minimum and denied three spades, so your game try has fizzled.

2. **Any minimum bid** is natural and indicates the final denomination. This is invitational if below game.

Partner	You		
		♠	Q 10 6 3
1 ♦	1 ♡	♡	A 9 8 6
1 ♠	2 ♣	♦	8 3
2 ♡	<u>2 ♠</u>	♣	A 10 2

You are inviting game in spades.

Partner	You		
		♠	9 7
1 ♣	1 ♡	♡	K Q J 10 6 3
1 ♠	2 ♦	♦	9 3
2 NT	<u>3 ♡</u>	♣	A 5 2

Your 3 ♡ bid is invitational.

Partner	You		
		♠	A Q 6
1 ♣	1 ♦	♡	9 3
1 ♡	1 ♠	♦	A J 10 8 7
2 ♠	<u>2 NT</u>	♣	10 7 3

You are inviting game in notrump; this also confirms that you do not have four spades.

Partner	You		
		♠	J 5 3
1 ♦	1 ♡	♡	A Q 8 6
2 ♣	2 ♠	♦	K 9 8 7 6
2 NT	<u>3 ♦</u>	♣	4

Your 3 ♦ bid is invitational.

3. **Any jump bid** is natural and forcing (if below game).

Partner	You		
		♠	A K Q 8 7
1 ♡	1 ♠	♡	9 3
2 ♣	2 ♦	♦	9 7 3
2 ♡	<u>3 ♠</u>	♣	A 10 2

Your jump to 3 ♠ is forcing to game.

Partner	You		
		♠	Q J 9 8
1 ♣	1 ♡	♡	A 9 8 7 3
1 ♠	2 ♦	♦	8 3
3 ♣	<u>4 ♠</u>	♣	K 5

You originally planned to invite game in spades, but partner's 3 ♣ rebid has improved your hand.

SHOWING A REAL TWO-SUITER

When fourth suit forcing is adopted, responder must be aware of the proper methods of describing *two-suited* hands (at least five-five shape) containing the fourth suit. These are explained as follows:

1. **With a *weak* two-suiter,** responder may (a) choose from among the available weak rebids; or (b) pass. Do *not* bid the fourth suit.

Partner	You		
		♠	8
		♡	A J 6 4 3
1 ♣	1 ♡	◇	Q 10 9 6 4
1 ♠	1 NT	♣	10 2

Your slightly distorted 1 NT rebid is the most sensible alternative. Do not bid 2 ◇.

2. **With an *invitational* two-suiter,** responder may (a) bid, then rebid, the fourth suit below 3 NT; or (b) bid 2 NT to invite game.

Partner	You		
		♠	A J 10 9 5
1 ♡	1 ♠	♡	3
2 ♣	2 ◇	◇	K Q 9 6 5
2 NT	3 ◇	♣	5 4

Your 3 ◇ rebid is invitational, which blends very well with the normal use of fourth suit forcing.

3. **With a *game-forcing* two-suiter,** responder may (a) jump in the fourth suit below 3 NT; (b) bid, then rebid, the fourth suit above 3 NT; or (c) bid 3 NT to sign off.

Partner	You		
		♠	K J 10 9 7
		♡	A K Q 8 3
1 ◇	1 ♠	◇	3 2
2 ♣	3 ♡	♣	6

You show at least five-five in the majors with enough strength to reach game.

New Minor Forcing ★ ★ ★

In traditional bidding, a new suit rebid by responder is *not* forcing after opener has rebid 1 NT, as in these two auctions:

Partner	You		Partner	You
1 ♣	1 ♡		1 ♡	1 ♠
1 NT	2 ◇		1 NT	2 ♣

Your last bid normally shows a weak two-suited hand, and partner is permitted to pass if he prefers that suit. While this works well on weak two-suiters, it puts a tremendous burden on responder when he holds a better hand. Consequently, most modern experts have some agreement in which the bid of a new *minor* suit is forcing on opener.

Commonly called "new minor forcing," this tool is very much like "fourth suit forcing" (see page *56*) in that it is a convenient forcing bid that may be artificial. Responder is thus able to explore game possibilities without having to jump into the stratosphere. Here is the basic understanding:

Two of a new minor suit (after a 1 NT rebid by opener) may be a short suit, and is forcing for one round. It promises at least game-invitational strength (about 11 or more points), and is most frequently used when responder has a *five*-card major suit, as a means of inquiring about three-card support.

Partner	You		♠ A 8 5
			♡ A K 8 7 3
1 ◇	1 ♡		◇ 9 8 2
1 NT	<u>2 ♣</u>		♣ 8 5

Your 2 ♣ bid serves as a check-back to locate three-card heart support.

Partner	You		♠ K J 9 6 5
			♡ K 3
1 ♡	1 ♠		◇ A Q 7
1 NT	<u>2 ◇</u>		♣ 8 7 2

With a choice of minor suits, prefer to bid the longer or stronger; this suggests a stopper.

New minor forcing is also effective when responder has *five* spades and *four* hearts (after a minor-suit opening). It asks opener for a four-card heart suit, as well as for three-card spade support. Carefully compare the following three examples:

Partner	You		♠ A K 8 7 5
			♡ A Q 9 7
1 ◇	1 ♠		◇ 4
1 NT	<u>2 ♣</u>		♣ J 9 3

You have the strength for game, but first wish to explore for a major-suit fit.
NOTE: *A jump to 3 ♡ is best used to show five-five shape (see page 66).*

Partner	You		♠ A Q 7 4 2
			♡ A J 7 5
1 ♣	1 ♠		◇ 9 4
1 NT	<u>2 ◇</u>		♣ 8 5

With invitational strength, you also go through the check-back procedure.

Partner	You		♠ K J 8 7 5
			♡ Q J 10 5
1 ◇	1 ♠		◇ 8
1 NT	<u>2 ♡</u>		♣ 9 3 2

Here you show a weak hand. Partner should either pass or correct to 2 ♠; only with a superb dummy may partner bid 3 ♡ or 3 ♠.

New minor forcing may also be used as a temporizing bid when responder wishes to *invite* game in his own suit, or in opener's suit. This is the only means of describing such hands of invitational strength, assuming that responder's second-round *jump* bids are forcing (as we recommend). For example:

Partner	You		♠ A 3
			♡ K J 10 9 7 5
1 ♣	1 ♡		◇ 7 5 2
1 NT	<u>2 ◇</u>		♣ Q 8

You are too strong for 2 ♡ but not strong enough for 3 ♡. Therefore, mark time with 2 ◇.

Partner	You		♠ A Q 7 5
			♡ 8 6 3
1 ◇	1 ♠		◇ K J 7 6 5
1 NT	<u>2 ♣</u>		♣ 8

To show an invitational diamond raise you must follow this devious route.

IN COMPETITION: If either opponent has *bid,* the new-minor-forcing convention is *off;* responder's rebid in a new minor (after opener's 1 NT rebid) shows a real suit and is not forcing.

OPENER'S THIRD BID

After the new-minor-forcing bid, opener must further describe his distribution, so as to help responder locate the best contract. In most cases, opener may also indicate whether he holds minimum or maximum strength for his 1 NT rebid. Listed below, in the exact order of *priority,* are the available options from which opener must choose:

1. **Two hearts** (the unbid suit) shows a four-card suit.

		You	Partner
♠	A 3 2	1 ♢	1 ♠
♡	K J 8 5	1 NT	2 ♣
♢	Q 9 8 2	2 ♡	
♣	K 5		

    Showing four hearts is the first priority.

2. **Two or three of responder's major** shows three-card support, and indicates a minimum or maximum, respectively.

		You	Partner
♠	K 7 5	1 ♣	1 ♠
♡	A 7 3	1 NT	2 ♢
♢	K 8 4	2 ♠	
♣	Q J 4 3		

    You show a minimum hand with three spades.

		You	Partner
♠	A 8	1 ♢	1 ♡
♡	Q J 9	1 NT	2 ♣
♢	A 10 7 2	3 ♡	
♣	K 9 6 3		

    You show a maximum hand with three hearts.

3. **Two or three notrump** confirms a stopper in the unbid suit and indicates a minimum or maximum, respectively.

		You	Partner
♠	J 7	1 ♡	1 ♠
♡	A Q 8 5 2	1 NT	2 ♢
♢	J 9 5	2 NT	
♣	A J 4		

    You show a minimum hand with clubs stopped and, of course, deny three spades.

		You	Partner
♠	K 10 6	1 ♢	1 ♡
♡	K 7	1 NT	2 ♣
♢	K 10 7 5	3 NT	
♣	A J 7 2		

    You show a maximum hand with spades stopped.

4. **Rebid of original suit or raise of responder's minor** is natural and denies the ability to make any other rebid.

♠	K 3		You	Partner
♡	K Q 10 8 5		1 ♡	1 ♠
◇	10 7 3		1 NT	2 ♣
♣	A 9 6		<u>2 ♡</u>	

You cannot support spades, or rebid notrump without diamonds stopped, so 2 ♡ is all that remains.

♠	9 8 5		You	Partner
♡	A 6		1 ◇	1 ♡
◇	K J 9 8		1 NT	2 ♣
♣	A Q 6 2		<u>3 ♣</u>	

Your "raise" to 3 ♣ is the only choice; this does not *agree clubs, but just shows that you have four.*

RESPONDER'S THIRD BID

After using new minor forcing, responder need *not* bid again if opener's third bid is at or below 2 NT. The following options are available to responder at his third turn:

1. **Pass** if opener's third bid is the logical final contract.

Partner	You	♠	A J 5 4 3
1 ♣	1 ♠	♡	Q 7 5
1 NT	2 ◇	◇	A 7 5
2 ♠	<u>P</u>	♣	9 7

Partner has confirmed a minimum, and nothing about your hand suggests being aggressive, so pass at a safe level.

Partner	You	♠	A 9 3
1 ◇	1 ♡	♡	K J 8 6 3
1 NT	2 ♣	◇	J 7
2 NT	<u>P</u>	♣	Q 9 7

Partner has shown a minimum without three hearts, so pass and hope you are not already too high.

2. **Any minimum bid** is natural and indicates the final denomination. This is invitational if below game.

Partner	You	♠	A Q 9 7 6 5
1 ◇	1 ♠	♡	9 5
1 NT	2 ♣	◇	7 5
2 NT	<u>3 ♠</u>	♣	A 6 3

Your 3 ♠ bid is invitational.

Partner	You	♠	K Q 8
1 ◇	1 ♡	♡	A 10 8 4 3
1 NT	2 ♣	◇	6 5
2 ◇	<u>2 NT</u>	♣	Q 10 3

You are inviting game in notrump.

Partner	You		♠	7 3 2
1 ♣	1 ♡		♡	K J 6 3
1 NT	2 ◇		◇	7
2 ♡	3 ♣		♣	A Q 9 8 4

You are inviting game in clubs. This implies only a four-card heart suit, since partner has shown three hearts.

Partner	You		♠	A K 7 6 3
1 ♡	1 ♠		♡	Q J 4
1 NT	2 ◇		◇	J 7 3
2 NT	3 ♡		♣	8 4

Your 3 ♡ bid is invitational.

There is one specific situation that requires special treatment. If opener's third bid is 2 ♡ (showing four hearts), responder does not yet know whether opener has three-card spade support. In that event, a 2 ♠ continuation by responder is *forcing* for one round, but still promises only invitational strength. Basically, this is just a check-back for three spades. Observe these auctions:

Partner	You		♠	A Q 6 5 4
1 ◇	1 ♠		♡	A 3
1 NT	2 ♣		◇	J 10 7
2 ♡	2 ♠		♣	7 6 3

Your 2 ♠ rebid shows five spades and is forcing. With a minimum, partner may bid 2 NT or 3 ♠, according to his spade length. With a maximum, he may bid 3 NT or 4 ♠.

Partner	You		♠	A K 6 5 3
1 ♣	1 ♠		♡	9 3
1 NT	2 ◇		◇	9 8
2 ♡	2 ♠		♣	K J 8 3
2 NT	3 ♣			

Your 3 ♣ rebid is not forcing. Partner has denied three spades and shown a minimum, so game appears doubtful.

Partner	You		♠	A 8 7 4
1 ◇	1 ♠		♡	7
1 NT	2 ♣		◇	Q 10 7 5 3
2 ♡	3 ◇		♣	A 9 3

You are inviting game in diamonds (as usual), but deny five spades, since you made no attempt to check back.

3. **Any jump bid** is natural and forcing (if below game).

Partner	You		♠	A K 10 8 5
1 ♡	1 ♠		♡	A 3
1 NT	2 ◇		◇	K 9 6 5
2 ♡	3 ♠		♣	9 5

Your jump to 3 ♠ is forcing. As partner has no club stopper, 3 NT is out. Partner should raise with a doubleton honor (he denied three); otherwise, you will try 4 ♡.

SHOWING A REAL TWO-SUITER

If the new-minor-forcing convention is adopted, responder must know the proper methods of describing *two-suited* hands (at least five-five shape) after opener's 1 NT rebid. These are explained below:

1. **With a *weak* two-suiter,** responder may (a) rebid a reasonably good five-card major; or (b) pass. Do *not* bid a new minor suit. NOTE: With a *major* two-suiter, responder, of course, is able to bid both suits.

Partner	You		
		♠	Q J 10 8 6
		♡	3
1 ◇	1 ♠	◇	7 3
1 NT	2 ♠	♣	K 9 8 5 4

   Your 2 ♠ rebid is a sign-off, and should be a satisfactory, if not ideal, contract.

Partner	You		
		♠	A 10 8 6 3
		♡	Q 9 8 6 3
1 ♣	1 ♠	◇	4
1 NT	2 ♡	♣	J 2

   Here you can show both suits; partner should either pass or correct to 2 ♠.

2. **With an *invitational* two-suiter,** responder should bid a new minor, even when holding both majors! Then on the next round, responder may bid his second suit (unless opener's third bid has indicated an obvious final contract).

Partner	You		
		♠	8 5
1 ◇	1 ♡	♡	A Q 10 7 4
1 NT	2 ♣	◇	5
2 NT	3 ♣	♣	K J 7 5 3

   Your 3 ♣ rebid is natural and invitational.

Partner	You		
		♠	Q J 9 8 7
1 ♣	1 ♠	♡	Q 10 8 7 4
1 NT	2 ◇	◇	A 3
2 NT	3 ♡	♣	8

   This clever maneuver invites game. Notice that you had to bid 2 ◇ over 1 NT, since 2 ♡ would show a weak two-suiter.

3. **With a *game-forcing* two-suiter,** responder should *jump* in his second suit.

Partner	You		
		♠	K J 9 7 5
		♡	6
1 ♡	1 ♠	◇	A K Q 7 3
1 NT	3 ◇	♣	8 3

   Your jump to 3 ◇ is natural and forcing to game.

3

Interference after One of a Suit

♣　　♦　　♥　　♠　　♣　　♦　　♥　　♠

In this third chapter, we are still concerned with auctions beginning with an opening bid of one of a suit by *your* side. The conventions herein are those that can occur *only* when the enemy interferes with your bidding. That is, we will be working strictly with competitive auctions.

In this chapter:

Negative Doubles

Truscott Two Notrump
(over an enemy takeout double)
with
New suit forcing at the one-level
and the Redouble

Limit Bidding after an Enemy Overcall

Eastern Cue-Bid
with
Eastern 3 NT bid

Invisible Cue-Bids
with
Invisible splinter bids

Competitive Doubles

Maximal Overcall Double

Negative Doubles ★

Based on the original "Sputnik," as devised by Alvin Roth of New York City, one of the world's greatest players and foremost bridge theoreticians

When partner's opening bid is overcalled by an opponent, a double by responder is for penalty in standard methods. This is simple and playable, but hardly an efficient use of the double. Thus, the "negative double" was born. The negative double is just another form of the takeout double, and is used by practically all of the better players today. Here is the basic understanding:

After a suit overcall of partner's one-level suit opening, an immediate double (through 4 ◇) is for takeout. The strength required is at least 7 points at the one- or two-level, or at least 9 points at the three- or four-level. In any case, there is no upper limit on strength.

NOTE: The level of 4 ◇ is an arbitrary limit, which we recommend. However, some partnerships prefer a lower limit, such as 3 ◇ or 3 ♠.

The distributional requirements for a negative double are somewhat controversial, but we suggest the following agreements:

1. **If there is exactly one unbid major,** doubler promises at least four cards in that major.

2. **If there are two unbid majors,** doubler promises at least four cards in one of the majors. EXCEPTION: After a 1 ◇ overcall of partner's 1 ♣ opening, a negative double shows at least four cards in each major.

3. **If both majors have been bid,** doubler promises at least four cards in each minor suit.

Now let's look at some examples:

Partner	Opp.	You		
			♠	A 3
			♡	K 9 8 5
1 ♣	1 ♠	DBL	◇	10 9 4 3
			♣	9 7 5

Your double guarantees four hearts.

Partner	Opp.	You		
			♠	A J 8 4
			♡	9 3
1 ◇	2 ♣	DBL	◇	K 10 8 7
			♣	5 4 3

You promise only one major here; but if that is the case, you should have a diamond fit (as above), or a stronger hand, to avoid later problems.

Partner	Opp.	You		
			♠	10 2
			♡	9 3
1 ♠	2 ♡	DBL	◇	K J 8 7
			♣	A 10 9 5 4

Here you show both minors.

Partner	Opp.	You		
			♠	K 10 5 3
			♡	A 3
1 ♣	1 ♡	DBL	♢	A K J 2
			♣	10 4 2

Obviously, you will reach game with this hand, and the negative double to show four spades is the right first step.

Partner	Opp.	You		
			♠	5
			♡	A 9 7 5 4
1 ♢	2 ♠	DBL	♢	K J 4
			♣	10 7 5 2

A negative double with a five-card major is perfectly all right when you are not strong enough to bid your suit.

Partner	Opp.	You		
			♠	K Q 10 3
			♡	J 5
1 ♡	3 ♢	DBL	♢	4 3
			♣	A 9 8 4 2

At the higher levels, the principle is the same; here you show four spades.

The primary function of the negative double is to locate a four-four major-suit fit, which can otherwise be difficult in a competitive auction. Therefore, when responder *bids* a major (instead of doubling), he promises at least a five-card suit, except after a 1 ♢ overcall. Witness these examples:

Partner	Opp.	You		
			♠	A 9 8 5 2
			♡	8 3
1 ♣	1 ♡	1 ♠	♢	K 7 2
			♣	10 7 3

You promise at least five spades, since you would double with just four.

Partner	Opp.	You		
			♠	A 7 3
			♡	K J 9 4 3
1 ♣	2 ♢	2 ♡	♢	4 3
			♣	Q J 8

Here you show at least five hearts.

Partner	Opp.	You		
			♠	K J 8 5
			♡	4 3
1 ♣	1 ♢	1 ♠	♢	K 10 2
			♣	J 8 6 5

This is the exception; a double would show both majors, so your 1 ♠ (or 1 ♡) bid may be just four cards.

REBIDS BY OPENER

After a negative double, opener should strive to bid a new suit, especially an unbid major suit. There are no "reverse" bid restrictions; with a minimum hand, opener simply bids the suit he wants to bid, regardless of the level necessary. Here are the meanings of opener's rebids:

1. **Any minimum bid** (below game) is natural and indicates a minimum opening bid (up to about 15 points). This is not forcing, and often ends the bidding.

	You	Opp.	Partner	Opp.
♠ A 4 3				
♡ K J 4 3				
♢ 10 7 3	1 ♣	1 ♠	DBL	P
♣ K Q 8	2 ♡			

You are just supporting partner's promised major.

	You	Opp.	Partner	Opp.
♠ A J 8 3				
♡ 4 3				
♢ A J 10 4 3	1 ♢	1 ♠	DBL	P
♣ K 4	1 NT			

Your 1 NT rebid is far superior to 2 ♢, since partner must have the heart suit protected.

On rare occasions, opener may even rebid in a strong *three*-card suit (preferably a major), when faced with unattractive alternatives. For example:

	You	Opp.	Partner	Opp.
♠ A Q 8				
♡ 9 2				
♢ Q 8 7 5 2	1 ♢	2 ♡	DBL	P
♣ A J 3	2 ♠			

Partner has promised four spades, so the known four-three spade fit offers more security than venturing into 3 ♢.

2. **Any jump bid** is natural and shows about 16 to 18 points. This is *not* forcing, but invitational if below game.

	You	Opp.	Partner	Opp.
♠ K 4				
♡ K J 5 4				
♢ A K J 9 5	1 ♢	2 ♣	DBL	P
♣ 6 5	3 ♡			

You must jump to 3 ♡ to show your extra values.

	You	Opp.	Partner	Opp.
♠ 10 4				
♡ K Q 9				
♢ K 3	1 ♣	2 ♡	DBL	P
♣ A K J 5 4 3	3 NT			

Your jump to 3 NT is the logical choice. Notice that you cannot bid just 2 NT, as that would indicate a minimum.

3. **Cue-bid of the enemy suit** (two- or three-level) shows about 19 or more points and is forcing to game. This bid has no relation to your holding in the enemy suit. All further bidding is natural.

	You	Opp.	Partner	Opp.
♠ A K 3				
♡ 4 3				
♢ A 9	1 ♣	1 ♡	DBL	P
♣ A Q J 10 8 6	2 ♡			

Your 2 ♡ cue-bid simply creates a game force; you are too strong for a 3 ♣ rebid.

4. **Pass** (rare) converts the negative double into penalty. At the one-level, this is almost unheard of; but at the two-level, opener may pass with at least four good trumps. At the higher levels, opener may judge to pass with lesser trump holdings if his hand is relatively balanced and the alternatives are unattractive.

```
♠  3                          You    Opp.    Partner    Opp.
♡  A J 6 4 3
◇  K Q 10 8                   1 ♡    2 ◇     DBL        P
♣  A 6 3                      P
```

You should be able to defeat 2 ◇, perhaps severely, so the penalty pass stands out.

```
♠  A J 6                      You    Opp.    Partner    Opp.
♡  K 9 5
◇  A 10 9 5                   1 ◇    4 ♣     DBL        P
♣  J 4 2                      P
```

Despite your poor trumps, passing is the only sensible action at this level; however, with a four-card major, tend to bid.

REBIDS BY NEGATIVE DOUBLER

After making a negative double, responder is *not* obliged to bid again (unless opener has cue-bid the enemy suit). If responder is content with opener's rebid or the enemy contract, he may certainly pass. If responder does bid again, the following meanings apply:

1. **One notrump, new suit, or simple preference** is natural and indicates a maximum of 10 points. This is not forcing.

```
Opp.    Partner    Opp.    You          ♠  9 4
                                        ♡  3
        1 ♡        1 ♠     DBL          ◇  K Q 10 5
P       1 NT       P       2 ♣          ♣  K 10 9 6 5 4
```

Having shown both minors, you now indicate longer clubs and the desire to sign off in 2 ♣.

```
Opp.    Partner    Opp.    You          ♠  K 9 6 3
                                        ♡  A 4
        1 ◇        2 ♣     DBL          ◇  J 10 8 4
P       2 ♡        P       3 ◇          ♣  7 4 3
```

You were hoping partner could bid spades; but, failing that, all you can do is give a preference back to 3 ◇.

2. **Two notrump, single raise, or jump preference** is natural and shows 11 or 12 (or a good 10) points. This is invitational if below game, but *not* forcing.

```
Opp.    Partner    Opp.    You          ♠  K J 9 5
                                        ♡  10 2
        1 ♡        2 ♣     DBL          ◇  Q 10 9 2
P       2 ♡        P       2 NT         ♣  A J 7
```

Your 2 NT bid is invitational.

```
Opp.    Partner    Opp.    You          ♠  10 3
                                        ♡  A J 8 5
        1 ♣        1 ♠     DBL          ◇  K 9 7 3 2
P       2 ♡        P       3 ♡          ♣  Q 10
```

You are inviting game in hearts, just as your bidding sounds.

Opp.	Partner	Opp.	You	♠ A 9 7 5
				♡ 9 8
	1 ◇	1 ♡	DBL	◇ K Q 8 6
P	2 ♣	P	3 ◇	♣ Q 9 2

Your 3 ◇ bid is invitational.

3. **Cue-bid of the enemy suit** (two- or three-level) shows at least 13 points and is forcing to game. As usual, this bid has no relation to your holding in the enemy suit. All further bidding is natural.

Opp.	Partner	Opp.	You	♠ K 5
				♡ A Q 8 4
	1 ◇	2 ♣	DBL	◇ K J 10 3
P	2 ♠	P	3 ♣	♣ 5 4 2

You will eventually reach game, but at this stage, you are not sure where. Perhaps partner's next bid will help you.

4. **Any game bid** is, obviously, a natural sign-off attempt.

PENALIZING THE ENEMY

It may seem that the use of negative doubles prevents responder from "wielding the ax" when an opponent steps into trouble. For example, say the bidding proceeds as follows:

Partner	Opp.	You	♠ 7 3
			♡ A 5 2
1 ◇	2 ♣	?	◇ 4 3 2
			♣ K Q 10 8 4

You would like to double 2 ♣ for penalty, then head for the bank, but alas, you are playing negative doubles!

Can the opponents get away with this? Usually not. When responder has a normal penalty double of overcaller's suit, he should *pass,* even with a very good hand. To compensate for this, opener must cooperate as follows:

If an enemy suit overcall is followed by two passes, opener should make every effort to reopen the bidding, preferably with a *double,* if he holds a doubleton or fewer cards in the enemy suit. This does *not* require additional strength.

♠ A J 6 4	You	Opp.	Partner	Opp.
♡ K 8 3				
◇ K J 7 6 5	1 ◇	2 ♣	P	P
♣ 3	DBL			

Your double is for takeout, but it allows partner to pass if he has a hand like the previous example.

♠ A 7 3	You	Opp.	Partner	Opp.
♡ —				
◇ K Q J 8 7 6	1 ◇	1 ♡	P	P
♣ J 8 5 4	2 ◇			

Your heart void and minimal defense make it unattractive to double, but you should still reopen with 2 ◇.

```
    ♠  A J 8 5            You     Opp.    Partner    Opp.
    ♡  K 7
    ◇  J 10 3             1 ♣     1 ♠      P         P
    ♣  K Q 5 4            P
```

In view of your spade length, partner could hardly have trap passed over 1 ♠.
He passed because he had nothing, so it is time to give up.

After a *jump* overcall, opener must be slightly more cautious about reopening the bidding due to the increased level. The pros and cons of each situation must be carefully weighed. Here is an example:

```
    ♠  A J 9 3            You     Opp.    Partner    Opp.
    ♡  3
    ◇  A K 9 5            1 ◇     3 ♡      P         P
    ♣  J 6 5 3            DBL
```

Your ideal shape makes this double desirable, but change a small spade to a
heart, and you should pass.

Truscott Two Notrump

Introduced to America by Alan Truscott of New York City, a leading
expert and bridge editor of the New York Times. *This convention was*
popularized by Robert Jordan of suburban Cincinnati, Ohio, and has
thus also come to be known as "Jordan."

The "Truscott 2 NT" convention is a very useful understanding after a *takeout double* of partner's opening bid of one of a suit. Essentially, it hinges on the use of a 2 NT bid, which is otherwise meaningless, to indicate a "limit raise" of opener's suit. After a double of a *major*-suit opening, the following two agreements apply:

1. **Two notrump** shows a *raise* of 10 to 12 points with at least four trumps (rarely, three good trumps) and is, obviously, forcing to at least three of opener's major.

```
    Partner    Opp.    You          ♠  4 3
                                     ♡  K J 7 5
     1 ♡       DBL     2 NT          ◇  A 9 8 2
                                     ♣  J 10 3
```

You show a limit raise in hearts.

After the 2 NT bid, opener may (a) sign off in three or four of his major; or (b) bid a new suit to try for game or slam. For example:

```
    ♠  Q J 5             You     Opp.    Partner    Opp.
    ♡  A Q 8 6 3
    ◇  7 3               1 ♡     DBL      2 NT       P
    ♣  K Q 7             3 ♣
```

Your 3 ♣ bid is a game try and forcing. With the previous example hand,
partner should reject by bidding 3 ♡.

2. **Jump raise** shows 6 to 9 points, typically with four trumps. It denies the ability to bid 2 NT, and is basically preemptive.

Partner	Opp.	You
1 ♠	DBL	3 ♠

♠ K 6 5 3
♡ 7 4 2
♢ 7
♣ J 7 6 5 3

Your 3 ♠ raise is no stronger than a 2 ♠ raise, but indicates better trump support.

NOTE: To show a *forcing* major raise, we recommend "splinter bids" (see page *31*) and the "3 NT balanced forcing raise" (see page *32*). If adopted, these methods apply equally well after an enemy takeout double.

MINOR-SUIT VARIATION

The Truscott convention may also be applied to minor suits, but in a slightly different way. It is undesirable to employ the 2 NT bid artificially, because of the inherent danger of reaching 3 NT from the wrong side. Of the several variations in use, we recommend the following three agreements after a takeout double of a *minor*-suit opening:

1. **Two notrump** is *natural* and shows about 9 to 11 high card points, but based on at least four cards (typically, five or six cards) in opener's minor. This denies a four-card or longer major, and is invitational to game. It is *not* forcing.

Partner	Opp.	You
1 ♢	DBL	2 NT

♠ K 4
♡ K Q 5
♢ Q 10 7 5 3
♣ 10 6 2

Your 2 NT bid invites 3 NT, but guarantees a diamond fit. With a minimum, partner may pass or sign off in 3 ♢.

2. **Three notrump** is like 2 NT, but shows about 12 to 14 high-card points.

Partner	Opp.	You
1 ♣	DBL	3 NT

♠ Q 9 5
♡ K 10
♢ A 7 3
♣ K 8 5 4 2

Your club fit and scattered stoppers strongly suggest that 3 NT will be the right contract, so bid it.

3. **Jump raise** shows about 6 to 9 points, at least five trumps (or four good trumps), and is not forcing. It is basically preemptive.

Partner	Opp.	You
1 ♣	DBL	3 ♣

♠ 8 6 3
♡ 7
♢ Q 8 7 2
♣ Q 10 8 4 2

You are hoping to shut out the opponents, or at least give them a problem.

NOTE: We also recommend that you adopt "inverted minor raises" (see page *41*), in which case, a *single* minor raise would be forcing, even after a takeout double.

NEW SUIT FORCING AT THE ONE-LEVEL

Although it is not actually a part of the Truscott convention, most experts realize the advantage in playing that a new suit response after an enemy takeout double is *forcing* at the one-level. To be sure, the bidding rarely dies there anyway, so it makes a lot of sense to allow greater freedom in responding. We suggest this understanding:

New suit at the one-level is the same as if the takeout double had not occurred. This response is *unlimited* and forcing for one round (by an unpassed hand), and the auction proceeds as in your normal methods.

Partner	Opp.	You	
			♠ 9 3
			♡ K J 5 3
1 ♣	DBL	1 ♡	♢ A 6 4
			♣ K 9 8 6

It would be imprudent to redouble, as enemy spade bids may prevent you from showing your heart suit.

Partner	Opp.	You	
			♠ A J 10 8 6
			♡ 7
1 ♢	DBL	1 ♠	♢ 9 8
			♣ K Q 10 7 4

You would like to show both of your suits, so don't waste time with a redouble.

NOTE: Remember, this applies only at the *one*-level. A new suit at the two-level is *not* forcing over an enemy takeout double.

THE REDOUBLE

Because of the availability of the previously described fit-showing bids, and the opportunity to make a forcing bid at the one-level, the *redouble* of an enemy takeout double takes on a different perspective, as follows:

Redouble shows at least 10 high-card points, and suggests a defensively oriented hand. This creates a "forcing" auction; i.e., your side must either outbid or double the enemy.

Partner	Opp.	You	
			♠ 7 3
			♡ A J 8 6
1 ♠	DBL	RDBL	♢ Q 10 7
			♣ K 9 8 7

A classic redouble; your main interest is in defense (penalizing the enemy) rather than offense.

Partner	Opp.	You	
			♠ A J 8 3
			♡ J 7 4
1 ♡	DBL	RDBL	♢ K Q 5 2
			♣ 9 7

With just three-card heart support, the redouble, followed by a later heart raise, is preferable to a bid of 2 NT.

Partner	Opp.	You	
			♠ K 8 6
			♡ Q 9 8 2
1 ♣	DBL	RDBL	♢ K 8 5
			♣ A 10 8

The balanced, undistinguished nature of this hand makes a redouble more desirable than a 1 ♡ bid.

Partner	Opp.	You	♠ 9
			♡ 10 8 3
1 ♢	DBL	RDBL	♢ K 8 2
			♣ A K J 10 8 4

A 2 ♣ response would not *be forcing, so the redouble is necessary, despite its awkward appearance.*

Limit Bidding after an Enemy Overcall ★ ★

After an opponent's overcall of partner's opening bid of one of a suit, responder occasionally is faced with an awkward bidding problem. For example, how would you bid the following hand?

Partner	Opp.	You	♠ A 6 3
			♡ A J 8 2
1 ♢	1 ♡	?	♢ 10 8 5
			♣ Q 9 6

A response of 1 NT is a distinct underbid, yet you are not strong enough for a forcing jump to 2 NT. Perhaps you should temporize with 2 ♣, but you must admit that would be very peculiar bidding. Partner may raise to 3 ♣, and there you are, forced to play 3 NT anyway.

The point we are trying to make is that some adjustment is necessary in your bidding strategy to cope successfully with enemy interference. Essentially, this involves changing from a "forcing" style to a "limit" style of bidding. After an enemy *overcall* of partner's opening bid of one of a suit, the following two agreements apply:

1. **Jump to 2 NT** shows 11 or 12 (or a very good 10) points, and is invitational to game. This simply shows a hand that is too strong for a 1 NT response.

Partner	Opp.	You	♠ A 6 3
			♡ A J 8 2
1 ♢	1 ♡	2 NT	♢ 10 8 5
			♣ Q 9 6

The original problem is now easily solved with the limit jump to 2 NT. Partner should pass with a bare minimum opening.

Partner	Opp.	You	♠ K 10 7
			♡ 9 8 5
1 ♣	1 ♠	2 NT	♢ K 8
			♣ A 9 8 6 5

Here your excellent club fit allows you to bid 2 NT with just 10 points.

2. **Jump raise** shows 11 or 12 (or a very good 10) points, and is invitational to game. EXCEPTION: If you use "inverted minor raises" (see page *41*), as we recommend, this agreement does *not* apply in the minor suits.

Partner	Opp.	You	♠ A 8 5 3
			♡ K 10 2
1 ♠	2 ♢	3 ♠	♢ 9 6
			♣ K 9 4 3

Your jump to 3 ♠ is a limit raise. Of course, if you play "limit major raises" (see page 31), this is true with or without interference.

Partner	Opp.	You		
			♠	A 6 2
			♡	10 5 4
1 ♡	1 ♠	3 ♡	♢	A J 9 7
			♣	Q 10 3

The competitive limit major raise does not require four trumps; any three will do.

When responder has the values to make a *forcing* raise or notrump bid, he must obviously find some other response. This usually presents no problem, as with stronger hands there is less concern about getting too high. Among the options available, responder may (a) temporize by bidding a new suit; (b) jump to 3 NT; or (c) cue-bid the enemy suit. NOTE: To improve your methods in this area, we recommend the "Eastern cue-bid" (see page *79*).

SECOND-ROUND JUMP BIDS

The foregoing principles should also be extended to responder's *second* bid. If either opponent has *bid*, and responder has made a *one*-level suit response, the following agreement applies:

Second-round jump bids in notrump or previously bid suits are natural and invitational to game, but *not* forcing.

Opp.	Partner	Opp.	You		
				♠	9 4
				♡	A Q 9 5
	1 ♣	1 ♢	1 ♡	♢	K 10 4 2
P	1 ♠	P	2 NT	♣	Q 9 5

You are inviting game in notrump.

Opp.	Partner	Opp.	You		
				♠	6 3
				♡	J 10 9 6
	1 ♢	P	1 ♡	♢	K Q 10 5
1 ♠	2 ♣	P	3 ♢	♣	K J 3

Your 3 ♢ bid is invitational.

Opp.	Partner	Opp.	You		
				♠	K Q J 9 8 5
				♡	8 3
	1 ♣	1 ♡	1 ♠	♢	A 9 6
2 ♡	P	P	3 ♠	♣	10 2

You are inviting game in spades.

Opp.	Partner	Opp.	You		
				♠	K 9 7 4
				♡	6 4
	1 ♣	P	1 ♢	♢	A Q 9 8 3
1 ♡	1 ♠	P	3 ♠	♣	4 3

Your 3 ♠ bid is invitational.

To *force* the bidding on the second round, responder may (a) bid a new suit, which is forcing for *one* round; or (b) cue-bid the enemy suit, which is forcing to game. Witness these examples:

Opp.	Partner	Opp.	You		
				♠	A Q 9 8 4
				♡	5 4
	1 ♣	1 ♡	1 ♠	◇	A J 9 6
P	2 ♣	P	2 ◇	♣	6 5

Your 2 ◇ rebid is natural and forcing for one round.

Opp.	Partner	Opp.	You		
				♠	A Q 10 9 6 5
				♡	8
	1 ◇	1 ♡	1 ♠	◇	A 7 3
P	2 ♣	P	2 ♡	♣	Q J 2

You are too strong for a limit jump to 3 ♠. Your 2 ♡ cue-bid creates a game force, and you can repeat your spades later.

Opp.	Partner	Opp.	You		
				♠	A 9 4
				♡	K Q 10 8 4
	1 ♣	P	1 ♡	◇	10 3
2 ◇	P	P	3 ◇	♣	A J 2

Your 3 ◇ cue-bid has no relation to your diamond holding, but merely guarantees the values to reach game.

TWO-OVER-ONE RESPONSES

Without interference, many players have high standards for a new suit response at the two-level, especially after a major-suit opening when the "1 NT forcing" convention is played (see page *33*). With that, we entirely agree. Unfortunately, however, it is not practical to impose that same strategy after enemy interference. There are just too many borderline hands on which an immediate response is best. Consequently, we suggest this agreement after an enemy suit *overcall* of partner's opening bid of one of a suit:

Two-over-one response may be made with as few as 9 or 10 points, provided a good five-card or longer suit is held. This is forcing for only *one* round, and does not promise a rebid.

Partner	Opp.	You		
			♠	7 6 4
			♡	10 2
1 ♡	1 ♠	2 ♣	◇	K 10 7
			♣	K Q J 9 7

Without the 1 ♠ overcall, you would respond 1 NT, but that is lunacy now. Bid 2 ♣ to show your good suit.

Partner	Opp.	You		
			♠	A 3
			♡	K J 10 8 4
1 ◇	2 ♣	2 ♡	◇	10 9 5 4
			♣	4 2

Your diamond fit makes this hand well worth a 2 ♡ response.

To compensate for these lower standards, opener must make certain adjustments in his rebidding tactics. Opener may (a) bid 2 NT; (b) raise responder's suit; or (c) rebid his original suit, each of which confirms a minimum opening and is not forcing. To force the bidding, opener may (d) bid a new suit, which is ambiguous in strength and forcing for one round; or (e) jump the bidding; or (f) cue-bid the enemy suit, either of which is forcing to game. Here are two examples:

	You	Opp.	Partner	Opp.
♠ K 10 2				
♡ A J 9 8 3				
◇ A 9 8	1 ♡	1 ♠	2 ♣	P
♣ 10 3	2 NT			

Your 2 NT rebid shows minimum values and is not forcing. The same would be true had you rebid 2 ♡ or 3 ♣.

	You	Opp.	Partner	Opp.
♠ A 3				
♡ 5 2				
◇ A Q 6	1 ♣	1 ♡	2 ◇	P
♣ K Q J 7 6 2	2 ♡			

You are too strong for a simple 3 ♣ or 3 ◇ bid, so cue-bid 2 ♡ to create a game force.

Responder's rebids after the two-over-one response follow identical strategy. He may (a) bid 2 NT; (b) raise opener's suit or give a preference; or (c) rebid his original suit, each of which is not forcing. Responder may also (d) bid a new suit; (e) jump the bidding; or (f) cue-bid the enemy suit, each of which is forcing to game. For example:

Opp.	Partner	Opp.	You	
				♠ 4 3
				♡ K Q 10 8 3
	1 ◇	2 ♣	2 ♡	◇ 10 4 2
P	2 ♠	P	2 NT	♣ A J 7

Your 2 NT rebid invites game, but is not forcing.

Opp.	Partner	Opp.	You	
				♠ A Q J 9 3
				♡ Q 4
	1 ♡	2 ◇	2 ♠	◇ 7 4 3
P	3 ♣	P	3 ♡	♣ J 5 2

Your simple preference to 3 ♡ is not encouraging. Partner should pass with a minimum opening.

Eastern Cue-Bid ★ ★ ★

Based on the ideas of Alvin Roth, and other scientific bidding theoreticians·

Prerequisites:
NEGATIVE DOUBLES
LIMIT BIDDING AFTER AN ENEMY OVERCALL

After an overcall of partner's opening bid of one of a suit, advocates of limit jump responses must find an alternate means of describing game-going hands. Often responder must choose between a misleading temporizing bid and an awkward jump to game. Either way, there is ambiguity. The "Eastern cue-bid," so named to contrast with the "Western cue-bid" (see Glossary), provides an effective solution to this problem. Here is how it works:

Immediate cue-bid (of a natural suit overcall through 2 ♠) shows 13 to 16 points (or more), a stopper in the enemy suit, and a balanced hand. More specifically, this indicates either a "forcing 2 NT" response with no unbid four-card major, or a "forcing raise" with control (ace or king) of the enemy suit.

Partner	Opp.	You		♠ K 5 4
				♡ A 8 6
1 ♢	1 ♠	2 ♠		♢ K J 3
				♣ A 9 8 2

Without the overcall, you would respond 2 NT, but that would be invitational in competition.

Partner	Opp.	You		♠ A 5
				♡ K J 7
1 ♠	2 ♣	3 ♣		♢ K J 9 8
				♣ Q 8 4 3

Your eye is on 3 NT, of course, but there is an advantage in allowing partner to become declarer.

Partner	Opp.	You		♠ K Q 4
				♡ K J 9 6
1 ♡	2 ♢	3 ♢		♢ A 8 6 3
				♣ 10 7

Your cue-bid is the first step toward showing a forcing heart raise with diamond control.

REBIDS BY OPENER

After the Eastern cue-bid, opener should assume that responder has made a forcing 2 NT bid. It is unnecessary to introduce an unbid four-card major, as responder would have made a negative double if interested in locating one. Opener should strive to make himself declarer in notrump whenever sensible, in order to put the overcaller on lead (often worth an extra trick in the play). Here are the meanings of opener's rebids:

1. **Minimum notrump bid** shows a maximum of about 15 or 16 points, and suggests a relatively balanced hand (no void or small singleton, although a singleton honor is quite permissible). Opener does *not* require a stopper in the enemy suit.

♠ A 8	You	Opp.	Partner	Opp.
♡ 10 5 3				
♢ A Q 8 5	1 ♢	1 ♡	2 ♡	P
♣ K 9 7 2	2 NT			

Partner has promised a heart stopper, so you do not need one.

♠ K Q 10 7 5	You	Opp.	Partner	Opp.
♡ A K J 2				
♢ 10 3	1 ♠	2 ♣	3 ♣	P
♣ J 8	3 NT			

There is no point in showing your heart suit, since partner did not make a negative double.

2. **Jump to 3 NT** is similar to above, but shows 16 or 17 points.

♠ K 4	You	Opp.	Partner	Opp.
♡ A J 8 7 5				
♢ K J	1 ♡	1 ♠	2 ♠	P
♣ A 9 8 2	3 NT			

You show extra values by jumping.

If opener is unable to jump to 3 NT, a further cue-bid of the enemy suit may be employed to show the same strength. For example:

	You	Opp.	Partner	Opp.
♠ A K J 7 6				
♡ 10 3				
◇ A K 4	1 ♠	2 ♡	3 ♡	P
♣ J 10 8	4 ♡			

Your 4 ♡ cue-bid shows 16 or 17 points. Partner can still sign off in 4 ♠ or 4 NT.

3. **Jump to 4 NT** shows 18 or 19 points. This is *not* Blackwood, but merely shows a stronger hand than the preceding notrump bids.

	You	Opp.	Partner	Opp.
♠ A 10 3				
♡ K 9 6				
◇ Q 8 7	1 ♣	2 ◇	3 ◇	P
♣ A K Q 10	4 NT			

Your 4 NT bid is a quantitative invitation to 6 NT.

4. **New suit or rebid of original suit** is natural and indicates an unbalanced hand.

	You	Opp.	Partner	Opp.
♠ A K J 6 5				
♡ 9 5				
◇ K J 9 7 4	1 ♠	2 ♣	3 ♣	P
♣ 5	3 ◇			

You have a pronounced two-suiter, so show it.

	You	Opp.	Partner	Opp.
♠ A 7 5				
♡ 2				
◇ A 10 7	1 ♣	1 ♡	2 ♡	P
♣ K J 10 8 7 4	3 ♣			

Although 3 NT may be the proper contract, you do not wish to become declarer with a small singleton heart.

	You	Opp.	Partner	Opp.
♠ 9 4				
♡ A K 10 4				
◇ A 5	1 ♣	1 ♠	2 ♠	P
♣ K Q 10 8 4	3 ♡			

Partner has denied four hearts, but your extra strength and consequent slam potential make it desirable to describe your shape.

NOTE: If the Eastern cue-bid is *doubled,* opener may, in addition to the previous options, pass with nothing useful to say. This will enable responder to become declarer in notrump to protect his stopper.

REBIDS BY CUE-BIDDER

After using the Eastern cue-bid, responder must bid again unless game has been reached. The meanings of responder's rebids are based on the premise that he has *already* bid notrump, even though, in fact, he hasn't. The possibilities are described here:

1. **Any notrump bid** (including 4 NT) is natural, irrespective of opener's rebid. In other words, Blackwood cannot be used immediately after the Eastern cue-bid.

Opp.	Partner	Opp.	You
	1 ◇	1 ♠	2 ♠
P	2 NT	P	<u>3 NT</u>

♠ A 8 4
♡ K 9 2
◇ K 10 3
♣ Q J 10 5

You are simply closing out the bidding.

Opp.	Partner	Opp.	You
	1 ♠	2 ♡	3 ♡
P	4 ◇	P	<u>4 NT</u>

♠ 6 5
♡ A Q J
◇ J 8 7 6
♣ K Q J 7

Your 4 NT bid is not Blackwood, but a natural denial of interest in partner's suits. It is not forcing.

Opp.	Partner	Opp.	You
	1 ♡	2 ♣	3 ♣
P	3 NT	P	<u>4 NT</u>

♠ K Q 5
♡ Q 7 3
◇ A K 7 5
♣ K J 10

Here you would pass 3 NT with interest only in game, so your 4 NT bid is a quantitative slam invitation showing about 17 or 18 points.

2. **Raise or preference** (in a suit bid by opener) shows support for that suit. Furthermore, if this action follows any notrump bid by opener, responder confirms *control* (ace or king) of the enemy suit.

Opp.	Partner	Opp.	You
	1 ♠	2 ♣	3 ♣
P	3 NT	P	<u>4 ♠</u>

♠ Q J 8 7
♡ A K 7
◇ 10 9 7 3
♣ K 8

Your 4 ♠ bid is clearly voluntary, so you show an original "forcing raise" with the ace or king of clubs.

Opp.	Partner	Opp.	You
	1 ♡	1 ♠	2 ♠
P	3 ◇	P	<u>3 ♡</u>

♠ Q J 9
♡ J 7 3
◇ K Q 8
♣ A 10 9 5

Here you do not promise spade control, since your 3 ♡ bid is a simple preference (it did not follow a notrump bid by opener).

3. **Any new-suit (or enemy-suit) bid** is a *cue-bid* and shows trump support for a suit bid by opener. This is a slam try and suggests about 16 or more points.

Opp.	Partner	Opp.	You
	1 ♡	2 ◇	3 ◇
P	3 NT	P	<u>4 ♣</u>

♠ A J 8
♡ K 9 8 5 3
◇ K 7 6
♣ A 8

Your bidding shows the ace of clubs, a good heart fit, and the ace or king of diamonds.

Opp.	Partner	Opp.	You
	1 ♣	1 ♠	2 ♠
P	2 NT	P	<u>3 ◇</u>

♠ A 5 4
♡ K 8
◇ A 9 3 2
♣ K Q J 5

Here you show the ace of diamonds, a good club fit, and the ace or king of spades.

EASTERN THREE-NOTRUMP BID

With the availability of the Eastern cue-bid after an enemy suit overcall, responder need never *jump* to 3 NT just to show a balanced hand. Therefore, such a bid can be put to better use, and might appropriately be called the "Eastern 3 NT bid." Here is how it works:

1. **Jump to 3 NT after a *major* opening** shows 13 to 16 points or more, good support for opener's major, and *denies* control of the enemy suit. This, of course, is forcing to at least game in opener's major.

Partner	Opp.	You		
			♠	A J 8 5
			♡	K J 8 3
1 ♡	2 ♣	3 NT	◇	A 10 8
			♣	5 4

You show a "forcing raise" in hearts without club control. Partner may sign off in 4 ♡, or try for slam (which obviously requires club control).

NOTE: After a major-suit opening, the Eastern 3 NT bid might be considered an extension of the "3 NT balanced forcing raise" (see page *32*) used in conjunction with limit major raises. When both of these gadgets are used, it is simple to remember that *all direct jumps* to 3 NT (with or without interference) show support for opener's major.

2. **Jump to 3 NT after a *minor* opening** shows 10 to 12 high-card points, at least five cards in opener's minor, and a stopper in the enemy suit. This is a natural bid and is not forcing.

Partner	Opp.	You		
			♠	K 7
			♡	A 8 3
1 ◇	1 ♠	3 NT	◇	A 10 9 8 3
			♣	9 8 5

Your strong diamond fit makes it very reasonable to gamble on 3 NT with your spade stopper.

Invisible Cue-Bids ★ ★ ★

Of increasing popularity are the so-called *two-suited* overcalls of partner's opening bid of one of a suit. They come in all varieties; so many that it is too tedious to develop specific defenses to each one. Instead, we recommend a general defense, which we have named "invisible cue-bids." This applies to *all* two-suited overcalls, the most common of which are listed below:

Michaels cue-bid	*Colorful cue-bid
Unusual notrump overcall	*Higher-suits cue-bid
Roman jump overcall	*Top-and-bottom cue-bid
Astro cue-bid	*variations of Michaels cue-bid

It is *not* necessary to be familiar with all of the above (although each can be found in the Glossary). The common denominator is that they all promise *two* suits, at least *one* of which is known. Clearly, responder would be foolish to bid naturally one of the suits promised by the enemy, and this logic provides the foundation for invisible cue-bids. Here is the basic agreement:

1. **Cheapest available cue-bid** (of a known enemy suit) shows at least 10 points and support for opener's suit. This is completely artificial, and has nothing to do with your holding in the suit actually bid.

Partner	Opp.	You		
			♠	A Q 4
			♡	9 8 7 3
1 ♡	2 NT*	3 ♣	♢	A 7 6 2
			♣	10 3

*Unusual NT (minors)

You show at least a limit raise in hearts.

Partner	Opp.	You		
			♠	K J 7
			♡	8 7 4
1 ♠	2 ♠*	3 ♡	♢	K 8 7 6 2
			♣	A 8

*Michaels cue-bid (hearts + minor)

Here you must cue-bid 3 ♡, as hearts is the only known suit.

Partner	Opp.	You		
			♠	J 9 5
			♡	A 9 3
1 ♢	2 ♢*	2 ♠	♢	A Q 10 7
			♣	8 4 3

*Colorful cue-bid (black suits)

You show a diamond fit, but nothing in particular about spades.

After this "cheapest" cue-bid, opener may (a) return to the agreed trump suit (or possibly 2 NT) with a bare minimum; (b) bid game; or (c) make any other bid to explore for game or slam.

In most instances, the two-suited overcall will designate *both* of the suits held. In that event, responder has a second cue-bid at his disposal, which is put to use as follows:

2. **Higher cue-bid** (when both enemy suits are known) shows at least 10 high-card points and at least five cards in the *"unbid"* suit. In other words, responder indicates a "forcing bid in the fourth suit," but the suit actually bid is completely artificial.

Partner	Opp.	You		
			♠	A 3
			♡	K J 9 8 7 4
1 ♠	2 NT*	3 ♢	♢	8 7
			♣	A 7 3

*Unusual NT (minors)

You show a "forcing 3 ♡ bid," but nothing about diamonds. Observe that 3 ♣ would show a spade fit.

Partner	Opp.	You	
			♠ 7
			♡ 6 5 4
1 ♣	2 ♣*	2 ♠	◇ A J 10 9 5 4
			♣ A J 3

*Michaels cue-bid (majors)

You show a forcing diamond bid; a 2 ♡ cue-bid would indicate club support.

After the "higher" cue-bid, opener should assume that responder has *bid* the suit shown. Opener may (a) bid 2 NT; (b) "raise" responder's suit; or (c) rebid his original suit, each of which confirms a minimum opening and is not forcing; or (d) make any other bid, which is forcing if below game.

INVISIBLE SPLINTER BIDS

If you can have invisible cue-bids, you can also have invisible *splinter* bids! Here is how:

Any jump cue-bid (of a known enemy suit) shows a game-forcing raise of opener's suit, with a singleton or void in the suit bid. This is yet another application of the "splinter bid" (see pages *31* and *199*).

Partner	Opp.	You	
			♠ K J 7 5
			♡ A K 8 3
1 ♠	2 NT*	4 ♣	◇ 10 6 5 2
			♣ 3

*Unusual NT (minors)

Your 4 ♣ bid shows a "4 ♠ raise" with a club splinter; you would bid 4 ◇ with a diamond splinter.

Partner	Opp.	You	
			♠ A 9 7
			♡ —
1 ◇	2 ◇*	3 ♡	◇ A Q 9 8 4 3
			♣ 9 8 5 3

*Astro cue-bid (clubs + hearts)

You show a forcing diamond raise with a heart splinter; a 4 ♣ bid would show a club splinter.

OTHER RESPONSES

The use of invisible cue-bids and invisible splinter bids has an effect on the interpretation of other responses after an enemy two-suited overcall. These remaining responses all have natural meanings, as described below:

1. **Double** shows at least 10 high-card points, and suggests *defensive* strength. This is analogous to a redouble of an enemy takeout double.

Partner	Opp.	You	
			♠ K J 9 7
			♡ 5
1 ♡	2 ♡*	DBL	◇ Q 10 7 5 4
			♣ A 9 7

*Michaels cue-bid (spades + minor)

Your double alerts partner to the fact that the opponents may be in trouble.

Partner	Opp.	You
1 ◇	2 ◇*	DBL

♠ A 8 7
♡ K J 7 5
◇ A Q 3
♣ 9 8 7

*Top-and-bottom cue-bid (black suits)

The double is also the correct action on strong balanced hands.

2. **All raises** (any level) show about 6 to 9 points. These are limited by the failure to make an invisible cue-bid. Even *jump* raises are mostly preemptive.

Partner	Opp.	You
1 ♡	2 NT*	3 ♡

♠ A 8 7 5
♡ K 8 3
◇ 8 7
♣ 10 8 5 2

*Unusual NT (minors)

Your 3 ♡ raise is not very encouraging.

Partner	Opp.	You
1 ♠	2 ♠*	4 ♠

♠ 10 9 7 5 3
♡ 3
◇ J 8 5
♣ K 7 5 4

*Higher-suits cue-bid (red suits)

Your jump to 4 ♠ is weak.

3. **All new suit bids** (not promised by the enemy) show a maximum of about 9 high-card points and are *not* forcing. *Jumps* in new suits are preemptive.

Partner	Opp.	You
1 ♠	2 ♠*	3 ◇

♠ 7 4
♡ A 7 4
◇ K 10 9 8 7 4
♣ 4 3

*Michaels cue-bid (hearts + minor)

Your 3 ◇ bid is not forcing; to force the bidding, you must double first, then bid diamonds.

Partner	Opp.	You
1 ◇	2 ◇*	3 ♡

♠ 7
♡ K J 8 7 6 5 3
◇ 8 6 5
♣ 10 2

*Colorful cue-bid (black suits)

You are preempting. Observe also that 2 ♡ would be nonforcing, and 3 ♣ would show a "forcing heart bid."

4. **Two or three notrump** indicates a stopper in the suit (or suits) shown by the enemy and is not forcing. This suggests an offensive type hand, often with a fit for opener's minor suit, or a source of tricks of your own.

Partner	Opp.	You	♠ Q 10 7
			♡ K 9
1 ♣	2 ♣*	2 NT	◇ J 7 3
			♣ A 10 8 7 5

*Michaels cue-bid (majors)

Your 2 NT bid is invitational to 3 NT; the club fit makes it undesirable to try for a penalty.

HOW TO SHOW AN ENEMY SUIT

It will inevitably happen that responder's *own* long suit will be one of those promised by the enemy two-suited overcall. When this occurs, there are two very obvious possibilities: Either your suit will be heavily stacked on your right, or your opponent has forgotten his own convention! What to do? Well, the first rule is, "Don't panic!" Responder must *not* bid at this turn, but should either pass or double, as explained here:

1. **Pass** with a weak hand. On the next round, if both convenient and desirable, you may bid your real suit (not forcing).

Partner	Opp.	You	♠ A J 9 8 5 4
			♡ 9 3
1 ◇	2 ◇*	P	◇ 8 7
			♣ Q 10 7

*Michaels cue-bid (majors)

Do not make the mistake of bidding 2 ♠ now; that would really lead to disaster. Chances are, left-hand opponent will bid 2 ♡, after which you can balance with 2 ♠.

2. **Double** with a good hand. On the next round, you may bid your real suit (forcing if below game).

Partner	Opp.	You	♠ A K 4
			♡ K J 10 9 7 4
1 ♣	2 NT*	DBL	◇ 9 8 5
			♣ J

*Unusual NT (red suits)

Indeed, you smell a rat, but be patient. Only at your next turn can you bid hearts naturally.

Competitive Doubles

Certain low-level doubles, while defined as penalty in standard bidding, are so improbable as such that they are virtually useless. This is especially true when the opponents have raised a suit. For example:

Opp.	Partner	Opp.	You
	1 ◇	1 ♡	1 ♠
2 ♡	P	P	DBL

When was the last time you wanted to double 2 ♡ for penalty on an auction like this? Can't remember, right? The penalty application of such a double is so unlikely that many experts have opted for a different interpretation. The idea of "competitive doubles" is far more realistic.

A competitive double leans heavily toward takeout, and might be described as a cooperative takeout double. In effect, it says, "I have the values to compete, but am unsure what action to take." It asks for partner's help in choosing the best contract. Let's look at our example auction again, and give responder a typical hand:

Opp.	Partner	Opp.	You
	1 ◇	1 ♡	1 ♠
2 ♡	P	P	DBL

♠ A J 9 4 3
♡ 5 4
◇ 10 9 4
♣ A 10 2

You wish to compete against 2 ♡, but are unsure where. Your double relegates this decision to partner.

The competitive double cannot be pulled out of a hat every time you don't know what to bid. Like any convention, its use must be governed by partnership agreement to avoid misunderstandings. We recommend this rule:

If partner has previously acted, you acted at your last turn, and your side has neither bid notrump nor established a suit fit, the double of a *raised* enemy suit (through 2 ♠) is a competitive double. This complex rule can best be understood through some more examples:

Opp.	Partner	Opp.	You
	1 ♣	P	1 ◇
1 ♠	P	2 ♠	DBL

♠ 9 5
♡ A 10 8
◇ K J 9 7 3
♣ Q 8 5

Your double asks partner to select the contract.

Opp.	Partner	Opp.	You
	1 ♣	1 ◇	DBL*
2 ◇	P	P	DBL

*Negative

♠ J 9 8 7
♡ K J 9 5
◇ A 6 3
♣ Q 2

Here too, you need partner's cooperation to compete successfully.

The opening bidder may also make a competitive double:

♠ A 8
♡ J 10 5
◇ 7 6 3
♣ A K Q 10 2

You	Opp.	Partner	Opp.
1 ♣	1 ◇	1 ♡	2 ◇
DBL			

You desire to compete; however, you are not sure whether to raise hearts or rebid your clubs.

♠ A 6 5
♡ K J 8
◇ A K 9 8 4
♣ A 3

You	Opp.	Partner	Opp.
1 ◇	1 ♠	DBL*	2 ♠
DBL			

*Negative

You are strong enough to reach game, but the competitive double is the most flexible first move.

Even the *defensive* side may make a competitive double, although the situations are less common. Here is a possibility:

Opp.	Partner	Opp.	You	♠ 9 5
				♡ Q 8
1 ♣	1 ♡	1 ♠	2 ◇	◇ A K 9 7 5 4
2 ♠	P	P	DBL	♣ J 10 3

Your double is an attempt to get partner to choose between 3 ◇ and 3 ♡, the obvious alternatives.

In order to reinforce your understanding, witness the following three auctions, which, according to the rule, do *not* illustrate competitive doubles:

You	Opp.	Partner	Opp.
1 ♣	1 ♡	1 NT	2 ♡
DBL			

For penalty; your side has bid notrump.

Opp.	Partner	Opp.	You
	1 ◇	P	1 ♡
1 ♠	2 ♡	2 ♠	DBL

For penalty; you have established a fit.

Opp.	Partner	Opp.	You
	1 ♣	1 ◇	P
2 ◇	P	P	DBL

For penalty; you passed at your last turn.

DOUBLES OF NON-RAISED SUITS

There are a few circumstances in which a competitive double may be made of a non-raised suit. Here is a useful agreement:

If a double (through 2♠), that would normally be for penalty, is *impossible* as such from the previous bidding, then it becomes a competitive double.

Opp.	Partner	Opp.	You	♠ A J 8
				♡ 8 5 3
	1 ◇	P	1 NT	◇ K 10 3
2 ♡	P	P	DBL	♣ Q 9 5 4

Your 1 NT response denied four hearts, so this cannot be a penalty double; you show maximum values and a desire to compete.

Opp.	Partner	Opp.	You	♠ 9 3
				♡ J 10 9 3
	1 ◇	P	P	◇ Q 8 4
1 ♠	P	P	DBL	♣ J 10 4 3

What else could this double mean? Partner will go easy, since your strength (?) is severely limited.

		You	Opp.	Partner	Opp.
♠ 8 7		1 ♣	P	1 ♡	P
♡ K J 3		2 ♣	P	P	2 ♠
◇ A 3		DBL			
♣ A J 10 9 8 3					

Since you have limited your hand, and denied four spades, your double is competitive.

WARNING: Do not forget that the penalty interpretation must be truly *impossible,* not just improbable, in order to apply this kind of competitive double.

THREE-LEVEL DOUBLES

Although something can be said for extending all competitive doubles to the three-level, an equally good point can be made for penalty doubles. Therefore, we recommend only a very limited use of competitive doubles beyond 2 ♠, as stated in the following rule:

If partner has acted, and you have made a *negative* double, *takeout* double, or *responsive* double, a double of the *same* suit at your next turn (through 3 ♠) is a competitive double.

Opp.	Partner	Opp.	You		
				♠	K Q 9 5
				♡	5 4
	1 ◇	1 ♡	DBL*	◇	A 7 6
3 ♡	P	P	DBL	♣	Q 10 7 2

*Negative

Your second double is competitive. After all, your hand hasn't changed since your first double.

Opp.	Partner	Opp.	You		
				♠	A Q 8
				♡	A K 9 7
		1 ◇	DBL	◇	7 5
2 ◇	2 ♠	3 ◇	DBL	♣	K Q 9 8

You show a strong takeout double with only mediocre spade support; you do not *show diamond strength.*

Opp.	Partner	Opp.	You		
				♠	A 5
				♡	K 10 8 5 4
1 ♣	1 ♠	2 ♣	DBL*	◇	Q J 9 8 5
3 ♣	P	P	DBL	♣	10

*Responsive

Having shown hearts and diamonds with your first double, you now emphasize your desire to compete.

BIDDING AFTER A COMPETITIVE DOUBLE

Responding to a competitive double is very much like responding to a takeout double; hence the following agreement:

If partner has made a competitive double, the principles of limit bidding apply. That is: (a) Minimum bids are not forcing; (b) jump bids show extra values and are invitational if below game; and (c) a cue-bid of the enemy suit is the only force.

		You	Opp.	Partner	Opp.
♠	10 7				
♡	9 8 7	1 ◇	1 ♠	DBL*	2 ♠
◇	A K 10 5	P	P	DBL	P
♣	K Q 8 3	3 ♣			

*Negative

Partner has asked for your cooperation, so 3 ♣ is the logical choice.

Opp.	Partner	Opp.	You	♠ Q J 10 8 7
				♡ A Q 9
	1 ♣	1 ◇	1 ♠	◇ 8 7 2
2 ◇	DBL	P	3 ♠	♣ 7 3

Your jump to 3 ♠ shows extra strength and invites game. Partner's double has implied secondary spade support.

Passing a competitive double (converting it to penalty) is a real possibility, and should be considered when you have at least *three* trumps, good defensive potential, and no attractive bid. The very nature of the competitive double itself signifies no clear-cut action, so doubler should contribute on defense. For example:

Opp.	Partner	Opp.	You	♠ K 9 7
				♡ A Q 8 3
	1 ◇	1 ♠	DBL*	◇ 7 5
2 ♠	DBL	P	P	♣ Q 8 7 2

*Negative

Apparently no suit fit exists, and notrump prospects look bleak, so the pass is indicated.

Maximal Overcall Double

Prerequisite:
PREEMPTIVE RERAISES

During a competitive auction, the enemy bidding may prevent opener from making a game try after he has been raised. For example:

♠ A K J 7 4	You	Opp.	Partner	Opp.
♡ A 5				
◇ K 8 4 3	1 ♠	2 ♡	2 ♠	3 ♡
♣ 10 9	?			

You would like to invite game, but if you bid 3 ♠, partner will construe that as competitive. Without the 3 ♡ bid, of course, you could bid 3 ◇ as a trial bid, but now that is impossible. In short, it seems that you must guess between 3 ♠ and 4 ♠ at this juncture.

Never fear; another gadget is here. The "maximal overcall double," which has attained considerable popularity, provides an effective solution. It is defined by the following rule:

If both opponents have acted, and their bidding prevents opener from making any game-trial suit bid after a single raise, a *double* of the enemy suit is *not* for penalty, and becomes a game try.

♠ A K J 7 4	You	Opp.	Partner	Opp.
♡ A 5				
◇ K 8 4 3	1 ♠	2 ♡	2 ♠	3 ♡
♣ 10 9	DBL			

The problem is now solved. Your double asks partner to bid 3 ♠ with a minimum, or 4 ♠ with a maximum.

♠ A 7 4
♡ A Q J 8 5
◇ 5
♣ A 9 8 7

You	Opp.	Partner	Opp.
1 ♡	DBL	2 ♡	3 ◇
DBL			

Your double is like a "3½ ♡" bid. Observe that both opponents have acted (a takeout double is an "act").

WARNING: A word of caution seems in order here. As with any new gadget, it is tempting to apply the maximal overcall double when inappropriate. Witness the following two auctions, and note that your double is for *penalty:*

You	Opp.	Partner	Opp.
1 ♡	2 ♣	2 ♡	3 ♣
DBL			

For penalty; 3 ◇ is available as a game try.

You	Opp.	Partner	Opp.
1 ♠	P	2 ♠	3 ♡
DBL			

For penalty; only one opponent has acted.

EXTENDED APPLICATIONS

The maximal overcall double is not restricted to use by the opening bidder. We recommend the following general agreement:

If both opponents have acted, and "preemptive reraises" apply (see page 55), the maximal overcall double may be used if no game-trial suit bid is available.

Opp.	Partner	Opp.	You
	1 ♣	P	1 ♠
2 ♡	2 ♠	3 ♡	DBL

♠ A J 8 5
♡ 7 4
◇ 10 7 5 3
♣ K Q 8

Since a 3 ♠ bid would be competitive, your double serves as a game try in spades.

Even the defensive side may get in on the action, as illustrated in these two final examples:

Opp.	Partner	Opp.	You
		1 ◇	1 ♡
1 ♠	2 ♡	3 ◇	DBL

♠ A 7 5
♡ K Q 8 7 5
◇ 7
♣ A J 10 7

Your double is a game try in hearts.

Opp.	Partner	Opp.	You
		1 ♠	2 ♣
2 ♠	3 ♣	3 ♠	DBL

♠ 5
♡ 9 3
◇ A Q J 4
♣ A K 10 9 8 2

You have legitimate game interest, but do not want to punish partner for competing. Your double is equivalent to bidding "4½ ♣."

4

Other Opening Bids

♣   ◆   ♥   ♠   ♣   ◆   ♥   ♠

Thus far, we have covered conventions dealing with strong balanced openings (Chapter 1) and opening bids of one of a suit (Chapters 2 and 3). In this fourth chapter, we will discuss the conventional agreements associated with other kinds of opening bids. More specifically, this includes opening bids of *two* of a suit, and the specialized 3 NT opening.

In this chapter:

Strong Artificial Two-Club Opening

Weak Two-Bids

Acol Three-Notrump Opening

Strong Artificial Two-Club Opening

> *Invented by the late David Bruce (formerly Burnstine), a leading American player of the early years of contract bridge, and Life Master #1 of the A.C.B.L.*

This extremely popular convention is responsible for the demise of the strong two-bid. The "strong artificial 2 ♣ opening" is used on *all* very strong hands, thereby releasing the bids of 2 ◇, 2 ♡, and 2 ♠ for other purposes, such as "weak two-bids" (see page *101*). Here is the basic understanding:

Two-club opening is strong, artificial, and forcing for one round. With a balanced hand, at least 23 high-card points are required. With an unbalanced hand, opener needs at least 21 high-card points, or a one-suited hand within *one* trick of game (but with at least 17 high-card points). The following hands are minimum examples of 2 ♣ openings:

♠ A K 8 5
♡ K Q 9   *Open 2 ♣. You are too strong for 2 NT.*
♢ A Q 7
♣ A J 4

♠ A K Q 8 7
♡ 5   *Open 2 ♣. You are too strong for 1 ♠.*
♢ K 9 7
♣ A K Q 5

♠ A 4
♡ A K Q 9 8 7 3   *Open 2 ♣. You have nine solid tricks in your own*
♢ A 10 3   *hand.*
♣ 3

We hasten to emphasize that the above stated requirements are only guidelines. A certain amount of overlap exists either way. Good judgment is often the key in deciding the proper opening bid in borderline cases, as illustrated by the following examples:

♠ A J 8
♡ K Q J 10 4   *Open 2 ♣. This balanced hand has superb play-*
♢ A K 3   *ing potential, despite only 22 HCP.*
♣ A 3

♠ K Q
♡ K J 6 5 4   *Open 1 ♡. Wasted spade values and poor suit*
♢ A K J 5 2   *texture reduce the value of this hand.*
♣ A

♠ A K J 10 7
♡ A K 10 8 4   *Open 2 ♣. With both major suits and promising*
♢ A 7 3   *shape, you can stretch a little.*
♣ —

♠ 5
♡ A J 3   *Open 1 ♢. Minor suit hands require ten tricks*
♢ A K Q 9 8 7 3 *to be within one trick of game.*
♣ A 5

♠ A 4
♡ A K Q J 8 7 3 2 *Open 1 ♡. Despite the nine solid tricks, you*
♢ 3   *have too few high cards to open 2 ♣.*
♣ 7 4

RESPONSES

After the 2 ♣ opening, responder cannot pass, no matter how weak his hand is. He must choose from the following responses:

1. **Two of a major or three of a minor** is a *positive* response showing 8 or more high-card points (or 1½ honor tricks) and at least a five-card suit. Furthermore, if suit is only five cards long, it must be headed by the *queen* or better.

Partner	You		
		♠	Q J 7 4 3
		♡	A 9 5
2 ♣	2 ♠	◇	Q 9 2
		♣	5 4

You show at least five spades.

Partner	You		
		♠	K 9 3
		♡	10 7 5 2
2 ♣	3 ♣	◇	3
		♣	A J 10 4 3

Here you show a club suit.

Partner	You		
		♠	7 5
		♡	5 4
2 ♣	3 ◇	◇	A Q 9 8 4 2
		♣	9 4 2

This hand qualifies by virtue of its honor tricks.

2. **Two notrump** is a *positive* response showing 8 or more high-card points and a balanced hand.

Partner	You		
		♠	A 8 7 5
		♡	10 3
2 ♣	2 NT	◇	Q 9 7 5
		♣	Q 8 7

You show a hand of "notrump" shape, usually with scattered high cards.

3. **Two diamonds** is the *negative* response. Typically, this shows a maximum of 7 high-card points, but responder could have more if his hand is unsuitable for any positive response.

Partner	You		
		♠	9 8 6
		♡	K 9 7 2
2 ♣	2 ◇	◇	6 3
		♣	J 8 5 3

Your 2 ◇ response implies a weak hand; you would make the same bid with no points at all.

Partner	You		
		♠	K 8 5 3
		♡	9 8 5 4 2
2 ♣	2 ◇	◇	A J 3
		♣	4

Your heart suit is not strong enough to bid 2 ♡, so you must mark time with 2 ◇, awaiting partner's rebid.

REBIDS AFTER A NEGATIVE RESPONSE

After the negative 2 ◇ response, opener will make the first *natural* bid of the auction. Opener must state the nature of his 2 ♣ opening through one of the following rebids:

1. **Two of a major or three of a minor** shows at least a five-card suit and is forcing for another round. EXCEPTION: Holding 4-4-4-1 shape, opener may bid a strong four-card suit, for lack of an alternative.

	You	Partner
♠ A K 7 4		
♡ K Q 10 9 6		
◇ A K	2 ♣	2 ◇
♣ K 3	<u>2 ♡</u>	

You show at least five hearts.

	You	Partner
♠ A 3		
♡ A		
◇ A Q J 9 8	2 ♣	2 ◇
♣ A Q J 8 4	<u>3 ◇</u>	

As always, with two five-card suits bid the higher ranking suit first.

2. **Two notrump** shows a balanced hand of 23 or 24 points and is not forcing. Responder should continue just as if 2 NT had been the opening bid, but with appropriate point-count adjustments.

	You	Partner
♠ A K J		
♡ K J 9 6		
◇ A K 8	2 ♣	2 ◇
♣ A 9 8	<u>2 NT</u>	

   You show better than a 2 NT opening bid. Partner may now use Stayman, Jacoby, etc., or whatever your normal methods are over 2 NT.

3. **Three notrump** shows a balanced hand of 25 to 27 points and is not forcing. We recommend that responder may continue (if at all) with the same methods used over 2 NT, except one level higher.

	You	Partner
♠ A K Q 5		
♡ K Q J		
◇ K Q 10 3	2 ♣	2 ◇
♣ A Q	<u>3 NT</u>	

   Here you show an even stronger hand. Partner, of course, must decide whether to bid any further.

4. **Four or five notrump** shows a balanced hand of 28 to 30, or 31 to 32 points, respectively. Seen any lately?

THE SECOND NEGATIVE

After a negative 2 ◇ response to the 2 ♣ opening, it is necessary to expand on those auctions where opener rebids in a *suit*. Responder is then required to bid again, which can be very awkward, especially when responder has a worthless hand.

   To solve this problem, many experts advocate a "second negative," or "double negative," as it is sometimes called. Of the several methods in practice, we recommend the following:

Cheaper minor rebid, or 3 NT over 3 ◇ (by responder) shows 0 to 4 high-card points (but never an ace) and is completely artificial. Essentially, this is a "nothing" bid, made simply to respect opener's force.

Partner	You
2 ♣	2 ◇
2 ♡	3 ♣

♠ J 9 7 4
♡ 9 5
◇ Q 9 8 5
♣ 8 7 4

Your 3 ♣ rebid is the second negative; it does not show a real club suit.

Partner	You
2 ♣	2 ◇
3 ♣	3 ◇

♠ 9 5
♡ 8 5 3
◇ 9 8 4 2
♣ J 10 9 6

Here you must bid 3 ◇ as the second negative.

Partner	You
2 ♣	2 ◇
3 ◇	3 NT

♠ J 8 4
♡ 8 4 3
◇ 9 5 2
♣ 10 8 6 5

This is a clumsy sequence, to be sure, but it is the most practical solution.

Further bidding after the second negative is natural. Game must be reached, unless opener immediately *rebids* his previously shown suit. Carefully observe the following two examples:

♠ A K Q J 9 8 3
♡ A J 3
◇ K J
♣ 7

You	Partner
2 ♣	2 ◇
2 ♠	3 ♣
3 ♠	

Your 3 ♠ rebid shows a nine-trick hand, and partner may pass with a worthless dummy.

♠ A K J 8
♡ 4
◇ A 2
♣ A K Q 10 5 2

You	Partner
2 ♣	2 ◇
3 ♣	3 ◇
3 ♠	

Here your 3 ♠ rebid is forcing, since you are mentioning a new suit.

FAILURE TO USE THE SECOND NEGATIVE

The main advantage of the second negative is obtained when it is *not* employed. Any other rebid by responder promises useful values, as explained below:

Failure to use the second negative confirms at least 4 high-card points and is forcing to game. Responder, of course, should rebid as naturally as possible.

Partner	You
2 ♣	2 ◇
2 ♠	2 NT

♠ 9 3
♡ K 9 7 3
◇ K 8 3
♣ 10 7 5 4

Your 2 NT rebid is constructive, since you would bid 3 ♣ with a very weak hand.

Partner	You
2 ♣	2 ◇
2 ♡	3 ♡

♠ 10 5 2
♡ A 10 3
◇ 7 4
♣ 9 8 7 5 4

You show a useful hand with support for partner's heart suit.

Partner	You		
		♠	Q 9 7 6 5
		♡	K 10 5
2 ♣	2 ◇	◇	8 4 3
3 ♣	<u>3 ♠</u>	♣	10 2

Your 3 ♠ rebid shows a natural suit, usually of at least five cards.

After an original negative response, opener should always assume that responder has *less* than 8 high-card points (or 1½ honor tricks). In the rare event that this is not the case, responder *himself* must take the initiative to drive the bidding beyond game. For example:

Partner	You		
		♠	J 8 7 5 3
2 ♣	2 ◇	♡	A J 7
3 ◇	3 ♠	◇	2
3 NT	<u>4 NT</u>	♣	Q 10 9 7

Your 4 NT bid is a natural slam invitation; do not pass 3 NT, as partner is unaware of your 8 HCP. Notice that you could not respond 2 ♠ with such a weak suit.

AUCTIONS AFTER A POSITIVE RESPONSE

After a positive response to the 2 ♣ opening, opener continues in the following manner:

1. **Three clubs** (after a 2 NT response only) is "Stayman." This asks responder to show a four-card major suit, in much the same way as Stayman is used over a 2 NT opening bid (see page 5). NOTE: To show a real club suit, opener must make this same rebid, then bid 4 ♣ at his next turn.

	You	Partner
♠ A K J 6		
♡ A 2		
◇ A K 8 7	2 ♣	2 NT
♣ K J 9	<u>3 ♣</u>	

Your 3 ♣ bid is Stayman. Partner must reply 3 ◇, 3 ♡, or 3 ♠, according to usual practice.

2. **Any other minimum rebid** is natural and logical in meaning. Opener may (a) bid a five-card or longer suit; (b) raise responder's suit with good trump support; or (c) bid notrump with a balanced hand.

Following any positive response, both players must keep in mind that *slam* is the main concern. There is no need to jump the bidding, since all bids are forcing to at least game. Any bid by either partner that *completes* game (in 3 NT or a previously bid suit) indicates *minimum* values and discourages slam. Witness these two auctions:

Partner	You		
		♠	Q 10 8 5 4
		♡	A 8 3
2 ♣	2 ♠	◇	9 4
3 ♡	<u>4 ♡</u>	♣	Q 7 6

Your raise to 4 ♡ is not forcing, and announces that your positive response was minimal. With a better hand, you must find some other rebid.

```
♠  A Q 8                     You      Partner
♡  K J 7
♢  A K J 6          2 ♣       2 NT
♣  K Q 10           3 NT
```

By raising to 3 NT, you indicate a minimum 2 ♣ opening; partner should pass with just 8 HCP.

SPECIALIZED RESPONSES

All of the basic sequences after the 2 ♣ opening have been discussed. You may have noticed, however, that no meaning was given to jump responses of 3 ♡, 3 ♠, 3 NT, and higher. Because such bids are awkward and space-consuming, most experts attach very specific meanings to them. We recommend the following specialized responses to the 2 ♣ opening:

1. **Three of a major** shows a six-card suit headed by two of the top three honors, and denies holding any outside ace or king.

```
Partner     You              ♠  10
                             ♡  A Q 10 7 6 5
2 ♣         3 ♡              ♢  J 8 2
                             ♣  9 5 4
```

Your jump to 3 ♡ is very informative, and will often enable partner to bid a slam.

2. **Four of any suit** shows a seven-card or longer suit headed by two of the top three honors, and denies holding any outside ace or king.

```
Partner     You              ♠  9
                             ♡  4 3
2 ♣         4 ♢              ♢  K Q J 9 8 5 4
                             ♣  9 8 2
```

You must jump to 4 ♢, since 3 ♢, remember, is just a normal positive response.

3. **Three notrump** indicates an *undisclosed* solid suit (headed by the A-K-Q) of at least six cards, and denies holding any outside ace or king. This response is artificial; however, opener should know the identity of responder's suit at least 99% of the time, simply by examining his own hand.

```
Partner     You              ♠  A K Q 9 8 5
                             ♡  8 4 2
2 ♣         3 NT             ♢  7 4 3
                             ♣  9
```

Your 3 NT bid is forcing and virtually assures a slam; partner will surely know you have spades.

WARNING: The preceding specialized responses are entirely optional, and for obvious reasons should *not* be used without prior partnership discussion.

After any of the specialized responses, opener may (a) rebid naturally; or (b) bid 4 NT as Blackwood (except over 3 NT, when Blackwood is useless). Also, to inquire about *suit quality,* opener may (c) bid five of responder's suit to invite a small slam; or (d) bid 5 NT (forcing) to invite a grand slam. For example:

```
♠  A K 4 3              You      Partner
♡  K
◇  A K Q 2              2 ♣      3 ♡
♣  K Q J 8             5 ♡
```

*You are inviting slam; partner should pass with A-Q-X-X-X-X, or bid 6 ♡
with A-Q-J-X-X-X. If your clubs were instead A-K-8-3, you would bid 5 NT,
forcing partner to bid either 6 ♡ or 7 ♡ on similar principles.*

INTERFERENCE BY THE OPPONENTS

The days when the enemy would always go quietly on your strong hands are probably
gone forever. Indeed, the more formidable your opponents, the more likely it is they
will find a way to interfere after your 2 ♣ opening, especially when the vulnerability is
favorable to them. Thus, it is desirable to have certain understandings regarding this.

The simplest method of coping with interference, practiced by many players, is
summed up as follows: "Pass with a negative response, and bid with a positive response." If you favor simplicity, you may as well adopt that strategy. Nevertheless, we
feel that slightly more detail is required, and recommend the following agreements:

1. **If the 2 ♣ opening is doubled,** which usually shows a club suit, responder may (a)
   make his normal response; (b) pass with four clubs; or (c) redouble with five clubs
   or four good clubs.

   ```
   Partner    Opp.     You        ♠  10 3
                                  ♡  K 9 5 2
   2 ♣        DBL      P          ◇  9 5 3
                                  ♣  10 5 4 3
   ```

   *Your pass shows four clubs. With fewer clubs, you would bid 2 ◇ (normal
   negative response). With longer or stronger clubs, you would redouble.*

2. **If the 2 ♣ opening is overcalled** (through 4 ◇), responder may (a) bid a reasonably
   good five-card or longer suit with at least 5 high-card points; (b) bid notrump with
   a balanced positive response containing a stopper; (c) cue-bid with a positive response and a singleton or void in the enemy suit; (d) double for penalty; or (e) pass
   otherwise.

   ```
   Partner    Opp.     You        ♠  9 3
                                  ♡  9 5 3
   2 ♣        2 ♠      3 ♣        ◇  10 7 2
                                  ♣  A J 9 8 6
   ```

   *You do not have a normal positive response, but there may never be another
   opportunity to show your suit.*

   ```
   Partner    Opp.     You        ♠  A 9 8 4
                                  ♡  2
   2 ♣        2 ♡      3 ♡        ◇  10 8 6 5 3
                                  ♣  K J 7
   ```

   Your 3 ♡ cue-bid shows heart shortness; slam is a strong favorite.

3. **If the 2 ♣ opening is overcalled *beyond* 4 ◇,** responder obviously has much less
   freedom. Basically, he should (a) bid only with a good six-card or longer suit; (b)
   double to warn opener against bidding; or (c) pass to encourage opener to bid his
   suit.

Partner	Opp.	You		♠ 7 5 3
				♡ 9 7 2
2 ♣	4 ♡	<u>DBL</u>		◇ 9 7 5 2
				♣ J 9 4

Your double does not promise strong hearts, but cautions partner not to ex-pect any help from your hand. In contrast, a pass would suggest a useful dummy.

4. **When the opening 2 ♣ bidder is confronted by interference,** it is desirable to have a few general understandings. The 2 ♣ opener may (a) make his normal rebid; **(b)** double or redouble for penalty; (c) cue-bid the enemy suit as a strong three-suit takeout; or (d) pass to force responder to act.

		You	Opp.	Partner	Opp.
♠ A 6					
♡ A K 3					
◇ A Q 9 7		2 ♣	P	2 ◇	DBL
♣ A Q 5 4		<u>RDBL</u>			

Your redouble is for business; partner should be able to scrounge eight tricks in spite of the enemy trump stack.

		You	Opp.	Partner	Opp.
♠ A K J 7					
♡ 3					
◇ A Q 8 6		2 ♣	2 ♡	P	P
♣ A K Q 8		<u>3 ♡</u>			

You show a singleton or void in hearts and support for three suits; a double, remember, is always for penalty.

		You	Opp.	Partner	Opp.
♠ K J 9 6					
♡ A 6					
◇ K Q J		2 ♣	P	2 ◇	3 ♡
♣ A K Q 9		<u>P</u>			

Your pass is like a takeout double; partner must either bid or double for penalty. Had the overcall been 3 ♠, you would double yourself.

Weak Two-Bids ★

Developed by the late Howard Schenken, once voted by his peers as the greatest bridge player of all time

The primary objective of the strong artificial 2 ♣ opening is to allow the use of *other* two-level openings for different purposes. Strong two-bids just do not occur often enough to waste four bids on them. Consequently, the popular treatment is to use an opening bid of 2 ◇, 2 ♡, or 2 ♠ as a "weak two-bid," i.e., sort of a mini-preemptive opening. Alternatively, some experts play only *major*-suit weak two-bids, thus reserving 2 ◇ for some other purpose, such as "Flannery" (see Glossary). The basic agreement is explained below:

Two of a suit opening (except 2 ♣) shows 5 to 11 high-card points and a reasonably good six-card suit. Furthermore, hand should not contain an outside major suit of four or more cards.

We are not as adamant about suit quality as are some authorities. Not vulnerable, a suit as weak as Q-10-X-X-X-X might be opened; but if vulnerable, we would recommend better texture, such as Q-10-9-8-X-X. Remember, however, these are just mini-mum holdings; typically, the suit is better. Now let's look at some examples:

♠ K J 10 8 5 4
♡ 4
♦ A 9 3   *Open 2 ♠. A classic weak two-bid.*
♣ 9 8 2

♠ 9 7
♡ K 10 7 6 5 4
♦ 10 2   *Open 2 ♡ if not vulnerable, but pass if vulnerable.*
♣ K J 8

♠ K 3
♡ 9 2
♦ A Q J 9 8 5   *Open 2 ♦. A maximum weak two-bid.*
♣ 10 9 3

♠ A Q 10 8 7 3
♡ A J 2   *Open 1 ♠. Never open a weak two-bid if your*
♦ 9 7 4   *hand qualifies for a one-bid.*
♣ 3

♠ —
♡ Q J 10 8 7 2   *Open 2 ♡. The void suit, or secondary minor suit,*
♦ K 10 9 6   *is not a deterrent.*
♣ 7 4 3

♠ A J 10 6 5 4 3
♡ 3   *Open 2 ♠ if vulnerable, but 3 ♠ if not vulnerable.*
♦ 7 6 4   *The seven-card suit is rare, but permissible.*
♣ 9 8

THIRD- AND FOURTH-SEAT WEAK TWO-BIDS

Once partner is a passed hand, greater flexibility is permitted in opening a weak two-bid. That is:

In third and fourth seat, the requirements for a weak two-bid may be tactfully set aside. Such conditions as point count, suit quality, and the lack of a side four-card major are no longer critical. Even a good five-card suit may be opened if you are willing to take the risk. NOTE: In *fourth* seat, avoid opening minimum-range weak two-bids, especially in hearts or diamonds; just pass the hand out.

♠ A 6
♡ J 10 9 6   *Open 2 ♦ in third seat; pass in any other position.*
♦ Q 10 9 8 5 4
♣ 4

♠ 9 3
♡ A K J 9 6 2   *Open 2 ♡ in third or fourth seat, but open 1 ♡ in*
♦ K 9 2   *first or second seat.*
♣ 4 3

♠ K Q J 9 6
♡ 3   *Open 2 ♠ in third or fourth seat; pass in first or*
♦ A 6 2   *second seat.*
♣ 9 8 4 3

THE TWO-NOTRUMP RESPONSE

The methods of responding to a weak two-bid are varied. While all experts agree that a 2 NT response is forcing, their opinions diverge from there. Some play a new-suit response forcing; others do not. We recommend the use of 2 NT as the *only* forcing response, as explained below:

Two-notrump response (to a weak two-bid) shows interest in game and is forcing for one round (even by a passed hand). This bid typically requires at least 14 points, but may be shaded slightly when you are vulnerable, or if your hand contains good support for opener's suit.

Partner	You		
		♠	A 5
		♡	A K 6 5
2 ♠	2 NT	◇	K 10 7 5
		♣	8 4 3

Your 2 NT bid is a game try.

Partner	You		
		♠	A 9 8
		♡	10 7 6 3
2 ♡	2 NT	◇	A K 8 7
		♣	9 2

Here your excellent heart fit allows you to be more aggressive.

After the forcing 2 NT response, the weak two-bidder must describe his hand more accurately. Two methods have found considerable popularity. We recommend the most widely used "feature-showing" method; however, a popular alternative is the "Ogust" method (see Glossary). Here are the meanings of opener's rebids:

1. **Three of original suit** indicates a minimum weak two-bid, typically in the range of 5 to 8 high-card points. This is the only way to show a minimum.

		You	Partner
♠	9 8		
♡	Q J 10 7 6 5		
◇	10 2	2 ♡	2 NT
♣	K 10 6	3 ♡	

   Your 3 ♡ rebid discourages game.

2. **Three notrump** indicates a suit headed by the A-K-Q, or possibly the A-K-J. This does not suggest the desire to play notrump, but merely promises a solid, or nearly solid, suit.

		You	Partner
♠	A K Q 9 5 4		
♡	5		
◇	9 6 5	2 ♠	2 NT
♣	10 8 7	3 NT	

   Partner will not pass 3 NT unless he can provide stoppers in the three unbid suits.

3. **Three of a new suit** shows a "feature" (A, K, or Q) in that suit and a good weak two-bid. Opener should have in the range of 8 to 11 high-card points.

♠ 8
♡ K 8 5
◇ A Q 10 8 6 2
♣ 9 5 3

You	*Partner*
2 ◇	2 NT
3 ♡	

You show a high honor in hearts, not a real suit (your 2 ◇ opening denied a four-card major). Perhaps this will help partner decide on the final contract.

4. **Four of a new minor suit** shows a four- or five-card side suit and a good weak two-bid. If just four cards, minor suit must be headed by at least the *queen*.

♠ 7
♡ A Q 9 8 4 3
◇ 9 2
♣ Q J 10 3

You	*Partner*
2 ♡	2 NT
4 ♣	

Your 4 ♣ bid shows a real club suit; 3 ♣ would show only a feature, remember. Occasionally, this will uncover a superior game or slam.

REBIDS BY TWO-NOTRUMP RESPONDER

After the 2 NT response and opener's descriptive rebid, responder will often have enough information to place the final contract. Typically, this is done by passing (when opener rebids his suit), or by returning to opener's suit at the desired level. The following rebids are available to responder:

1. **Three of opener's suit** (or 4 ◇ after a 2 ◇ opening) is not forcing, but mildly invitational. Opener should bid again only with a tiptop maximum.

Partner	*You*		
		♠	A 8
		♡	A 7 4 3
2 ♠	2 NT	◇	J 7 2
3 ◇	3 ♠	♣	K Q 8 5

Your 3 ♠ bid is not forcing, but partner is not barred, since your 2 NT bid promised game interest.

2. **Any other suit bid** (below game) shows at least a five-card suit and is forcing. Opener should raise with any three cards or a doubleton honor.

Partner	*You*		
		♠	A K J 7 5
		♡	6 5 3
2 ◇	2 NT	◇	A 7
3 ◇	3 ♠	♣	A Q 10

Your 3 ♠ bid is forcing; you had to bid this way, since an original 2 ♠ response would not be forcing.

3. **Three notrump** is a natural sign-off bid. After a *major*-suit weak two-bid, this is an optional sign-off; i.e., opener is permitted to correct to game in his major if his hand is unsuitable for notrump.

Partner	*You*		
		♠	A K 6 3
		♡	J 4
2 ♡	2 NT	◇	K Q 8 5
3 ♣	3 NT	♣	K 10 2

You suggest playing 3 NT, but partner is free to return to 4 ♡ if he chooses.

4. **Game in any suit** is a natural sign-off bid. This includes opener's suit—or any other suit, for that matter.

Partner	You		
		♠	J 8
		♡	K Q 7 3
2 ♠	2 NT	◇	A 9 4 2
3 ♡	4 ♠	♣	A 7 3

Partner's heart feature (obviously, the ace) removes all your doubts about bidding game.

NONFORCING RESPONSES

As previously stated, we recommend the use of 2 NT as the only forcing response to a weak two-bid. The remaining *nonforcing* responses are described below:

1. **Raise to three** is a preemptive blocking maneuver. This is *not* an invitation to game; weak two-bidder is expected to pass.

Partner	You		
		♠	J 6 3
		♡	10 8 5
2 ♠	3 ♠	◇	A Q 8 4 3
		♣	9 6

Your 3 ♠ bid is an attempt to impede the enemy, as they have more strength than your side.

2. **New suit** is natural and not forcing. This suggests at least a six-card suit and no fit with opener's suit. Weak two-bidder should usually pass, but may raise with support for responder's suit.

Partner	You		
		♠	A Q J 9 7 6
		♡	9 5 4
2 ◇	2 ♠	◇	7
		♣	A 9 3

Your 2 ♠ bid is not forcing; you would make the same bid without the ace of clubs.

3. **Jump in a new suit** (rare) is natural and invitational if below game. This shows a self-sufficient suit and about *one* playing trick short of the actual bid.

Partner	You		
		♠	K Q J 10 8 5 4
		♡	2
2 ♡	3 ♠	◇	A Q
		♣	J 5 4

You show about eight tricks, so partner should continue to 4 ♠ if he can provide two.

4. **Three notrump** is a complete sign-off. Opener has no decision to make, and must pass regardless of his hand. NOTE: If responder wishes weak two-bidder to exercise his opinion, he must bid 2 NT, then rebid 3 NT (as previously explained).

Partner	You		
		♠	—
		♡	K J 7
2 ♠	3 NT	◇	A K Q J 8 7 5
		♣	Q J 10

You are bidding what you expect to make, and do not care to hear any more about partner's spades.

5. **Game in any suit** is a sign-off bid. This may be either expecting to make, or intended as an advance sacrifice.

Partner	You		
		♠	Q 9
		♡	A K J 8
2 ♠	4 ♠	◇	A K 7 3
		♣	10 8 3

Your 4 ♠ raise may be based on high cards . . .

Partner	You		
		♠	J 9 7 5
		♡	3
2 ♠	4 ♠	◇	8 7
		♣	A 8 6 5 3 2

. . . or it may be weak; let the opponents guess!

INTERFERENCE BY THE OPPONENTS

If the opening weak two-bid elicits competition from the enemy, as it often does, there are surprisingly few changes. Insofar as they are possible, all previously described responses (including 2 NT and the rebids thereafter) apply equally well after interference. Nevertheless, there are a few additional agreements necessary. Our recommendations follow:

1. **If the weak two-bid is doubled** (for takeout), responder may (a) make his normal response; or (b) redouble to show a defensively oriented hand of at least 14 high-card points.

2. **If the weak two-bid is overcalled,** responder may (a) make his normal response; (b) double for penalty; or (c) cue-bid the enemy suit as an all-purpose slam try. EXCEPTION: After a 2 ◇ opening, a three-level cue-bid may be an attempt to reach 3 NT, asking for a stopper in the enemy suit.

Partner	Opp.	You		
			♠	9 7
			♡	A J 7
2 ◇	2 ♠	3 ♠	◇	K 10 8 5
			♣	A Q J 6

If partner has a spade stopper, he will rebid 3 NT; otherwise, you will gamble on 5 ◇.

3. **If opener's right-hand opponent overcalls after the 2 NT response,** opener may (a) pass with a minimum weak two-bid; (b) double to show a "feature" in the enemy suit; (c) bid three of his original suit with a "feature" that cannot be shown at the three-level; or (d) make his normal rebid.

♠	7 3		You	Opp.	Partner	Opp.
♡	A Q 10 9 5 4					
◇	7 2		2 ♡	P	2 NT	3 ◇
♣	K 9 8		3 ♡			

You show a club feature. With a diamond feature, you would double; with a minimum weak two-bid, you would pass. Higher bids would retain their usual meanings.

Acol Three-Notrump Opening ★ ★

Prerequisite:
STRONG ARTIFICIAL 2 ♣ OPENING

An important feature of the Acol system, the British counterpart of "Standard American"

There are several versions of the so-called "gambling 3 NT opening" in popular use nowadays. All show a long strong minor suit, but the outside strength varies from (a) nothing outside; to (b) one outside stopper; to (c) at least two outside stoppers. We do not favor type (a), since it places the declaration in the wrong hand, leaving dummy's stoppers exposed to the opening lead. Type (b) is perhaps better, but how is partner supposed to know *which* suit is protected?

Consequently, we recommend type (c), or the "Acol 3 NT opening." It is made with the expectation of succeeding far more often than not. In other words, the "gambling" element is greatly reduced. Here are the requirements:

Three-notrump opening shows 16 to 21 high-card points, a solid or semi-solid minor suit of at least six (usually seven) cards, and outside stoppers in at least two (often all three) suits. Furthermore, opener should never have a void or a small singleton.

♠	A 3	
♡	K 5	*Open 3 NT. A classic example.*
◇	A K Q 9 8 7 3	
♣	Q 5	

♠	K 8	
♡	A Q	*Open 3 NT. With only a six-card suit, you should*
◇	A 10 7	*have about 19 to 21 HCP.*
♣	A Q J 10 8 5	

♠	Q J 3	
♡	K	*Open 3 NT. A singleton honor is permissible.*
◇	A K J 10 8 7 5	
♣	A 3	

♠	A 8 5	
♡	3	*Open 1 ♣. If partner responds 1 ♡, then jump to*
◇	K 7	*3 NT.*
♣	A K Q J 9 8 4	

RESPONSES

The methods of responding to the various types of gambling 3 NT openings have found little standardization. Therefore, we will present those that we feel are most effective for the Acol 3 NT. It is not necessary that you adopt our recommendations, but we hesitate to offer simpler ones, as they are just inadequate.

First of all, responder must never rescue the 3 NT bid. Opener can often win nine tricks all by himself, so it would be an insult to proclaim otherwise. When slam is out of the question, responder should generally pass. The meanings of the responses are explained below:

1. **Four clubs** is a general slam try, promising 9 or more high-card points, with at least an *ace* and a *king* (or three kings). This is completely artificial and is forcing to at least 4 NT.

Partner	You		
		♠	A 9 8 7 5
		♡	Q J 5
3 NT	4 ♣	♢	K 10 3
		♣	8 6

You have mild slam interest, but wish to leave the decision up to partner.

After the 4 ♣ response, opener may (a) return to 4 NT or five of his minor to reject the slam try; (b) cue-bid a major-suit ace; or (c) bid 4 ♢ as "Gerber" to ask for aces. Here are two examples:

♠	K 4	You	Partner
♡	A 3		
♢	9 8	3 NT	4 ♣
♣	A K Q 10 9 5 3	4 NT	

You have a minimum for your 3 NT bid, so sign off in 4 NT; don't bid the same values twice.

♠	Q	You	Partner
♡	K J 10		
♢	K J	3 NT	4 ♣
♣	A K Q J 7 5 3	4 ♢	

Your 4 ♢ rebid is Gerber. If partner has: three aces, you will bid a grand slam; two aces, you will bid a small slam; one ace, you can stop safely in 4 NT.

2. **Four diamonds** (in response to 3 NT) is also "Gerber." This is how responder can take control.

Partner	You		
		♠	Q 10 7
		♡	K Q 8
3 NT	4 ♢	♢	A Q 8 5
		♣	5 4 2

You have enough strength to bid a slam, but first want to check about aces.

NOTE: From the above, you should observe that *all* 4 ♢ bids are ace-asking after the 3 NT opening; i.e., either a direct response or a rebid of 4 ♢ asks for aces in Gerber fashion. Normal step responses are used: 4 ♡ shows *zero* aces, 4 ♠ shows *one* ace, etc. If Gerber bidder rebids 5 ♢, that asks for *kings* in a similar manner.

3. **Four of a major** shows a good six-card or longer suit, but denies any outside ace. This is not forcing, but slam is still possible if opener has a maximum and good controls.

Partner	You		
		♠	A Q J 9 8 6
		♡	6 5 4
3 NT	4 ♠	♢	J 9 5
		♣	3

Your 4 ♠ bid is not a rescue but a constructive move; partner may bid again.

4. **Four notrump** is a natural slam invitation, but not forcing. This denies the controls needed to respond 4 ♣, and usually shows about 11 to 13 high-card points.

	Partner	You	♠ K J 8 7 6
			♡ Q J 9
	3 NT	4 NT	◇ 10 7
			♣ K Q 8

Your 4 NT bid is a mild slam try, and forewarns partner of your deficiency in controls.

5. **Five clubs** is an attempt to play game in opener's minor. This suggests a major-suit singleton (or void) and a weakish hand. Opener will pass or correct to 5 ◇.

	Partner	You	♠ 4
			♡ A 7 4 2
	3 NT	5 ♣	◇ J 9 5 3
			♣ 10 8 6 3

You are not sure of partner's minor, but whichever it is, five of a minor appears right.

NOTE: In similar fashion, a rebid of 5 ♣ (or 6 ♣) by responder *after* using the "Gerber" 4 ◇ response requests opener to pass or correct to 5 ◇ (or 6 ◇).

INTERFERENCE BY THE OPPONENTS

In the event that the Acol 3 NT opening is interfered with by the enemy, the following agreements should apply:

1. **If the 3 NT opening is doubled,** responder may (a) bid 4 ♣ as a *rescue* bid; (b) pass with a few scattered values; (c) redouble to indicate a normal "4 ♣ response"; or (d) make his normal response.

Partner	Opp.	You	♠ 8 5
			♡ 9 7 6 3
3 NT	DBL	4 ♣	◇ J 9 8 2
			♣ 8 3 2

Without the double you would pass, but now the risk is too great. Partner must pass or correct to 4 ◇.

2. **If the 3 NT opening is overcalled,** responder may (a) bid 4 NT as a *competitive* maneuver; (b) double for penalty; or (c) make his normal response.

Partner	Opp.	You	♠ K 3
			♡ K J 8 6
3 NT	4 ♠	4 NT	◇ J 10 8
			♣ 9 7 5 2

You would rather try for ten tricks at notrump than defend; but had the overcall been 4 ♡, you would double.

3. **If the 3 NT opening is overcalled, and responder has passed,** opener may (a) bid or double with a maximum hand; or (b) pass with a minimum hand.

♠ A 5	You	Opp.	Partner	Opp.
♡ K 8 3				
◇ A K Q 10 9 5 4	3 NT	4 ♠	P	P
♣ K	DBL			

Your double is optional. Partner must decide whether to bid or defend.

5

Defensive Bidding

Up until now you have been mostly on the *offensive* side, i.e., the side that has opened the bidding. In this chapter, we will cover the many *defensive* conventions that apply after the *enemy* has opened the bidding.

In this chapter:

★

Takeout Doubles
Optional Doubles
Double of One-Notrump Opening
Lead-Directing Doubles
Weak Jump Overcalls
Unusual Notrump Overcall

★ ★

Michaels Cue-Bid
Invitational Cue-Bid
Responsive Doubles
S-O-S Redouble
Astro

★ ★ ★

Jump Cue-Bid Overcall
Defense to One Club Forcing
Defenses to Two-Level and Higher Conventional Openings

including
Defense to strong artificial 2  opening
Defense to Flannery
Defense to three-suited openings
Defense to unusual 2 NT opening
Defense to gambling 3 NT opening
Defense to transfer preempts

Takeout Doubles ★

A concept developed (independently) by Charles Patton of New York City and Bryant McCampbell of St. Louis, Missouri, in 1912-13 (the days of auction bridge)

The takeout double has been around for so long that one is skeptical about including it in a book on bridge conventions. Nevertheless, there is so much more to its use than most players realize that we feel extensive coverage is most appropriate. We will begin with the most common, well-known application, i.e., after an opening bid of one of a suit by your right-hand opponent. The basic agreement is explained below:

Direct double of one-of-a-suit opening is a takeout double. Typically, this shows at least a minimum opening bid with *support* (three or more cards) for each of the unbid suits; but it may also be made with a hand *too strong* for an overcall (about 18 points or more).

Opp.	You		
		♠	A J 8 5
		♡	8 3
1 ♡	DBL	◇	K Q 6
		♣	K 9 8 4

You can support any suit partner bids; but had the opening bid been in any other suit, you would have to pass.

Opp.	You		
		♠	A K J 9 7
		♡	5 4
1 ◇	DBL	◇	A 5
		♣	A J 10 2

Your hand is slightly too strong for a 1 ♠ overcall. You would also double an opening bid of 1 ♣ or 1 ♡.

Enough of the classic textbook examples. Let us now study some of the characteristics and tendencies of the better players. The following guidelines should be helpful:

1. **With four cards in each major** (after a minor opening), it is permissible to double without support for the unbid minor.

Opp.	You		
		♠	A J 6 5
		♡	K J 10 7
1 ♣	DBL	◇	10 5
		♣	A 9 2

You are willing to gamble that partner will respond in a major suit rather than diamonds.

2. **With a singleton or void in the enemy suit and 4-4-4-1 or 5-4-4-0 shape,** the strength of a takeout double may be shaded slightly. Hands of this nature offer the best hope of locating a good fit and competing successfully.

Opp.	You		
		♠	K J 9 4
		♡	3
1 ♡	DBL	◇	A 9 6 4
		♣	Q 10 3 2

You would not open the bidding, to be sure, but your "perfect" shape makes a double attractive.

3. **With 4-3-3-3 shape,** use extreme caution. Avoid doubling on minimum strength, especially if your hand contains doubtful honors in the enemy suit.

Opp.	You	♠ A J 8 3
		♡ K 8 7
1 ◇	P	◇ K Q 8
		♣ 10 5 3

Your dismal shape and diamond honors will disappoint partner, so pass. Only after a 1 ♣ opening would a double be reasonable.

4. **With a five-card suit,** it is often a close decision whether to overcall or double. Generally, prefer the overcall if your hand contains a *good* five-card major suit, but otherwise double.

Opp.	You	♠ A J 9
		♡ A K 10 7 6
1 ◇	1 ♡	◇ 3
		♣ J 8 7 4

It is better to overcall to show your good heart suit. Had your hearts been, say, J-X-X-X-X, and your clubs A-K-X-X, then you should double.

RESPONSES

Responding to the takeout double is a very important task, and must be handled properly. Indeed, many players falter in this area, often causing the doubler to develop bad habits just to compensate. Responder must keep in mind that he is *forced* to bid, even with nothing! Therefore, it is necessary to *jump* (or cue-bid the enemy suit) to show that he really has something. Here are the meanings of the responses to a takeout double:

1. **Any minimum new-suit bid** shows 0 to 9 points. Responder simply bids his longest unbid suit, always preferring a major suit if he has one.

Opp.	Partner	Opp.	You	♠ 8 7 5
				♡ Q 9 5 4
1 ♡	DBL	P	2 ♣	◇ 5 3
				♣ J 7 5 3

You are bidding not *because you want to, but because partner has compelled you to.*

2. **One notrump** shows 6 to 9 (or a bad 10) points. This promises a stopper in the enemy suit, and denies holding a four-card or longer unbid major suit.

Opp.	Partner	Opp.	You	♠ A 8 7
				♡ 10 3
1 ◇	DBL	P	1 NT	◇ K 9 8 5
				♣ 10 9 4 2

Your 1 NT response is preferable to bidding a four-card club suit, since your hand is balanced.

3. **Jump in a new suit** shows 10 to 12 points and is invitational to game but *not* forcing. Responder does not require a long suit, since doubler implies support for each of the unbid suits. It is quite common to jump in a four-card major; however, minor-suit jumps tend to show at least five cards.

Opp.	Partner	Opp.	You		
				♠	J 10 9 6
				♡	A 3
1 ◇	DBL	P	2 ♠	◇	A J 4
				♣	7 6 4 3

You must jump to 2 ♠ to show your values; a simple response of 1 ♠ is a "nothing" bid.

4. **Two notrump** shows 11 or 12 (or a good 10) points and is invitational to game. Like the 1 NT response, this promises a stopper in the enemy suit, and implies no unbid four-card or longer major suit.

Opp.	Partner	Opp.	You		
				♠	K Q 10
				♡	A 4
1 ♠	DBL	P	2 NT	◇	Q 9 8 3
				♣	10 6 5 4

Your 2 NT bid is not forcing. With a minimum takeout double, partner should pass.

5. **Cue-bid** (of the enemy suit) usually shows 13 or more points, but may be made with 10 to 12 points if holding *two* unbid four-card majors. This shows nothing in particular about your holding in the enemy suit, but is just a convenient forcing bid. Responder promises to bid again (if below game). In fact, game must be reached, unless a suit is subsequently *raised* under game.

Opp.	Partner	Opp.	You		
				♠	A J 9 8 5
				♡	A 5 4
1 ♣	DBL	P	2 ♣	◇	K 3
				♣	9 7 6

Your 2 ♣ cue-bid shows a good hand; later you will bid your spade suit (forcing).

Opp.	Partner	Opp.	You		
				♠	Q J 9 4
				♡	K J 8 7
1 ◇	DBL	P	2 ◇	◇	9 3
				♣	K 8 2

You are not sure whether to jump to 2 ♡ or 2 ♠, so cue-bid 2 ◇. Partner will undoubtedly bid two of a major, which you will raise to three to invite game; with a stronger hand, you would raise to game.

6. **Three notrump** shows 13 to 16 points, or slightly less if your hand contains a five-card or longer minor suit that you expect will provide tricks. Responder must have little doubt that 3 NT is the proper contract.

Opp.	Partner	Opp.	You		
				♠	A Q 7
				♡	9 8
1 ♠	DBL	P	3 NT	◇	K Q 10 8 6 4
				♣	10 3

Your long diamond suit compensates for the slight deficiency in points. Notice that partner can be counted on for stoppers in every suit except the enemy suit.

7. **Double jump (or higher) in a new suit** shows *less* than 10 points, but at least a six-card suit. This response is basically preemptive. EXCEPTION: If this bid completes game, responder *may* have a stronger hand (and less than a six-card suit) when there is some tactical reason for becoming declarer.

Opp.	Partner	Opp.	You
1 ◇	DBL	P	3 ♠

♠ Q J 10 8 7 5
♡ 4
◇ J 5 4
♣ 8 6 2

You show a weak hand with long spades.

Opp.	Partner	Opp.	You
1 ♠	DBL	P	4 ♡

♠ K 5
♡ A J 9 6 4
◇ K 10 7 5
♣ 6 3

You would normally cue-bid 2 ♠ with this kind of hand, but do not wish to take the chance that partner may bid hearts. With K-X in spades, you want to be declarer, not dummy!

8. **Passing** (a takeout double) is rare, and should be avoided whenever possible. This converts the double into penalty, and requires at least *five* trumps, from which you can win at least *three* trump tricks.

Opp.	Partner	Opp.	You
1 ◇	DBL	P	1 ♡

♠ 4 3
♡ J 5 4
◇ Q J 7 6 3
♣ 6 5 4

Do not make the mistake of passing 1 ◇ doubled; that will surely be a disaster. Bid your best "suit" and pray.

Opp.	Partner	Opp.	You
1 ♡	DBL	P	P

♠ 8 3
♡ K Q 10 9 7
◇ 9 7 4
♣ J 6 4

Now you can pass. Incidentally, partner should usually lead trumps when you convert his double, so be prepared.

RESPONSES IN COMPETITION

When right-hand opponent bids or redoubles after the takeout double, responder is obviously relieved of the obligation to bid. The following agreements then go into effect:

1. **Over a redouble,** responder may (a) pass to allow doubler to rescue himself; or (b) make his normal response. NOTE: Passing the redouble is *not* an attempt to convert the double into penalty, but merely expresses the lack of any clear-cut preference among the unbid suits.

Opp.	Partner	Opp.	You
1 ◇	DBL	RDBL	1 ♡

♠ 5 3
♡ 9 8 6 5
◇ 10 7 5 3 2
♣ 10 2

Your 1 ♡ bid does not promise any strength, but just shows four hearts. Change a small heart to a spade, and you would pass.

2. **Over an intervening bid,** responder may (a) bid a new suit with 6 to 9 points (may be shaded slightly at the one-level); (b) double for penalty; (c) make his normal response; or (d) pass. NOTE: In competition, it is still necessary to jump the bidding in a new suit to show 10 to 12 points, even if this must be done at a higher level than normal (but not beyond game, of course).

Opp.	Partner	Opp.	You	
				♠ K J 8 6
				♡ Q 6 3
1 ◇	DBL	2 ◇	<u>2 ♠</u>	◇ 8 7 5 4
				♣ 10 2

Your free bid of 2 ♠ shows 6 to 9 points; with 10 to 12 points, you must jump to 3 ♠ to invite game.

Opp.	Partner	Opp.	You	
				♠ 8 5
				♡ A Q 9 7
1 ♣	DBL	1 ♡	<u>DBL</u>	◇ J 10 8
				♣ 7 5 4 3

*Your double is for penalty. Partner, remember, should have at least **three** hearts for his double.*

REBIDS BY TAKEOUT DOUBLER

On most occasions, the takeout doubler will encounter a *minimum* suit response from partner. In that event, doubler must remember that he has *already* shown approximately an opening bid, and thus should not bid again except with considerably **extra** strength. Here are the meanings of doubler's rebids:

1. **Pass** with *all* hands of 15 points or less. Also, takeout doubler should usually pass with 16 or 17 points if his hand is unsuitable for a raise of responder's suit.

Opp.	Partner	Opp.	You	
				♠ A J 8 5
				♡ Q J 7 5
		1 ◇	DBL	◇ 4 3
P	1 ♠	P	<u>P</u>	♣ K Q 9

   Do not succumb to the amateur bid of 2 ♠. You have a minimum takeout double, so don't compound the situation with a gross overbid.

2. **Single raise** shows about 16 to 18 points with at least four-card support for responder's suit. EXCEPTION: A single raise to the three-level in a non-competitive auction should be slightly stronger, about 18 to 20 points.

Opp.	Partner	Opp.	You	
				♠ A 7 5
				♡ K Q 9 7
		1 ♣	DBL	◇ A Q 8 3
P	1 ♡	P	<u>2 ♡</u>	♣ 9 2

   Your raise to 2 ♡ shows extra values and a good fit. In contrast, had partner responded 1 ♠, you should pass.

Opp.	Partner	Opp.	You	
				♠ K 10 8 5
				♡ A 3
		1 ♡	DBL	◇ Q J 7 5
P	2 ◇	2 ♡	<u>3 ◇</u>	♣ A J 4

   You show a similar hand. Without the 2 ♡ bid, however, you should pass.

Opp.	Partner	Opp.	You	
				♠ 7 5
				♡ K J 9 8
		1 ♠	DBL	◇ A K 8
P	2 ♣	P	<u>3 ♣</u>	♣ A K 6 3

   Here you show 18 to 20 points, since you are raising to the three-level in the absence of competition.

3. **Jump raise to three** shows about 19 or 20 points (or a good 18 points) with at least four-card support for responder's suit.

Opp.	Partner	Opp.	You		
				♠	K 10 9 8
				♡	A K Q 4
		1 ♦	DBL	♦	3
P	1 ♠	P	3 ♠	♣	A 9 8 3

You show a hand too strong for 2 ♠, but you must not jump to game; partner may have nothing, remember.

4. **New suit** shows about 18 to 20 points and a five-card or longer suit. This is invitational, but not forcing. NOTE: The strength requirement may be shaded slightly when doubler's hand contains an *unbid* four-card major.

Opp.	Partner	Opp.	You		
				♠	A K J 9 3
				♡	A 9 3
		1 ♡	DBL	♦	K 7
P	2 ♦	P	2 ♠	♣	K 10 8

You show a hand that was too strong for an original overcall of 1 ♠.

Opp.	Partner	Opp.	You		
				♠	6
				♡	A K 8 4
		1 ♠	DBL	♦	A Q J 7 6 5
P	2 ♣	P	2 ♦	♣	10 8

With a side four-card heart suit, you need not be quite so strong. Obviously, you were hoping partner might bid hearts over your double.

5. **Jump in a new suit** shows a strong hand and at least a six-card self-sufficient suit. Essentially, doubler is bidding what he expects to make, so this is not forcing.

Opp.	Partner	Opp.	You		
				♠	A 4
				♡	A K Q 10 9 7
		1 ♦	DBL	♦	5 3
P	1 ♠	P	3 ♡	♣	A Q 9

You show about 8½ or 9 tricks; if partner can provide a trick, he must bid again.

6. **All notrump bids** show very strong hands, with a stopper in the enemy suit. Typical ranges are: (a) 1 NT shows 18 to 20 points; (b) jump to 2 NT shows 21 or 22 points; (c) non-jump 2 NT shows 19 to 21 points; and (d) 3 NT shows better than 2 NT, or the expectation of winning nine tricks.

Opp.	Partner	Opp.	You		
				♠	A K 9 7
				♡	A 8 4
		1 ♦	DBL	♦	K 3
P	1 ♡	P	1 NT	♣	K J 9 5

You should not raise hearts with just three-card support, so your 1 NT bid is indicated.

Opp.	Partner	Opp.	You		
				♠	A Q 8
				♡	K 9 8
		1 ♠	DBL	♦	K J 6
P	2 ♦	P	2 NT	♣	A Q 10 9

You show a hand too strong for a 1 NT overcall.

Opp.	Partner	Opp.	You		
				♠	A K 6 5
				♡	K 10
		1 ♡	DBL	◇	A K Q 10 8 5
P	2 ♣	P	<u>3 NT</u>	♣	3

Here you have a "trick-taking" hand. With a heart lead, and partner's club stopper, the road to nine tricks is clear.

7. **Cue-bid** (of the suit originally doubled) shows 21 or more points, but has no relation to doubler's holding in the enemy suit. This forces responder to bid again, but does *not* promise a rebid. Therefore, responder is well-advised to jump the bidding if he has any real values to show.

Opp.	Partner	Opp.	You		
				♠	9 7
				♡	A Q 8
		1 ♠	DBL	◇	A K J 9
P	2 ♡	P	<u>2 ♠</u>	♣	A K 9 2

You show a powerhouse double. Nonetheless, if partner rebids only 2 NT or 3 ♡, a pass is recommended.

The above outlined rebids by takeout doubler are based on the presumption that responder has made a *minimum new-suit* response, the most frequent case. They also would apply, insofar as possible, when responder has *not bid at all* because of an intervening bid over the double.

Nevertheless, these same rebids *cannot* be applied when responder has *jumped* the bidding, *cue-bid,* or bid *notrump* in response to the double. In that event, responder's strength is more clearly defined and a common sense approach is best. Our recommendations are briefly explained below:

1. **If responder has *jumped*** (inviting game), doubler may (a) make any natural bid to accept the game invitation; or (b) pass to reject.

2. **If responder has *cue-bid*** (forcing), doubler may make any natural bid, preferring, of course, to bid an unbid four-card major. It is unnecessary to jump, as responder must bid again unless game is reached.

3. **If responder has bid *one notrump*** (6 to 10 points), doubler may (a) bid 2 NT to invite game; (b) sign off in game; (c) bid a five-card or longer suit, which is not forcing at the two-level but forcing at the three-level; (d) cue-bid the enemy suit (one-round force) to invite game and urge responder to bid a suit; or (e) pass.

OTHER FIRST-ROUND TAKEOUT DOUBLES

Up until now, we have concerned ourselves only with one specific application of the takeout double, i.e., the direct double of an opening bid of one of a suit. We will now examine the remaining situations in which a takeout double may be made on the first round of bidding. But first, *memorize* this rule:

If partner has not bid or doubled, the double of a *natural suit* bid through *four diamonds* is a takeout double.

Remember the key words, *"natural suit"* and *"four diamonds,"* and you know the rule. Let us see how this applies to some specific situations:

1. **Double of a higher-suit opening** is for takeout. Quite logically, the higher the opening bid, the more strength required. A good rule of thumb is to add *one* point (to

the doubler's requirements) for each level beyond the one-level. But in any event, do not be afraid to take a chance when you have the ideal shape for a takeout double, i.e., 4-4-4-1 or 5-4-4-0.

Opp.	You
	♠ A 4
	♡ K Q 9 5
2 ♠*	DBL ♢ A 8 7 4
	♣ J 9 8

*Weak two-bid

For all practical purposes, your double of 2 ♠ is just like a double of 1 ♠.

Opp.	You
	♠ K J 8 6
	♡ K 10 7 4
4 ♣	DBL ♢ A 9 6 4 3
	♣ —

Here your exciting shape allows you to be aggressive.

2. **Double of any suit response to any opening bid** is for takeout. Furthermore, if the enemy has bid *two* natural suits, this double virtually guarantees at least four cards in each of the two unbid suits (or else a very strong hand).

Opp.	Partner	Opp.	You
			♠ 7 5
			♡ K Q 8 5
1 ♣	P	1 ♠	DBL ♢ A K 10 2
			♣ 9 7 5

It would be very unusual not to have at least four hearts and four diamonds on this sequence.

Opp.	Partner	Opp.	You
			♠ K J 10 7
			♡ 4
1 ♡	P	2 ♣	DBL ♢ A K 9 8 6
			♣ 5 4 3

Even five-four shape is typical, especially when the enemy has shown considerable strength.

Opp.	Partner	Opp.	You
			♠ —
			♡ K 10 7 5 4
1 ♠	P	3 ♠	DBL ♢ A J 8 7
			♣ Q J 9 6

Here, of course, you are making a three-suit takeout.

Opp.	Partner	Opp.	You
			♠ A J 8 2
			♡ 4
1 NT	P	2 ♡	DBL ♢ J 9 7 6
			♣ K Q 10 8

As long as 2 ♡ is natural (not Jacoby), your double is a takeout for the unbid suits.

3. **Balancing doubles of all suit opening bids** are for takeout. These are just like direct doubles, but with the modification that balancer *overbids* by about two points. In other words, balancer adds a *"queen"* to his hand, then bids normally. Obviously, partner of balancer must compensate by underbidding by two points, or deducting that hypothetical queen.

Opp.	Partner	Opp.	You		
				♠	A 8 7
				♡	K J 4 3
1 ◇	P	P	DBL	◇	8 3 2
				♣	Q J 8

You would not have doubled 1 ◇ in direct seat, but the "queen" rule gives you enough to balance with a double.

Opp.	Partner	Opp.	You		
				♠	Q 10 8 5
				♡	3
3 ♡	P	P	DBL	◇	A 10 6 4
				♣	K 9 8 2

A direct double of 3 ♡ would be frightening, but the balancing double is all right, although not without risk.

The next application might be called the "oddball," since it is the *only* time that a double of a notrump bid is for takeout.

4. **Double of a 1 NT or 2 NT response to a natural suit opening bid** is for takeout. In effect, this is just like a takeout double of the suit opened.

Opp.	Partner	Opp.	You		
				♠	K Q 6 5
				♡	A Q 10 3
1 ◇	P	1 NT	DBL	◇	5 3
				♣	J 10 8

Your double of 1 NT is the same as a double of 1 ◇.

Opp.	Partner	Opp.	You		
				♠	A Q J 4
				♡	3
2 ♡*	P	2 NT	DBL	◇	A 10 8 7
				♣	Q 10 7 2

*Weak two-bid

You indicate a takeout double of 2 ♡.

5. **Doubles by a passed hand** (i.e., by a player who passed prior to any bidding) follow all the rules previously mentioned, but with the obvious high-card limitations imposed by the failure to open the bidding.

Opp.	Partner	Opp.	You		
				♠	K Q J 4
				♡	4
		P		◇	9 8 6
1 ♡	P	2 ◇	DBL	♣	K J 10 9 7

Even though you passed originally, this is indeed your first opportunity to double, so its usual meaning applies.

NOTE: Responding to *all* takeout doubles (including the "belated" doubles of the next section) closely parallels the methods described after a takeout double of an opening bid of one of a suit. The important principles are: (a) all minimum bids show minimum values; (b) all jump bids are invitational to game; and (c) a cue-bid of the enemy suit is the only forcing bid.

However, one slightly different aspect deserves mention. The *penalty* pass of a takeout double does *not* require as strong a trump holding if the auction is very high, or if you are *behind* the original bidder.

BELATED TAKEOUT DOUBLES

A "belated" takeout double is one that is made on the *second* round of bidding. There are many opportunities for such doubles. For instance, you might have overcalled, doubled, opened the bidding, or even *passed* on the first round of bidding, then make a takeout double on the second round.

It is impractical to create a rule that will determine exactly when a belated double is for *takeout* and when it is not; there are just too many variable factors. We can, however, recall some of the essential ingredients for a takeout double, each of which should already be familiar: (a) partner must never have bid or doubled; (b) the level of bidding must not be beyond 4 ◇; and (c) the double must be of a natural suit bid.

Bearing these qualifications in mind, the conditions under which a belated double is for takeout (or penalty) can now be determined by examining the following specific situations:

1. **After making a simple suit overcall,** overcaller may double for takeout through the level of 4 ◇. This suggests a maximum overcall with support for the unbid suit (or suits).

Opp.	Partner	Opp.	You
		1 ♠	2 ♣
P	P	2 ♠	DBL

    ♠ 6
    ♡ K J 8
    ◇ A 7 3
    ♣ A Q J 6 5 2

    Your double shows a good 2 ♣ overcall with tolerance for hearts and dia-monds. This action is far more flexible (and safer) than rebidding 3 ♣.

2. **After you have made a takeout double,** a second double is for takeout through 4 ◇ if the suit doubled was bid *prior* to your first double. When your second double is of a *new* suit, it is for takeout only if that suit was raised at the two-level, or in balancing position through 2 ◇. Otherwise, the double of a new suit is penalty oriented.

Opp.	Partner	Opp.	You
		1 ♠	DBL
2 ◇	P	2 ♠	DBL

    ♠ 7
    ♡ K Q J 8
    ◇ A 9 5
    ♣ A Q 9 7 5

    You just show a stronger-than-minimum takeout double.

Opp.	Partner	Opp.	You
		1 ♠	DBL
2 ♡	P	P	DBL

    ♠ 5 3
    ♡ A K J 9
    ◇ A 8 3
    ♣ A Q 10 3

    Here your double is for penalty, but had left-hand opponent bid 2 ♣ or 2 ◇, a reopening double would be for takeout.

Opp.	Partner	Opp.	You
		1 ♣	DBL
1 ♡	P	2 ♡	DBL

    ♠ K J 9 8
    ♡ A 5 4
    ◇ A K J 7
    ♣ 5 4

    Because of the raise, your double of 2 ♡ is for takeout; you obviously show spades and diamonds.

3. **After opening the bidding with one of a suit,** opener may double for takeout through the level of 4 ◇. This shows a good opening bid, and implies support for the unbid suit (or suits).

Opp.	Partner	Opp.	You	
				♠ 6
				♡ A K Q 5 4
			1 ♡	◇ K J 5 4
2 ♣	P	2 ♠	DBL	♣ A 10 3

Your double implies three or four diamonds. In contrast, a bid of 3 ◇ would suggest five diamonds.

4. **After a 1 NT opening or overcall,** only a *balancing* double (by 1 NT bidder) is for takeout through 2 ♠, provided the suit doubled was first bid *after* your 1 NT bid. Otherwise, all doubles are for penalty.

Opp.	Partner	Opp.	You	
				♠ A J 9 7
				♡ A 3
			1 NT	◇ Q J 9 6
2 ♡	P	P	DBL	♣ K Q 10

Your reopening double is for takeout; however, if right-hand opponent had bid 2 ♡, a double would be for penalty.

Opp.	Partner	Opp.	You	
				♠ A 8
				♡ A K 7
		1 ♣	1 NT	◇ A 8 4 3
2 ♣	P	P	DBL	♣ Q J 10 8

Here your double is for penalty, since clubs were first bid prior to your 1 NT overcall. Surely, if you wanted to double for takeout, you would have doubled 1 ♣!

5. **After you have passed an enemy bid,** the situation is more complex. It is helpful to break it down into two parts: (a) *direct* doubles; and (b) *balancing* doubles.

a. **A direct double** is for takeout through 2 ◇, or through 4 ◇ if a raised suit, provided the suit doubled was first bid *after* your last pass. Otherwise, direct doubles are for penalty. EXCEPTION: If opener rebids *two* of his original minor suit after a *suit* response, a double is for takeout.

Opp.	Partner	Opp.	You	
				♠ A 9 7 5
				♡ K Q 9 5
		1 ♠	P	◇ 3
1 NT	P	2 ◇	DBL	♣ K J 8 2

Your double is for takeout; but had opener's rebid been 2 ♡ (or higher), a double would be for penalty.

Opp.	Partner	Opp.	You	
				♠ K J 6 5
				♡ —
		1 ◇	P	◇ A K 7 5
1 ♡	P	3 ♡	DBL	♣ 10 9 8 6 5

Because of the raise, your double of 3 ♡ is for takeout; this is most uncommon.

Opp.	Partner	Opp.	You	
				♠ 9 3
				♡ K 10 9 6
		1 ♣	P	◇ A J 10 7
1 ♠	P	2 ♣	DBL	♣ A 9 3

This is the exception. Your double is for takeout, but note that had the response been 1 NT (instead of 1 ♠), a double would be for penalty.

NOTE: As is evident by the above examples, the *direct* takeout double (after passing an enemy bid) is a rare bird. It implies the full values to have acted previously, but suggests there was no attractive action to take at your last turn. In contrast, the *balancing* takeout double (described below) is quite common. It implies skimpier values, and is based on the deduction that partner is marked for some high cards by the enemy bidding.

   b. **A balancing double** is for takeout through 4 ◇, provided the suit doubled was first bid *after* your last pass, or has been *raised*. When the suit doubled was first bid *prior* to your last pass, and non-raised, a balancing double is for takeout only through 2 ♠.

Opp.	Partner	Opp.	You	
				♠ 7 5
				♡ K 10 9 5 3
		2 ♠*	P	◇ 3
3 ◇	P	P	DBL	♣ A Q 9 7 5

*Weak two-bid

Your double is for takeout, since diamonds were introduced after your pass.

Opp.	Partner	Opp.	You	
				♠ Q 8 5 4
				♡ 8 3
		1 ♡	P	◇ K 10 7 3
2 ♡	P	P	DBL	♣ A 10 9

   This is a very common situation for balancing with a takeout double, i.e., when the enemy has found a fit at the two-level. It is safer than it looks.

Opp.	Partner	Opp.	You	
				♠ K J 10 3
				♡ A 9 8 2
1 ◇	P	1 NT	P	◇ 5 2
2 ◇	P	P	DBL	♣ Q 7 5

   Your balancing double is for takeout; obviously you hope to compete in a major suit.

Opp.	Partner	Opp.	You	
				♠ A 5
				♡ Q J 10 8
1 ♡	P	1 NT	P	◇ A 8 3
3 ♡	P	P	DBL	♣ A 7 5 2

   At this level, your double is for penalty (hearts were bid prior to your last pass and non-raised), although very rare.

6. **After making a natural 2 NT or 3 NT bid,** all doubles are for *penalty*.

7. **After opening with a strong artificial 2 ♣ bid** (see page *93*), all doubles are for *penalty*.

8. **After doubling any notrump bid** (excluding the "oddball" case on page *119*), all further doubles are for *penalty*.

9. **After doubling any natural suit bid for penalty,** all further doubles are for *penalty*.

VERY BELATED TAKEOUT DOUBLES

Although uncommon, it is possible to make a takeout double on the *third* (or even the fourth) round of bidding. The following agreement is helpful:

On the third or fourth round of bidding, all of the rules for second-round (belated) doubles apply equally well, based on your *last* previous call.

Opp.	Partner	Opp.	You	
			1 ♡	♠ 4
				♡ A K 8 7 6
P	P	1 ♠	2 ♣	◇ K 7
2 ♠	P	P	DBL	♣ A K 9 5 3

Your double is for takeout, obviously with a strong preference for hearts or clubs. This action is more flexible than a 3 ♣ bid.

Opp.	Partner	Opp.	You	
			1 ◇	♠ A 6 5
			DBL	♡ A K 8 6
1 ♠	P	2 ◇	DBL	◇ 5
3 ◇	P	P	DBL	♣ A K 9 8 3

Your third double is still for takeout.

Opp.	Partner	Opp.	You	
			1 ♣	♠ Q 9 7 5
			P	♡ 4
1 ♡	P	2 ♣	P	◇ K J 8 6
2 ♡	P	P	DBL	♣ A 10 3 2

Even though you passed twice, your balancing double is for takeout.

Optional Doubles

An "optional double" is neither a takeout double nor a penalty double, but somewhere in between. Essentially, it shows a good hand and gives partner the option (hence, the name) of bidding or passing. The most practical use of this kind of double occurs after preemptive bids.

We recommend the optional double over enemy preemptive bids of 4 ♡ and 4 ♠ only. Lower preempts are best handled by takeout doubles (see page *117*), and higher ones suggest the need for penalty doubles. Here is the basic agreement:

Double of four of a non-raised major at your first turn (provided partner has not bid or doubled) shows about 3½ (or more) honor tricks. There is no particular shape requirement, but your hand is usually balanced or semi-balanced, and should not contain a singleton or void in an unbid suit.

Opp.	You	
		♠ A 7 5
		♡ A 8 6
4 ♡	DBL	◇ K Q 10 7
		♣ K J 8

You have a good hand, and there is little else you can do but double.

Opp.	Partner	Opp.	You	
				♠ 9 5
				♡ A Q 7 5
4 ♠	P	P	DBL	◇ A K 8 5 4
				♣ K 9

The same is true in balancing position . . .

Opp.	Partner	Opp.	You	
				♠ A 8
				♡ A 10 7
1 ◇	P	4 ♠	DBL	◇ A 10 6 3
				♣ K Q 4 3

. . . or if both opponents have bid.

WARNING: When optional doubles are used, you must *not* double with a **hand like** the following:

Opp.	You		
		♠	K Q 10 7
		♡	A 9 7
4 ♠	?	◇	Q 6 4 3
		♣	10 3

If you double, partner will most likely remove it, perhaps with disastrous results. Just pass and settle for a small profit.

RESPONSES

The decision whether to leave in or remove an optional double is by no means an exact science. Without doubt, it is a guessing game, but an intelligent guess can usually be made by adhering to this guideline:

Removing an optional double requires at least a *six*-card suit (or a five-card spade suit) and reasonably good distribution.

Opp.	Partner	Opp.	You		
				♠	J 8 7 5
				♡	9 3
4 ♡	DBL	P	<u>P</u>	◇	A 6 3
				♣	Q 10 7 4

Do not try to be a hero by bidding 4 ♠. Even if you find a four-four fit, the bad breaks may defeat you.

Opp.	Partner	Opp.	You		
				♠	Q J 9 5 3
				♡	3
4 ♡	DBL	P	<u>4 ♠</u>	◇	K 10 6
				♣	J 9 7 5

With a fifth spade and a singleton heart, 4 ♠ now becomes the percentage call.

Opp.	Partner	Opp.	You		
				♠	5 4
				♡	J 8
4 ♠	DBL	P	<u>P</u>	◇	A J 10 9 7 5
				♣	8 7 6

Despite your six-card suit, the balanced nature of your hand suggests defending. However, if you change a small spade to a club, then a 5 ◇ bid is appropriate.

OPTIONAL DOUBLES OF RAISED SUITS

The double of an enemy *raise* to four of a major is slightly different. We recommend this understanding:

Double of four of a raised major at your first turn (provided partner has not bid or doubled) is still an optional double but leans toward "takeout." That is, doubler suggests support for the unbid suits, often with a singleton in the enemy suit.

Opp.	Partner	Opp.	You		
				♠	K Q 9 6
				♡	3
1 ♡	P	4 ♡	<u>DBL</u>	◇	A K 8
				♣	K 10 9 8 4

Your double is almost like a takeout double.

Opp.	Partner	Opp.	You
3 ♠	P	4 ♠	<u>DBL</u>

♠ 7
♡ A Q 8 7
♢ K Q 10 4
♣ A Q 7 2

Your double encourages partner to bid, but he is still free to pass with no clear-cut bid.

Removing this kind of optional double requires only a *five*-card suit, or a four-card spade suit. For example:

Opp.	Partner	Opp.	You
		1 ♡	P
4 ♡	DBL	P	<u>4 ♠</u>

♠ J 8 7 3
♡ 9 4
♢ 7 6 5
♣ A J 3 2

Your 4 ♠ bid is now justified, as partner is an overwhelming favorite to hold four spades.

BELATED OPTIONAL DOUBLES

The optional double of four of a major suit may also be applied on the *second* round of bidding, as stated below:

If you have opened the bidding with one of a suit, overcalled in a suit, or made a takeout double, a double of four of a major at your next turn (provided partner has not bid or doubled) is an optional double.

Opp.	Partner	Opp.	You
		1 ♢	
4 ♡	P	P	<u>DBL.</u>

♠ A K 5
♡ A 7
♢ K Q 9 8 5
♣ K 10 7

Your double shows a very strong opening bid, but not necessarily heart strength; the decision is up to partner.

Opp.	Partner	Opp.	You
		1 ♠	DBL
2 ♢	P	4 ♠	<u>DBL</u>

♠ 8 3
♡ A K 8 7
♢ A 9 6
♣ A Q J 4

Your double is optional, showing that your original double was based on great high-card strength.

Opp.	Partner	Opp.	You
		1 ♣	
1 ♡	P	4 ♡	<u>DBL</u>

♠ A Q J 7
♡ 3
♢ A 10 8
♣ A K 10 9 7

Here your double is takeout oriented, because of the enemy heart raise.

Double of One-Notrump Opening

The direct double of a 1 NT opening bid is primarily for penalty, although partner has the option of removing it with a weak hand containing a long suit. We recommend this agreement, which closely parallels standard methods:

Direct double of a 1 NT opening shows at least 14 high-card points and a strong suit to lead. Without a good lead, at least 17 high-card points are required.

Opp.	You		
		♠	K Q J 10 4 3
		♡	A 8
1 NT	DBL	◇	A 7 3
		♣	9 2

You should have no trouble defeating 1 NT with your obvious spade lead. If partner can contribute anything, so much the better.

Opp.	You		
		♠	K J 8
		♡	A 7 6 5
1 NT	P	◇	K J 8 3
		♣	A 9

With no attractive lead, it is wiser to pass. With another point or two, a double is recommended, although it would be risky.

BALANCING DOUBLES

The balancing double of a 1 NT opening bid is more of a cooperative double than a penalty double. We suggest this agreement:

Balancing double of a 1 NT opening shows at least 14 high-card points, but the emphasis is different than a direct double. Since you are *not* on lead, an ideal double contains balanced distribution and all-around values, so that partner's opening lead (or escape bid) will not prove embarrassing.

Opp.	Partner	Opp.	You		
				♠	K 9 7
				♡	A J 8 3
1 NT	P	P	DBL	◇	K J 8
				♣	Q 10 2

Your balancing double is desirable, since you can support any suit partner leads (or bids).

Opp.	Partner	Opp.	You		
				♠	A J 8
				♡	K Q J 9 8 7
1 NT	P	P	2 ♡	◇	K 10 5
				♣	3

A direct double with this hand would be fine. But in balancing position, a double is unsound, since partner will not know to lead hearts. Just bid your suit.

NOTE: At matchpoint play, the requirements for a balancing double may be shaded slightly if you wish to gamble on a "top" score. This practice is dangerous, however, so do not complain if you wind up with an occasional "zero."

WEAK NOTRUMPS

Sometimes you will encounter opponents who play "weak notrumps" (see Glossary). In that event, we recommend this modification:

Double of a weak 1 NT opening (direct or balancing) may be made with about *one* or *two* points less strength than is normally required.

Opp.	You	
		♠ A J 9
		♡ 9 8 6 5
1 NT*	DBL	◇ A Q 6 5
		♣ A 8

*12 to 14 points

You would not double a strong 1 NT opening, to be sure, but now you should get your feet wet.

Just because your opponents use weak notrumps, however, does not give you a license to be reckless. Discretion is still called for. For example:

Opp.	Partner	Opp.	You	
				♠ 7 5
				♡ A J 8
1 NT*	P	P	P	◇ K Q 7 5
				♣ Q 10 9 2

*12 to 14 points

You should pass. Do not make borderline balancing doubles when a particular lead (here, a spade) could prove disastrous.

BIDDING AFTER A DOUBLE

After the double of a 1 NT opening (strong or weak, direct or balancing), the partner of doubler must decide whether to pass or remove the double. Many factors are involved, and no advice will always work, but most experts suggest the following guidelines:

1. **Pass the double** with balanced hands, no matter how weak. Even if it proves that 1 NT cannot be defeated, that result may not be as bad as the result you would have obtained by bidding. EXCEPTION: It is permissible to remove a *balancing* double with weak balanced hands of 4-4-3-2 or 5-3-3-2 shape, but not with 4-3-3-3 shape.

Opp.	Partner	Opp.	You	
				♠ J 7 5 4
				♡ 9 5 3
1 NT	DBL	P	P	◇ 4 3 2
				♣ 10 9 6

You have no safety in bidding, so pass. You should also pass a balancing double.

Opp.	Partner	Opp.	You	
				♠ 6 5
		1 NT	P	♡ Q 5 3 2
				◇ 6 4 2
P	DBL	P	2 ♣	♣ 10 9 8 3

Bid 2 ♣ (not 2 ♡) to allow the best chance of escaping undoubled. Observe that you would pass a direct double.

2. **Two of a suit** shows a *weak* distributional hand.

Opp.	Partner	Opp.	You	
				♠ 9 6 4 2
				♡ 2
1 NT	DBL	P	2 ◇	◇ Q 10 8 7 3
				♣ 6 4 3

Your singleton heart makes it unattractive to defend, so bid 2 ◇. You would similarly remove a balancing double.

3. **Any higher bid** shows a *good* distributional hand (6+ HCP after a strong notrump or 8+ HCP after a weak notrump). Responder may (a) jump in a six-card or longer suit (not forcing); or (b) "cue-bid" 2 NT with a two-suited hand to force doubler to bid.

Opp.	Partner	Opp.	You
1 NT	DBL	P	3 ♡

♠ 7 3
♡ Q 10 9 8 5 3
◇ A J 10 7
♣ 3

Your 3 ♡ bid is invitational to game. Change a small heart to a diamond and you would cue-bid 2 NT (forcing).

4. **If your right-hand *opponent* runs from 1 NT doubled,** you may (a) double for penalty; (b) make a "forcing pass" to see if partner can double for penalty; (c) cue-bid the enemy suit as a "good" three-suit takeout; or (d) make your normal response.

Opp.	Partner	Opp.	You
1 NT	DBL	2 ◇	P

♠ A J 9 4
♡ Q 9 5
◇ 10 8
♣ 10 6 4 3

You have more strength than you might have, but it is unnecessary to act now; your pass is forcing. Partner may be able to double 2 ◇, so give him a chance.

Lead-Directing Doubles

A "lead-directing double" is a form of penalty double. Although the penalty double, in itself, is not a convention, the *lead-directing* aspect of such a double may constitute a conventional agreement, and will be covered here.

Undoubtedly, the most common type of lead-directing double is the double of an artificial bid. With the multitude of conventions in use today, there are more and more opportunities for this kind of double. We suggest this agreement:

Double of an artificial suit bid (or a penalty double of a natural suit bid) asks for the lead of that suit. Essentially, this is based on the presumption that the enemy does not intend to play in the suit actually doubled.

Opp.	Partner	Opp.	You
1 NT	P	2 ♣*	DBL

♠ 9 5
♡ A 3
◇ J 5 4
♣ K J 10 8 6 4

*Stayman

The 2 ♣ bid is artificial, so your double shows clubs and asks for the lead of that suit.

NOTE: Against "weak notrumps" (see Glossary), many experts prefer to play the double of a Stayman 2 ♣ response as strength-showing rather than lead-directing.

Opp.	Partner	Opp.	You
1 ♡	P	1 ♠	P
2 ♣	P	2 ◇	DBL

♠ 9 8 5
♡ 8 5 3
◇ K Q 10 9 7
♣ A 8

The 2 ◇ bid may or may not be phony, but your double is clearly for penalty and so asks for a diamond lead.

Opp.	Partner	Opp.	You	♠ A Q 10 7
				♡ 7 4
1 ♣	P	3 ♣	P	♢ J 7 4 2
3 ♡	P	3 ♠	DBL	♣ 7 5 4

Here you request a spade lead.

Opp.	Partner	Opp.	You	♠ 3 2
				♡ K 9 7
		2 ♡*	P	♢ A Q J 6
2 NT	P	3 ♢**	DBL	♣ 9 7 5 3

*Weak two-bid
**Feature

So much for his feature! If you don't double, left-hand opponent may bid 3 NT, and steal it.

Almost as important as the lead-directing double is the *failure* to make one. On many occasions, negative inferences can be drawn. For instance, what would you lead against this slam?

Opp.	Partner	Opp.	You	♠ K 3
1 ♡	P	1 ♠	P	♡ 9 7 5
3 ♠	P	4 NT	P	♢ 10 9 7 4
5 ♢	P	6 ♠	(end)	♣ 10 8 6 5

It looks like a tossup between the minors, but is it? Partner could have doubled 5 ♢ to ask for a diamond lead, but he had no such opportunity for clubs. Hence, lead a club.

EXCEPTION: When your side has *bid*, the double of a low-level artificial bid by the enemy is *strength-showing*, rather than lead-directing. Witness the following two examples:

Partner	Opp.	You	♠ K 10 8 7
			♡ Q 8 5
1 NT	2 ♣*	DBL	♢ K 10 7
			♣ 9 8 5

*Landy (majors)

Your double shows general strength and indicates that the hand belongs to your side. It is not lead-directing.

Opp.	Partner	Opp.	You	♠ K Q 8
				♡ A J 9 4 3
			1 ♡	♢ 8
2 ♢	P	2 ♡*	DBL	♣ A K 7 2

*One-round force

You show a strong opening bid. After all, you already indicated a heart lead when you opened.

DOUBLES OF NOTRUMP BIDS

Previously in this book we explained two special cases involving doubles of notrump bids: a direct double of a 1 NT (or 2 NT) response to a natural suit opening bid (page

119), and a double of a 1 NT opening bid (page *125*). Except for these cases, all doubles of notrump bids are for penalty, and *may* be lead-directing. The exact lead-directing implications are not universally agreed upon, even among experts, so we will present our own recommendations below:

Double of any notrump bid is for penalty, and if made by the *non-leader,* asks for the lead of, in this order of priority: (a) leader's bid suit; (b) doubler's bid suit; (c) dummy's first bid (or shown) real suit; or (d) if no real suits have been bid, leader's *weaker* major suit.

Opp.	Partner	Opp.	You	
				♠ A 7 5
				♡ Q 9 7 5 4
			1 ♡	◇ K J 8
1 NT	2 ◇	3 NT	DBL	♣ A 10

Your double asks for a diamond lead (leader's suit). Without the double, partner would tend to lead your suit.

Opp.	Partner	Opp.	You	
			1 ♣	♠ 4
				♡ A 9 8 4
1 ♡	P	3 ◇	P	◇ K 10 6
3 NT	P	P	DBL	♣ A Q J 10 7

You demand a club lead (doubler's suit). You do not want partner finding any "brilliancies," like a spade lead.

Opp.	Partner	Opp.	You	
				♠ A Q 10 8 7
				♡ 3
1 ♡	P	1 ♠	P	◇ A K 7
1 NT	P	P	DBL	♣ A 8 7 3

Your double is for penalty, indicating a trap pass over 1 ♠. Clearly, you want a spade lead (dummy's suit).

Opp.	Partner	Opp.	You	
				♠ 6 5 4
1 NT	P	2 ◇*	P	♡ Q J 10 9 7
2 ♡	P	2 NT	P	◇ A 9
3 NT	P	P	DBL	♣ A 8 7

*Jacoby (showing hearts)

Your double asks for a heart lead (dummy's real suit). Had you wanted a diamond lead, you would have doubled 2 ◇.

Opp.	Partner	Opp.	You	
				♠ 9 4
				♡ K Q J 9 8 7
1 NT	P	3 NT	DBL	◇ A 5
				♣ 10 8 3

Here you demand partner's weaker (or shorter) major, which surely must be hearts in view of your hand.

NOTE: As suggested by the preceding examples, an enemy 3 NT bid is the most common target for this kind of lead-directing double. Quite logically, this is because 3 NT is the most frequently played contract. Nonetheless, the identical principles apply from 1 NT all the way through 7 NT.

THE LIGHTNER DOUBLE

Invented by Theodore Lightner of New York City, a leading player since the earliest days of contract bridge

The "Lightner double" applies when the enemy reaches a suit slam. Its intent is not so much to increase the penalty for defeating the slam, but to steer partner into the winning lead. Unfortunately, experts do not all agree as to *which* suit is requested. Our recommendation is explained below:

Double of a voluntarily bid suit slam is for penalty, and if made by the *non-leader*, asks for the lead of, in this order of priority: (a) a side suit bid by dummy or declarer; or (b) leader's longest suit; but never a suit bid by your side.

Opp.	Partner	Opp.	You		
1 ♠	P	2 ♣	P	♠	7 5 4
3 ♠	P	4 NT	P	♡	Q 6 5 3
5 ♡	P	6 ♠	DBL	◇	A 8 7 6 4 2
				♣	—

Your double asks for a club lead (dummy's suit), which, along with your diamond ace, should defeat 6 ♠.

Opp.	Partner	Opp.	You		
				♠	A K
				♡	Q J 10 8 7 5
1 ◇	P	3 ◇	3 ♡	◇	7
5 ◇	P	6 ◇	DBL	♣	9 8 7 4

Your double forbids a heart lead. Hopefully, partner will find a spade lead (probably his longer side suit).

In the majority of cases, the Lightner double is based on a *void*, often in an enemy suit. Consequently, opening leader may have to do some detective work when the enemy has bid more than one side suit. For example, what would you lead after the following auction?

Opp.	Partner	Opp.	You		
		1 ♠	P	♠	J 9 8 7 5 3
2 ♣	P	2 ♡	P	♡	7
4 NT	P	5 ♡	P	◇	Q J 9
6 ♡	DBL	(end)		♣	6 5 4

Partner's double suggests a club or spade lead, but which one? Plainly, your hand (and the bidding) indicates a spade lead, so don't blindly lead a club.

WARNING: The Lightner double applies only against *voluntarily* bid slams, so the double of an enemy *sacrifice* bid is not lead-directing. For example:

Opp.	Partner	Opp.	You		
			1 ♡	♠	8
4 ♠	5 ♡	5 ♠	6 ♡	♡	A Q J 8 7
P	P	6 ♠	DBL	◇	K Q 10 7
				♣	A J 8

You are not requesting any particular lead, just warning partner not to bid any higher.

Weak Jump Overcalls ★

Another of the many contributions of the great Oswald Jacoby

The "weak jump overcall" is now firmly ingrained into standard bidding, having replaced its counterpart, the "strong jump overall," decades ago. Consequently it is a moot point whether such a standard treatment should be included in a book on bridge conventions. Nonetheless, we have chosen to do so because of its widespread use, and frequent misuse.

The practice of weak jump overcalls dictates that a *single* jump overcall shows a weak hand. The *double* jump (or higher) overcall is also weak, but that is true in any system. For example, over an opponent's 1 ◇ opening bid a jump to 2 ♡, 2 ♠, or 3 ♣ is weak *only* when you play weak jump overcalls, but a jump to 3 ♡, 3 ♠, 4 ♣, or higher is always weak. *All* of these jumps are so related, however, that but one basic agreement is necessary. Here it is:

Any jump suit overcall shows a maximum of 10 high-card points, at least a six-card suit, and little, if any, defensive strength. The main emphasis is on *playing* tricks, as shown by the following table:

Vulnerability	Overbid by
Unfavorable	2 tricks
Equal	3 tricks
Favorable	3 to 5 tricks

When making a jump overcall, or any preemptive bid for that matter, it pays to bid the full extent of your hand in *one* bid. That is, if you intend to bid up to 3 ♠, then bid 3 ♠ directly; don't jump to 2 ♠, expecting to compete later. Once you preempt, you are finished bidding; the rest is up to partner. Now let's look at some examples:

Opp.	You		
		♠	K Q J 9 5 4
		♡	7 3
1 ◇	?	◇	8 6
		♣	9 5 2

You have five playing tricks. Bid 2 ♠ at equal or favorable vulnerability, but pass at unfavorable.

Opp.	You		
		♠	8
		♡	Q J 8 7 5 4
1 ♣	?	◇	10 6 3
		♣	8 7 5

Bid 2 ♡ at favorable only. Otherwise, pass.

Opp.	You		
		♠	9 8 7
		♡	3
1 ♡	?	◇	A 5
		♣	Q J 10 8 6 5 3

You have six tricks. Bid 3 ♣ at equal or favorable, but pass at unfavorable. An outside ace is permissible.

Opp.	You		
		♠	A J 10 8 7 5
		♡	8 5 3
1 ◇	1 ♠	◇	A 9 2
		♣	9

At any vulnerability, prefer the simple overcall if your hand qualifies and contains reasonable defense.

Opp.	You	
		♠ 10 8
		♡ 9 7
1 ♣	?	♢ K Q J 10 4 3 2
		♣ 4 3

You have six tricks. Bid 3 ♢ at equal or favorable, but only 2 ♢ at unfavorable.

Opp.	You	
		♠ 4
		♡ 7 5
1 ♠	?	♢ 8 6 2
		♣ J 10 9 7 5 4 3

Bid 3 ♣ at favorable only. At this vulnerability, you sometimes cast your fate to the wind.

Opp.	You	
		♠ 9
		♡ A K Q 10 7 6 5
1 ♠	?	♢ 10 3
		♣ 8 7 2

You have seven tricks. Bid 4 ♡ at equal or favorable, but just 3 ♡ at unfavorable.

Opp.	You	
		♠ —
		♡ 8
1 ♡	?	♢ K Q 10 9 8 5 4 3
		♣ J 10 5 2

With about eight tricks, bid 5 ♢ at equal or favorable, and 4 ♢ at unfavorable.

When jumping to game in your suit, it is permissible to exceed the limit of 10 high-card points, provided you are willing to give up on slam. Often, this is desirable for tactical reasons. For example:

Opp.	You	
		♠ A K Q J 9 8 6
		♡ —
1 ♢	<u>4 ♠</u>	♢ 7 6
		♣ Q J 10 5

Despite your 13 HCP, you want to make it as difficult as you can for the enemy to find a possible heart fit.

RESPONSES

When partner has made a weak jump overcall, most of the time you should pass. He has already overbid by a certain number of tricks, based on the vulnerability, hoping to steer the opponents off course. Having stepped out on a limb, the last thing partner needs is for *you* to saw it off!

Nevertheless, if you feel there is a chance for game, or if you have a good fit with partner's suit, there is reason for bidding. Here are the meanings of the responses to a weak jump overcall:

1. **All raises** (any level) are obstructive bids, not attempts to reach game or slam.

Partner should not bid any further. EXCEPTION: When both opponents have bid, a raise below the game level does *not* bar partner from sacrificing.

Opp.	Partner	Opp.	You		
				♠	J 8 7
				♡	A 7 5
1 ♣	2 ♠	P	3 ♠	◇	K 9 7 3
				♣	10 4 2

You are not inviting game, but extending the preempt to make it a little harder for the enemy to compete.

Opp.	Partner	Opp.	You		
				♠	9 7 5
				♡	A 9 7 5
1 ♠	3 ◇	3 ♠	4 ◇	◇	K 9 8
				♣	A 7 5

(none vul)

Partner is allowed to save in 5 ◇ (over 4 ♠), but only with especially good distribution.

When responder himself intends to sacrifice, it is almost always best to do so *immediately,* in order to put maximum pressure on the enemy. Witness these two examples:

Opp.	Partner	Opp.	You		
				♠	J 9 7 5
				♡	3
1 ◇	2 ♠	P	4 ♠	◇	9 8 7 6
				♣	A 9 5 2

(favorable)

You are sure the enemy can make 4 ♡, so the advance sacrifice is called for. Since you might also bid 4 ♠ on a good hand, the opponents have a difficult guess.

Opp.	Partner	Opp.	You		
				♠	9 8 3
				♡	K 10 7
1 ♠	3 ♡	3 ♠	5 ♡	◇	A 9 4 3 2
				♣	7 5

(none vul)

Your 5 ♡ bid steals the enemy's bidding room, and thus increases their chances of going wrong.

2. **New suit** is natural and not forcing. Ostensibly, this denies support for partner's suit, but it may also be made as a *lead-directing* maneuver when it is apparent that the enemy will outbid you. Partner should usually pass, but may raise with good support.

Opp.	Partner	Opp.	You		
				♠	A 8 5
				♡	9 8 5
1 ♣	2 ♡	3 ♣	3 ◇	◇	K Q 10 8 4
				♣	7 5

(favorable)

It looks as though you are outgunned, so at least try to get partner off to the right lead.

3. **Cue-bid** (of the enemy suit) is a game or slam try in partner's suit, and is forcing for one round. If partner has the worst possible hand, he must rebid his suit at the cheapest level. Otherwise, he may make any other rebid.

Opp.	Partner	Opp.	You	♠ A 7
				♡ A K 8 7
1 ♣	2 ♠	P	<u>3 ♣</u>	◇ A Q 10 3
				♣ 9 8 4

(favorable)

You are trying for game. If partner returns to 3 ♠, you should pass; remember, he may have quite a poor hand.

The remaining responses are rare, and since they all mean what they say, only the following brief mention is necessary:

4. **Two notrump** is natural and invitational to 3 NT. NOTE: An alternative treatment, preferred by many experts, is to use this as a *forcing* response, much like a 2 NT response to a "weak two-bid."

5. **Three notrump** is a natural sign-off attempt.

6. **Jump in a new suit** is natural, and invitational if below game.

EXCEPTIONAL SITUATIONS

Even though your partnership plays weak jump overcalls, there are four common situations where they should not be used, as stated here:

Weak jump overcalls do *not* apply (a) in balancing position; (b) after a nonforcing single raise; (c) after a 1 NT opening bid; or (d) after a preemptive bid. In these cases, a jump overcall shows at least a six-card self-sufficient suit, and within *one* playing trick (or 1½, in a pinch) of the bid actually made.

Opp.	Partner	Opp.	You	♠ 7 4
				♡ A K Q 10 9 5
1 ♣	P	P	<u>2 ♡</u>	◇ A 7
				♣ 8 7 4

Your 2 ♡ bid shows seven tricks; 3 ♡ would show eight tricks, etc. With a weaker hand, you must bid 1 ♡ or pass.

Opp.	Partner	Opp.	You	♠ K Q J 10 8 5
				♡ 3
1 ♡	P	2 ♡	<u>3 ♠</u>	◇ A Q 9
				♣ A 10 2

You show eight tricks. This is useful, since a simple 2 ♠ overcall is often shaded here.

Opp.	You	♠ A 6 5
		♡ K Q 10 9 8 6 5
1 NT	<u>3 ♡</u>	◇ —
		♣ K 10 8

With your opponent's hand well defined, this is not an opportune situation to preempt; so 3 ♡ shows a good hand.

Opp.	You	♠ —
		♡ 9 4
2 ♠*	<u>4 ◇</u>	◇ A Q J 9 8 7 6 5
		♣ A Q 10

*Weak two-bid

You imply a very distributional nine-trick hand.

Opp.	Partner	Opp.	You	♠	Q J 10 9 7 5 4
				♡	A 3
1 ◇	P	2 ♡*	3 ♠	◇	4
				♣	A K 5

*Weak jump shift

Since the enemy has preempted, your bid is strong. Had the 2 ♡ bid been strong, then your bid would be weak.

After any of these good jump overcalls, a different responding approach is dictated. Responder may (a) pass; (b) raise overcaller's suit (or bid 2 NT) to invite game; (c) bid a new suit, which is forcing if below game; (d) sign off in game; or (e) cue-bid the enemy suit, which is game-forcing and suggests slam interest. Here is an example:

Opp.	Partner	Opp.	You	♠	Q 8 6
				♡	9 8 2
		1 ♡	P	◇	A Q 9 7 3
P	3 ♣	P	3 ◇	♣	J 5

Your 3 ◇ bid is forcing and shows game interest. If partner rebids 4 ♣ (discouraging), you should pass.

Unusual Notrump Overcall ★

Devised by the renowned Alvin Roth, and developed in conjunction with Tobias Stone

After an opponent's opening bid of one of a suit, a direct jump to 2 NT is the "unusual notrump overcall." As any reader should know, this bid does not indicate the desire to play notrump (hence, the term "unusual"), but shows a two-suited type hand. Although some players retain this bid exclusively to show the minor suits, it is far better to agree that it shows the *two lower unbid* suits, as explained below:

1. **Over one club,** 2 NT shows at least five *diamonds* and five *hearts*.

2. **Over one diamond,** 2 NT shows at least five *clubs* and five *hearts*.

3. **Over one of a major,** 2 NT shows at least five *clubs* and five *diamonds*.

Before stating the exact requirements for this bid, it is helpful to look at *two-suited* hands, in general. For defensive bidding purposes, our recommendation is that two-suiters be roughly divided into three categories, as shown in the following table:

Type of Two-Suiter	High-Card Points
Weak	12 or less
Intermediate	13 to 16
Strong	17 or more

We hasten to assert that the above ranges are only approximate; there is a certain amount of overlap either way. Borderline hands may be either upgraded or downgraded according to your judgment. Nevertheless, commit these ranges to memory, as they will be referred to again and again in the following pages. The strength of the unusual notrump overcall may now be defined, as follows:

Two notrump over one of a suit shows either a *weak* or a *strong* two-suiter. In other words, do *not* make this bid with an intermediate two-suiter. NOTE: This "weak or strong" treatment is our recommendation, and is not universally accepted; many players impose no restrictions at all.

Opp.	You		
		♠	7
		♡	4 3
1 ♡	2 NT	◇	Q J 10 8 6
		♣	A Q J 9 5

A typical weak two-suiter.

Opp.	You		
		♠	8
		♡	K J 9 7 5
1 ♣	2 NT	◇	A 10 8 6 5 3
		♣	2

Another weak two-suiter, but here you show diamonds and hearts, because of the 1 ♣ opening.

Opp.	You		
		♠	A 3
		♡	4
1 ♠	2 NT	◇	A K 8 7 6
		♣	A Q J 5 4

You make the same bid with a strong two-suiter; you will distinguish this at your next turn.

Opp.	You		
		♠	9 8
		♡	6
1 ♡	2 ◇	◇	K Q J 9 8
		♣	A K J 9 3

The intermediate two-suiter is best handled with a simple overcall; you intend to bid again. If you bid 2 NT, you will have an awkward rebidding problem.

The vulnerability, of course, is an important consideration, especially when bidding a weak two-suiter. "How weak is weak?" is a question that is difficult to answer, because other factors, such as hand pattern, location of high cards, and suit texture all enter the picture. Our previous examples would be appropriate at *any* vulnerability, but now let's look at some less clear-cut hands:

Opp.	You		
		♠	9 5
		♡	K J 10 9 6
1 ◇	?	◇	3
		♣	K Q 9 8 3

Bid 2 NT at equal or favorable vulnerability. At unfavorable, overcall 1 ♡, then go quietly.

Opp.	You		
		♠	K 10
		♡	3
1 ♡	?	◇	K J 9 7 4
		♣	Q 9 5 4 2

Bid 2 NT at favorable only.

Opp.	You		
		♠	—
		♡	3
1 ♠	2 NT	◇	Q 10 8 7 5 4
		♣	K 9 8 5 4 3

Very freak hands are usually worth bidding at any vulnerability.

RESPONSES

After partner has made an unusual 2 NT overcall, responder should assume that it shows a *weak* two-suiter, and bid accordingly. It is responder's duty to choose the trump suit, as he knows exactly which two suits partner holds. The following responses apply, with or without further enemy competition:

1. **Takeout to a suit shown by partner** indicates a preference for that suit, with no interest in game. On rare occasions, this may even be a doubleton.

Opp.	Partner	Opp.	You		
				♠	A Q 9 8 5
				♡	J 7 4
1 ◇	2 NT	P	3 ♡	◇	Q 8 5
				♣	7 6

You must choose between clubs and hearts, the suits partner has shown.

Opp.	Partner	Opp.	You		
				♠	K J 9 7
				♡	A 9 8 6 5
1 ♠	2 NT	P	3 ♣	◇	10 3
				♣	9 8

With no clear preference, try to get out as cheaply as possible. Incidentally, if right-hand opponent had doubled 2 NT, you should pass to let partner choose the suit.

2. **Jump takeout to a suit shown by partner** indicates good support for that suit. If below game, this is *not* strength-showing but mostly preemptive. A jump to game may be either constructive (expecting to make) or preemptive.

Opp.	Partner	Opp.	You		
				♠	J 7 5 4
				♡	10 7 5 2
1 ♡	2 NT	P	4 ♣	◇	3
				♣	A 8 5 4

(none vul)

You wish to obstruct the enemy, but would not mind if partner continues to 5 ♣ with a suitable hand.

Opp.	Partner	Opp.	You		
				♠	6 5 4
				♡	J 8 7 3
1 ♠	2 NT	3 ♠	5 ◇	◇	K 9 8 4 2
				♣	3

(both vul)

Your jump to 5 ◇ is intended as an advance sacrifice, as the enemy is undoubtedly headed for game.

3. **Cue-bid** (of the enemy suit) is a game or slam try, and is forcing for one round. If partner has a *minimum* (for a weak two-suiter), he must bid the more economical of his two suits. With a *maximum*, he may make any other bid.

Opp.	Partner	Opp.	You		
				♠	A J 8 7
				♡	K 9 8
1 ♣	2 NT	P	3 ♣	◇	Q 6
				♣	9 8 7 5

(none vul)

You are worth a game try. If partner bids 3 ◇ (showing a minimum), you will sign off in 3 ♡.

The remaining responses to the unusual 2 NT overcall are logical in meaning and very rare, so deserve only the following brief mention:

4. **New suit not shown by partner** shows an independent suit, and is not forcing.

5. **Three notrump** is a place to play.

6. **Four notrump** is Blackwood (not quantitative, of course).

REBIDS BY UNUSUAL NOTRUMP BIDDER

When the unusual 2 NT bidder has a *weak* two-suiter, his rebid usually presents no problem; there isn't any. Unless partner has cue-bid (forcing), there is no obligation to bid again. Nevertheless, it is permissible to bid again, as shown in the following:

1. **Bid or raise of a previously shown suit** is natural and not forcing. This indicates more extreme shape (greater than five-five).

Opp.	Partner	Opp.	You		
				♠	6 3
				♡	—
		1 ♠	2 NT	♦	K J 9 8 7
P	3 ♣	3 ♡	4 ♣	♣	K Q 10 8 6 5
(favorable)					

Your 4 ♣ raise shows extra in the way of distribution, not high cards.

Opp.	Partner	Opp.	You		
				♠	5
				♡	K Q 8 6 3
		1 ♣	2 NT	♦	A J 10 9 7 6
3 ♣	P	P	3 ♦	♣	3
(none vul)					

You show six diamonds and five hearts.

When the *strong* two-suiter is held, the unusual 2 NT bidder must find some other rebid. Here is what to do:

2. **Any strange-sounding action** denotes a *strong* two-suiter. Unusual notrump bidder may (a) cue-bid the enemy suit; (b) bid notrump; (c) bid the fourth suit; or (d) double in a competitive auction.

Opp.	Partner	Opp.	You		
				♠	8 7
				♡	A K Q 7 5
		1 ♦	2 NT	♦	4
P	3 ♣	P	3 ♦	♣	A K J 10 4

Your 3 ♦ cue-bid shows a strong two-suiter; nonetheless, if partner returns to 4 ♣ (implying nothing), you should pass.

Opp.	Partner	Opp.	You		
				♠	K 5
				♡	10
		1 ♠	2 NT	♦	A K 9 8 5
P	3 ♦	P	3 NT	♣	A K Q 4 3

Your 3 NT bid logically shows a spade stopper, and gives partner the additional option of passing.

Opp.	Partner	Opp.	You		
				♠	A 3
				♡	3
		1 ♡	2 NT	♦	K Q 10 8 7
3 ♡	P	P	DBL	♣	A K Q 4 3

Here your double shows a strong two-suiter, leaving the decision up to partner.

FURTHER APPLICATIONS

Thus far, we have considered only a special case of the unusual notrump overcall, i.e., the direct jump to 2 NT over an opening suit bid. That is clearly the most frequent application, but not the only one. The remaining situations all presume that the enemy has opened the bidding, and that your side has never bid or doubled. Here they are:

1. **Two notrump over any strong two-bid** shows a *weak* two-suiter. NOTE: If the enemy suit bid is *artificial* (as with the strong artificial 2 ♣ opening), then that suit is still deemed to be *unbid*.

Opp.	You		
		♠	9
		♡	3
2 ♣*	2 NT	◇	J 10 9 7 5 4
		♣	K J 10 8 7

    *Strong and artificial

    Your 2 NT bid indicates the minors, since clubs have not truly been bid.

    WARNING: The above applies to *strong* two-bids only. After a weak or intermediate two-bid, a 2 NT overcall is natural, showing 16 to 19 points.

2. **Two notrump after any 1 NT bid** shows a *weak* (or better) two-suiter. In other words, as long as the enemy has bid 1 NT, an immediate or subsequent bid of 2 NT is unusual.

Opp.	Partner	Opp.	You		
				♠	9 3
				♡	K J 10 9 8
1 ♣	P	1 NT	2 NT	◇	A Q 10 7 3
				♣	3

    Your 2 NT bid shows diamonds and hearts, the two lower unbid suits.

Opp.	Partner	Opp.	You		
				♠	7
				♡	4
1 NT	P	2 ◇*	2 NT	◇	K 10 8 7 5
				♣	A J 9 8 5 4

    *Jacoby (showing hearts)

    Here you show both minors, since hearts is the only "bid" suit.

3. **Two notrump over any forcing response** shows a *weak* (or better) two-suiter.

Opp.	Partner	Opp.	You		
				♠	Q J 10 7 4
				♡	3 2
1 ♡	P	2 ◇	2 NT	◇	—
				♣	K J 10 7 5 3

    Since there are just two unbid suits, we have a rare case in which the unusual notrump shows spades.

4. **Two notrump over a single major raise** shows a *weak* (or better) two-suiter. NOTE: This is a controversial treatment. Some experts would consider this a natural bid, but the *unusual* treatment is far more practical.

Opp.	Partner	Opp.	You		
				♠	5
				♡	A 3
1 ♠	P	2 ♠	2 NT	◇	K J 8 7 6
				♣	Q J 9 5 2

    You show both minor suits.

5. **Two notrump in balancing position** shows a *weak* two-suiter only when you have *passed* and the enemy has shown but *one* suit. Otherwise, it is natural.

Opp.	Partner	Opp.	You	
		1 ♡	P	♠ 7 3
				♡ 9 4
2 ♡	P	P	2 NT	◇ K 10 9 6
				♣ A J 9 8 3

You show both minors. Notice the relaxed standards, typical of reopening bids.

Opp.	Partner	Opp.	You	
				♠ K J 9
				♡ A Q 8
1 ♠	P	P	2 NT	◇ A J 10 7
				♣ A 3 2

This is not unusual, since you haven't passed; most experts recommend about 18 to 20 points.

6. **One notrump in direct position** shows a *weak* two-suiter by a *passed* hand only. Observe that a balancing 1 NT bid is always natural.

Opp.	Partner	Opp.	You	
				♠ 8 5
				♡ K 9 8 7 5
			P	◇ 3
P	P	1 ◇	1 NT	♣ A J 10 5 3

Because of your pass, you can now show clubs and hearts without the risk of bidding 2 NT.

Opp.	Partner	Opp.	You	
				♠ K 8
				♡ A 10 3
P	P	1 ♣	P	◇ K 9 7 4
1 ♡	P	P	1 NT	♣ J 10 4 2

Here your 1 NT bid is natural, although risky.

7. **Three notrump over any 2 NT bid** (rare) shows a *weak* two-suiter.

8. **Three notrump by a passed hand** (rare) shows a *weak* two-suiter.

NOTE: After any of these further applications of the unusual notrump overcall, the same basic responding strategy should be used.

FOUR-NOTRUMP OVERCALL

If the enemy has opened the bidding and your side has never bid or doubled, an overcall of 4 NT makes little sense as a natural bid, and is so farfetched as Blackwood (with one exception to be noted), that virtually all experts treat this bid as another form of the unusual notrump overcall.

The strength of an unusual 4 NT overcall depends on the context. If the enemy has made a *preemptive* bid and you have never passed, it implies *intermediate* or better strength. Otherwise, it implies a *weak* hand. The specific meaning of the 4 NT overcall is based on the *last* bid by the enemy, as explained below:

1. **Over four spades,** 4 NT is a takeout for the *unbid* suits. This may also be done with a two-suiter in *hearts* and *diamonds,* with the intention to clarify later.

Opp.	You
4 ♠	4 NT

♠ —
♡ K Q J 7
♢ A K 7 6 5
♣ Q 10 9 7

The classic case; you have support for all unbid suits.

Opp.	Partner	Opp.	You
4 ♠	P	P	4 NT

♠ 5
♡ K Q 10 7 6
♢ A K J 7 4 3
♣ 2

If partner bids 5 ♣ as expected, you will correct to 5 ♢, thus showing both red suits.

2. **Over four hearts,** 4 NT is a takeout for the *minor* suits.

Opp.	You
4 ♡	4 NT

♠ 7 3
♡ —
♢ A Q J 7 6 5
♣ K Q J 7 2

You show an intermediate minor two-suiter.

3. **Over four of a minor,** 4 NT is *Blackwood.* This is the exception alluded to. Although very unlikely, no other meaning is logical.

4. **Over any lower bid,** 4 NT is a takeout for the *two lower unbid* suits.

Opp.	Partner	Opp.	You
1 ♠	P	3 ♠	4 NT

♠ —
♡ 9
♢ K J 10 9 5 2
♣ Q J 9 8 6 3

You suggest a weak minor two-suiter.

On some occasions, the unusual 4 NT bid may be employed *after* you have already bid or doubled. Here is the principal situation:

5. **If you (but not partner) have bid or doubled, and the enemy bids four of a major,** 4 NT is a takeout for the *unbid* suits over 4 ♠, or the *minor* suits over 4 ♡.

Opp.	Partner	Opp.	You
			1 ♢
1 ♠	P	4 ♠	4 NT

♠ —
♡ K J 10 7
♢ A Q 10 8 7 4
♣ K Q 8

Your 4 NT bid is a three-suit takeout, but with a strong preference for diamonds.

Opp.	Partner	Opp.	You
		1 ♡	2 ♣
4 ♡	P	P	4 NT

♠ 7
♡ 3
♢ K Q J 8
♣ A K 9 8 5 4 3

You show both minors with, obviously, longer clubs.

Opp.	Partner	Opp.	You
		3 ♠	DBL
4 ♠	P	P	4 NT

♠ —
♡ K Q 10 8
♢ Q J 8 5 2
♣ A K J 9

Your 4 NT bid forces partner to choose one of the unbid suits.

Michaels Cue-Bid ★ ★

Invented by the late Mike Michaels of Miami Beach, a bridge writer, lecturer, and prominent player

The direct cue-bid of an opponent's opening bid of one of a suit is traditionally employed as a "strong cue-bid" (see Glossary) and is forcing to game or thereabouts. Unfortunately, these hands occur so seldom (and can be handled otherwise when they do) that most experts put the cue-bid to better use. The most popular agreement is the "Michaels cue-bid," which promises a *two-suited* hand, as follows:

1. **Over one club,** 2 ♣ shows both *majors*.

2. **Over one diamond,** 2 ♦ shows both *majors*.

3. **Over one heart,** 2 ♡ shows *spades* and an undisclosed *minor*.

4. **Over one spade,** 2 ♠ shows *hearts* and an undisclosed *minor*.

NOTE: Inexperienced players may prefer one of the simplified variations of Michaels, such as the "colorful cue-bid," "higher-suits cue-bid," or "top-and-bottom cue-bid" (see Glossary).

The Michaels cue-bid typically shows at least five-five shape. Exceptionally, over a minor-suit opening, just five-four shape (in the majors) is permissible, so long as the four-card major is reasonably good.

The strength of the Michaels cue-bid will be defined by the same guidelines used for the "unusual notrump overcall" (see page *136*). We will continue to refer to the three ranges of two-suiters, which we emphasize are *approximate*. The table is repeated below for your convenience:

Type of Two-Suiter	High-Card Points
Weak	12 or less
Intermediate	13 to 16
Strong	17 or more

Direct cue-bid of one of a suit opening shows either a *weak* or a *strong* two-suiter. That is, do not make this bid with an intermediate two-suiter. NOTE: As with the "unusual notrump overcall," this "weak or strong" treatment is our recommendation, and is not universally accepted.

Opp.	You	
		♠ K J 9 8 5
		♡ K Q 10 7 3
1 ♣	2 ♣	♦ 5 3
		♣ 2

A typical weak two-suiter.

Opp.	You	
		♠ K Q J 8
		♡ A J 10 7 4
1 ♦	2 ♦	♦ 7
		♣ 9 4 3

Since your spades are good, you may cue-bid with only five-four shape.

Opp.	You	
		♠ Q J 10 8 7
		♡ 4 3
1 ♡	2 ♡	♦ A Q J 9 5
		♣ 2

Another weak two-suiter, but here only one of your suits (spades) is known.

Opp.	You
1 ♠	2 ♠

♠ —
♡ A Q J 7 5
◇ 6 5
♣ J 10 9 7 6 5

You show hearts and either minor suit.

Opp.	You
1 ◇	2 ◇

♠ A K J 9 5
♡ A K Q 8 2
◇ 6 4
♣ 5

The strong two-suiter is bid the same way; your next bid will describe this.

Opp.	You
1 ♡	1 ♠

♠ K Q 10 8 5
♡ 3
◇ 10 4
♣ A K Q 7 3

With an intermediate two-suiter, start with a simple overcall, then bid again.

As always, factors such as vulnerability, hand pattern, location of high cards, and suit texture all must be taken into account when bidding with a weak hand. The preceding examples would be suitable for Michaels at *any* vulnerability, but observe the following:

Opp.	You
1 ♡	?

♠ A Q 8 4 3
♡ 6 4
◇ 6
♣ K 10 6 5 3

Bid 2 ♡ at equal or favorable vulnerability. At unfavorable, an overcall of 1 ♠ is perhaps wiser.

Opp.	You
1 ♣	?

♠ J 10 8 7 5
♡ K J 8 4 2
◇ 7 2
♣ 3

Bid 2 ♣ at favorable only. Otherwise, pass.

Opp.	You
1 ♠	P

♠ K Q
♡ J 9 7 5 4
◇ 6
♣ A 9 5 4 3

Pass at any vulnerability.

WARNING: If the Michaels cue-bid is adopted, the rare "powerhouse" hand that is traditionally shown by a "strong cue-bid" must be handled differently. The correct procedure is generally to *double* first, then cue-bid on the next round. For example:

Opp.	Partner	Opp.	You
		1 ♠	DBL
P	2 ♡	P	2 ♠

♠ 4
♡ A K 6
◇ A K Q 9 5
♣ A Q 10 3

Your cue-bid after doubling shows your great strength and forces partner to keep bidding. Do not make the mistake of cue-bidding immediately.

RESPONSES

After partner has made a Michaels cue-bid, responder should assume that it shows a *weak* two-suiter and bid accordingly. It is responder's duty to select the trump suit, or possibly inquire as to partner's unknown minor (after a major-suit cue-bid). The following responses apply, with or without further enemy competition:

1. **Takeout to a suit shown by partner** indicates a preference for that suit, with no interest in game. Typically, this shows at least three trumps.

Opp.	Partner	Opp.	You		
				♠	9 5 4
				♡	K 7
1 ♢	2 ♢	P	2 ♠	♢	J 8 3
				♣	K J 7 5 4

Partner has both majors, so take your choice.

Opp.	Partner	Opp.	You		
				♠	K J 9 6
				♡	Q 6 3
1 ♠	2 ♠	P	3 ♡	♢	J 5
				♣	9 8 7 4

You do not know partner's second suit, but a heart fit is present, so sign off in 3 ♡.

2. **Two notrump after a major-suit cue-bid** asks for partner's *minor*. Responder may intend to drop partner in three of his minor suit, or perhaps make another bid to invite game.

Opp.	Partner	Opp.	You		
				♠	3
				♡	K 10 9 7 5
1 ♡	2 ♡	P	2 NT	♢	J 7 6 5
				♣	Q 8 3

You plan to pass whichever minor partner bids.

Opp.	Partner	Opp.	You		
				♠	J 9 8 6
				♡	K J 8
1 ♠	2 ♠	P	2 NT	♢	A J 9 7
				♣	8 7

(none vul)

If partner bids 3 ♣, you will bid 3 ♡ to invite game. However, if partner bids 3 ♢, you should jump to 4 ♡.

In a competitive auction, if 2 NT is unavailable, responder may (a) bid 4 ♣, which is not forcing; or (b) bid 4 NT, which is forcing, to locate the unknown minor. Observe, though, that 3 NT is always a *natural* bid. For example:

Opp.	Partner	Opp.	You		
				♠	Q 4
				♡	9 7 5 2
1 ♡	2 ♡	3 ♡	4 ♣	♢	K 9 8 6
				♣	Q J 7

You desire to compete to four of partner's minor; without clubs, he must correct to 4 ♢. If you wanted to play five of his minor, you would bid 4 NT.

3. **Jump takeout to a suit shown by partner** shows good support for that suit. If below game, this is *not* strength-showing, but mostly preemptive. A jump to game may be either constructive (expecting to make) or preemptive.

Opp.	Partner	Opp.	You	♠ K 7 6 3
				♡ 4 2
1 ♣	2 ♣	P	3 ♠	♢ 9 7
				♣ J 10 5 3 2

(none vul)

You are trying to blockade the enemy, but partner is not prevented from bidding 4 ♠ with a suitable hand.

Opp.	Partner	Opp.	You	♠ A 9 7 5
				♡ Q 10 7 4
1 ♠	2 ♠	P	4 ♡	♢ 6
				♣ K 10 7 4

You expect to make 4 ♡, so bid it.

4. **Cue-bid** (of the enemy suit) is a game or slam try, and is forcing for one round. If partner has a *minimum* (for a weak two-suiter), he must bid the more economical of his two suits. With a *maximum,* he may make any other bid.

Opp.	Partner	Opp.	You	♠ K Q 9 6
				♡ 7 4
1 ♢	2 ♢	P	3 ♢	♢ Q 7 4
				♣ A J 5 4

(favorable)

If partner bids 3 ♡ (showing a minimum), you will correct to 3 ♠. Otherwise, you will reach 4 ♠.

The remaining responses to the Michaels cue-bid are natural and quite rare, so are mentioned here only briefly:

5. **New suit not shown by partner** describes an independent suit and is not forcing.

6. **Two notrump after a minor-suit cue-bid** is invitational to game.

7. **Three notrump** is a place to play.

REBIDS BY MICHAELS CUE-BIDDER

At least 90% of the time, the Michaels cue-bidder will have a *weak* two-suiter. In that event, he must tread warily. Unless partner has made a forcing response (cue-bid or 2 NT), there is no obligation to bid again. Nevertheless, the Michaels cue-bidder *may* bid again, as stated below:

1. **Bid or raise of one of your two suits** is natural and not forcing. This indicates more extreme shape (greater than five-five).

Opp.	Partner	Opp.	You	♠ K 10 9 6 5
				♡ A Q 9 8 7 6
		1 ♣	2 ♣	♢ 9 7
P	2 ♡	P	3 ♡	♣ —

Your raise to 3 ♡ shows extra distribution, not additional high cards; game is a definite possibility.

Opp.	Partner	Opp.	You	♠ 5
				♡ K J 10 9 7
		1 ♠	2 ♠	♢ 4
3 ♢	P	3 ♠	4 ♣	♣ K Q J 9 8 3

(favorable)

You simply express the desire to compete further, with an eye on sacrificing.

When the *strong* two-suiter is held, Michaels cue-bidder follows the identical practice used by the "unusual notrump" bidder. Here is what to do:

2. **Any strange-sounding action** denotes a *strong* two-suiter. Michaels cue-bidder may (a) cue-bid the enemy suit; (b) bid notrump; (c) bid a suit he cannot possibly have; or (d) double in a competitive auction.

Opp.	Partner	Opp.	You		
				♠	K Q 10 7 5
				♡	A J 9 8 4
		1 ♣	2 ♣	◇	A K 4
P	2 ♡	P	3 ◇	♣	—

Your 3 ◇ bid suggests 5-5-3-0 shape, but if partner returns to 3 ♡ (implying nothing), you should pass.

Opp.	Partner	Opp.	You		
				♠	4
				♡	A Q 10 8 7
		1 ♠	2 ♠	◇	A K Q 8 2
P	2 NT	P	3 ♠	♣	K 7

Over your 3 ♠ cue-bid, partner may bid 3 NT (natural), sign off in 4 ♣ (which you will correct to 4 ◇), or bid 4 NT to ask for your minor.

NOTE: The last example brings out an important point. As long as Michaels cue-bidder's minor suit is *unknown*, the first duty of 4 NT is to ask for that suit. Otherwise, of course, 4 NT would be Blackwood.

FURTHER APPLICATIONS

The Michaels cue-bid, as discussed so far, has been limited to the direct cue-bid of an opening bid of one of a suit. Although most common, this is not the only use of Michaels. The remaining situations all presume that (a) the enemy has opened the bidding; (b) partner has never bid or doubled; (c) you are cue-bidding a *naturally* bid suit; and (d) it is your *first* opportunity to do so. Here they are:

1. **Over a one-notrump response,** a cue-bid of opener's suit shows a *weak* (or better) two-suiter.

Opp.	Partner	Opp.	You		
				♠	A 10 9 6 5
				♡	K J 9 7 6
1 ◇	P	1 NT	2 ◇	◇	3
				♣	10 2

You show both major suits.

2. **Over a new-suit response,** a cue-bid of *opener's* suit shows a *weak* (or better) two-suiter.

Opp.	Partner	Opp.	You		
				♠	6
				♡	J 10 9 7 3
1 ♣	P	1 ♠	2 ♣	◇	K J 10 7 5
				♣	A 6

You show hearts and diamonds, but compare this:

Opp.	Partner	Opp.	You		
				♠	—
				♡	J 10 9 7 3
1 ♣	P	1 ♠	2 NT	◇	K J 10 7 5 4
				♣	6 2

The unusual 2 NT overcall shows a weak freak when used in preference to Michaels.

NOTE: The cue-bid of *responder's* suit (e.g., 2 ♠ in the above auction) is a controversial matter. Because it is hardly necessary as a takeout device, many experts treat it **as** *natural* (at the two-level), showing a strong suit. With this practice, we agree.

3. **Over a Jacoby transfer bid,** a cue-bid of responder's *real* major shows a *weak* (or better) two-suiter.

Opp.	Partner	Opp.	You		
				♠	K Q 10 7 6
				♡	4
1 NT	P	2 ◇*	2 ♡!	◇	9 7
				♣	A J 10 4 3

*Jacoby (showing hearts)

You show spades and a minor; obviously, you would never bid this way with a heart suit.

4. **If an opening suit bid is followed by two passes,** a cue-bid of opener's suit shows an *intermediate* (or better) two-suiter. NOTE: With a *weak* two-suiter, it is necessary to overcall in the higher suit, then show the second suit later if the opportunity arises.

Opp.	Partner	Opp.	You		
				♠	5
				♡	K Q J 8 6
1 ♠	P	P	2 ♠	◇	A K 10 7 3
				♣	5 4

You show at least intermediate strength. With a weak hand, you would have to settle for a 2 ♡ bid.

5. **Any three-level or higher cue-bid** shows a two-suiter. If the enemy has made a *preemptive* opening bid and you have never passed, this suggests *intermediate* or better strength. Otherwise, it suggests a *weak* hand.

Opp.	You		
		♠	9
		♡	A K J 8 7
2 ♠*	3 ♠	◇	10 3
		♣	A Q J 10 4

*Weak two-bid

You show hearts and a minor, with at least intermediate strength.

Opp.	You		
		♠	K J 9 8 5
		♡	A K J 9 7 3
3 ◇	4 ◇	◇	—
		♣	5 3

You show both major suits.

Opp.	Partner	Opp.	You		
				♠	K 10 9 7 5
				♡	4
1 ♡	P	2 ♡	3 ♡	◇	A J 10 8 6 3
				♣	3

Here you imply a weak two-suiter.

Opp.	Partner	Opp.	You	♠	—
				♡	Q J 9 8 7 4
2 ♣*	P	2 ♠	<u>3 ♠</u>	♢	8 4
				♣	K Q J 9 7

*Artificial force

> *You show a weak two-suiter with hearts and* either *minor, as clubs have not truly been bid.*

6. **Any cue-bid by a passed hand** (i.e., a player who failed to open the bidding) follows all previous guidelines, but always shows a *weak* two-suiter, of course.

Opp.	Partner	Opp.	You	♠	K 10 9 6 4
				♡	Q J 9 8 5 3
			P	♢	8
1 ♣	P	1 NT	<u>2 ♣</u>	♣	3

> *Even though you passed, you are still cue-bidding at your first opportunity, so show a major two-suiter.*

After any of these further applications of Michaels, the responding strategy is essentially the same. For example, say the bidding proceeds as follows:

Opp.	Partner	Opp.	You
2 ♡*	3 ♡	P	?

*Weak two-bid

According to previous agreements, and a little common sense, your responses would have the meanings shown below:

3 ♠	*shows a weak hand with spade support (not forcing).*
3 NT	*is natural, to play.*
4 ♣	*shows a weak hand, hoping to play 4 ♣ or 4 ♢. Partner should pass or correct to 4 ♢, unless very strong.*
4 ♢	*shows an independent suit (not forcing).*
4 ♡	*is a slam try.*
4 ♠	*says you think you can make it.*
4 NT	*asks to play 5 ♣ or 5 ♢.*
5 ♣	*shows an independent suit (not forcing).*

Invitational Cue-Bid ★ ★

> *Developed by Lawrence Rosler and Roger Stern, leading experts and bridge theoreticians of the Northeast*

The "invitational cue-bid" is a method of responding to partner's overcall. Before going right into it, though, let's briefly discuss the overcall itself.

We recommend a range of about 10 to 17 points at the one-level, or about 13 to 17 points at the two-level (or higher), for a simple suit overcall. To be sure, other considerations enter the picture, such as suit quality and vulnerability, but it is neither our intention here, nor the main objective of this book, to teach judgment at the bridge table. The approximate point ranges will suffice.

In traditional methods, the cue-bid of the enemy suit in response to partner's over-call would be forcing to game. The "invitational cue-bid" simply engages the cue-bid more liberally, to include *invitational* hands (hence, the name) as well. Here is the way it works:

Cue-bid of the enemy suit in response to partner's suit overcall is forcing for one round. If responder has support for overcaller's suit, this bid may be made with as little as 11 (or a very good 10) points. Otherwise, responder typically shows at least 13 points. In either event, there is no upper limit.

Opp.	Partner	Opp.	You		
				♠	9 5
				♡	A K 3
1 ♠	2 ♣	P	2 ♠	◇	9 7 6 2
				♣	K 7 5 3

Your hand is too strong for a raise to 3 ♣, so start with an invitational cue-bid.

Opp.	Partner	Opp.	You		
				♠	K 4
				♡	A K J 10 8
1 ◇	1 ♠	P	2 ◇	◇	10 6 5 4
				♣	K 9

You would like to bid 2 ♡, but that is not forcing. You must first cue-bid 2 ◇, then bid your hearts later.

REBIDS BY OVERCALLER

After the invitational cue-bid, overcaller must not pass, except if his right-hand oppo-nent (opening bidder) bids or doubles—in which case, he may pass with nothing useful to say. Overcaller should try to rebid as *naturally* as possible, but within the following framework:

1. **Rebid of original suit** confirms a minimum overcall and is not forcing. This does not necessarily show more than a five-card suit.

♠ K J 8 7 5	Opp.	You	Opp.	Partner
♡ 9 6 3				
◇ K Q 10 9	1 ♡	1 ♠	P	2 ♡
♣ 2	P	2 ♠		

Your natural rebid would be 3 ◇, but that requires extra strength. Thus, you are forced to rebid 2 ♠.

2. **Any rebid *below* your original suit** is ambiguous in strength (could be a minimum or a maximum overcall) and is forcing.

♠ A Q 10 8 6	Opp.	You	Opp.	Partner
♡ K 10 9 3				
◇ 8 4	1 ◇	1 ♠	P	2 ◇
♣ 10 3	P	2 ♡		

Even though your overcall is minimum, it is possible to show your heart suit below the level of 2 ♠.

♠ K 10 5	*Opp.*	*You*	*Opp.*	*Partner*
♡ A 4				
◇ K Q 8 6 5 4	1 ♠	2 ◇	P	2 ♠
♣ 9 8	P	<u>2 NT</u>		

Your two-level overcall is rather minimum, but a 2 NT rebid is more descriptive than 3 ◇.

♠ A K 9 8 6	*Opp.*	*You*	*Opp.*	*Partner*
♡ 9 7				
◇ A K J 9	1 ♣	1 ♠	P	2 ♣
♣ 7 4	P	<u>2 ◇</u>		

Here your overcall is very good, but there is no need to jump, since 2 ◇ is forcing.

3. **Any rebid *beyond* your original suit** confirms a good or maximum overcall. This is forcing (if below game).

♠ K Q 9 7 6	*Opp.*	*You*	*Opp.*	*Partner*
♡ A Q 7				
◇ K 8	1 ♡	1 ♠	P	2 ♡
♣ 9 8 5	P	<u>2 NT</u>		

By rebidding past 2 ♠, you show extra values.

REBIDS BY CUE-BIDDER

The invitational cue-bidder is required to bid again, unless overcaller rebids his original suit or if game has been reached. Here are the meanings of these rebids:

1. **Preference to overcaller's first suit** shows 11 or 12 points and is not forcing.

Opp.	*Partner*	*Opp.*	*You*		
				♠ Q 10 8	
				♡ A 3	
1 ♣	1 ♠	P	2 ♣	◇ A 10 9 4	
P	2 ♡	P	<u>2 ♠</u>	♣ 7 6 4 2	

You show the common "limit raise" type hand; with a better hand, you must jump to 3 ♠ or 4 ♠.

Opp.	*Partner*	*Opp.*	*You*		
				♠ A 5 3	
				♡ 9 5	
1 ♡	2 ♣	P	2 ♡	◇ K 9 4 3	
P	2 ♠	P	<u>3 ♣</u>	♣ K 9 8 2	

You show a hand slightly too strong for an original 3 ♣ raise; partner need not bid again.

2. **Single raise** (below game) shows 13 or 14 points and is invitational to game.

Opp.	*Partner*	*Opp.*	*You*		
				♠ A Q 5	
				♡ K 9 6 3	
1 ◇	1 ♠	P	2 ◇	◇ 10 3	
P	2 ♠	P	<u>3 ♠</u>	♣ A 9 8 2	

You are inviting 4 ♠, even though partner has confirmed a minimum. With just 11 or 12 points, you would pass 2 ♠.

3. **New suit** shows at least 13 points and a five-card or longer suit. This is forcing for one round.

Opp.	Partner	Opp.	You
1 ♣	1 ♥	P	2 ♣
P	2 ♥	P	2 ♠

♠ A K 9 8 7
♥ A 3
♦ K 10 8 6
♣ 9 7

You show at least five spades, and partner must bid again.

4. **Two notrump** shows 13 or 14 points after a one-level overcall, but only about 11 or 12 points after a two-level overcall. In either case, this is not forcing, but invitational to game.

Opp.	Partner	Opp.	You
1 ♣	1 ♠	P	2 ♣
P	2 ♦	P	2 NT

♠ Q 7
♥ A K 9 5
♦ 9 5 2
♣ A 10 7 6

Partner's 2 ♦ bid has given you a clear-cut rebid. With a minimum overcall, partner should pass 2 NT.

5. **Repeat of the invitational cue-bid** (rare) shows a *natural* suit, and is invitational if below game.

Opp.	Partner	Opp.	You
1 ♣	1 ♠	P	2 ♣
P	2 ♠	P	3 ♣

♠ 3
♥ 7 6 5
♦ A 5
♣ K Q J 10 9 8 5

You show a real club suit. If you want to force partner to keep bidding, you must bid a new suit (diamonds or hearts, in this case).

NOTE: The above is the only way to bid the enemy suit naturally in response to partner's overcall, since we recommend a specialized meaning for a *jump* cue-bid response (see page *153*). Nevertheless, little is lost, as the situations where it is desirable to play in the enemy suit are rare indeed.

6. **Any game bid** is a natural sign-off attempt, just as it sounds.

Opp.	Partner	Opp.	You
1 ♦	2 ♣	P	2 ♦
P	2 NT	P	3 NT

♠ K 8
♥ A Q 8 3
♦ 10 5 3
♣ K J 4 2

Partner's 2 NT bid must show a diamond stopper, so forget about raising clubs, and try for the easier nine-trick game.

OTHER RESPONSES TO OVERCALLS

The invitational cue-bid is such a convenient and valuable weapon that the *failure* to use it can be very informative. A new light is shed on certain other responses, the most significant of which is the *jump raise,* which now becomes a weak, preemptive bid. We recommend the following meanings for responses to partner's overcall.

1. **Single raise** shows 6 to 10 points. This is slightly weaker than customarily played, due to the availability of the invitational cue-bid.

Opp.	Partner	Opp.	You		
				♠	J 10 5
				♡	9 4
1 ♣	1 ♠	P	2 ♠	◇	A J 8 4
				♣	9 8 7 2

Your 2 ♠ bid also serves as a mild obstruction should the hand happen to belong to the enemy.

2. **Jump raise** (any level) is weak and preemptive. This promises at least *four* trumps, and typically shows about 5 to 8 points if below game.

Opp.	Partner	Opp.	You		
				♠	9 7 5 4
				♡	3
1 ♠	2 ♣	P	4 ♣	◇	Q 9 8 6
				♣	J 10 9 6

(none vul)

Your 4 ♣ bid is not strength-showing, but an attempt to shut out the opponents.

3. **New suit** shows about 8 to 13 points, and is not forcing.

Opp.	Partner	Opp.	You		
				♠	8 3
				♡	K Q J 8 4
1 ◇	1 ♠	P	2 ♡	◇	7 4 3
				♣	A 10 7

You show at least five hearts, but not enough strength to force.

4. **Jump in a new suit** shows about 11 to 13 points and a good six-card or longer suit. This is invitational to game after a one-level overcall, but forcing to game after a two-level overcall.

Opp.	Partner	Opp.	You		
				♠	A 9 7
				♡	9 3
1 ♣	1 ♡	P	3 ◇	◇	A Q J 10 8 7
				♣	9 3

Your jump to 3 ◇, of course, denies support for partner's heart suit.

5. **Jump cue-bid** is a "mini-splinter bid." This shows a singleton or void in the suit bid, at least *four*-card support for overcaller's suit, and at least 13 points (no upper limit). This differs from the "splinter bid" (see page *31*) in that it is forcing only to the next higher level of partner's suit, *not* necessarily game.

Opp.	Partner	Opp.	You		
				♠	3
				♡	A 7 5
1 ♠	2 ♣	P	3 ♠	◇	K 9 7 5
				♣	Q J 10 7 2

You show a club fit and a spade splinter. If partner returns to 4 ♣ (discouraging), you should pass.

6. **All notrump bids** retain their usual meanings. For the record, we suggest the following ranges: (a) 1 NT shows 8 to 11 points; (b) 2 NT shows 12 to 14 points after a one-level overcall, or 9 to 11 points after a two-level overcall; and (c) 3 NT shows better than 2 NT, or the expectation of winning nine tricks.

INVITATIONAL CUE-BID IN COMPETITION

When the enemy poses further competition, we recommend this agreement:

If right-hand opponent bids or makes a negative double after partner's suit overcall, the principle of the invitational cue-bid, and its related responses, is still in effect. The level of bidding may sometimes be higher, perhaps even awkward, but it *still* pays to follow the structure whenever feasible.

Opp.	Partner	Opp.	You		
				♠	K J 7
				♡	7 2
1 ♢	1 ♠	2 ♢	<u>3 ♢</u>	♢	10 4 3
				♣	A Q 8 5 4

You show, in all probability, an 11- or 12-point spade raise. With a minimum, partner must rebid 3 ♠ (or 3 ♡), in which case game will be avoided. Had you instead jumped to 3 ♠, that would have been preemptive.

Opp.	Partner	Opp.	You		
				♠	8 7
				♡	A 7 5 4
1 ♡	2 ♢	DBL*	<u>2 ♡</u>	♢	K J 7 5
				♣	Q J 4

*Negative

Here your cue-bid guarantees a diamond fit. Without diamond support, you would redouble to show a good hand.

Opp.	Partner	Opp.	You		
				♠	9 6
				♡	A 10 6
1 ♠	2 ♡	2 ♠	<u>3 ♠</u>	♢	K 10 9 5
				♣	A 8 3 2

Your 3 ♠ cue-bid informs partner that you are bidding on high cards, whereas a jump to 4 ♡ would be preemptive. Should the enemy continue to 4 ♠, partner will be able to make a more intelligent decision.

If your right-hand opponent bids a *new* suit, you then have a choice of cue-bids. In that event, cue-bid the suit in which you are *stronger*. Partner can then judge the usefulness of any honors in that suit; he might even bid notrump, especially if his overcall was in a minor suit. For example:

Opp.	Partner	Opp.	You		
				♠	K Q 10
				♡	A 7 6 5
1 ♣	1 ♢	1 ♠	<u>2 ♠</u>	♢	Q 10 8 3
				♣	8 5

You could cue-bid either 2 ♣ or 2 ♠, so the inference is that your spades are stronger. Partner may now bid notrump without a spade stopper.

FURTHER APPLICATIONS

Thus far, we have assumed that partner has made a direct overcall of a first-seat opening bid, which is undoubtedly the most frequent overcalling position. The invitational cue-bid structure, however, is very flexible and should be used in a variety of similar situations. These are listed below, along with any special characteristics:

1. **If you passed *prior* to any bidding,** an invitational cue-bid *promises* support for partner's suit. This should be evident, as your hand could hardly be strong enough to cue-bid otherwise.

Opp.	Partner	Opp.	You		
				♠	K 9 4
				♡	Q J 7
		P	P	◇	A 8 6 5 3
1 ♣	1 ♡	P	2 ♣	♣	9 2

   Your cue-bid shows a heart fit and about 11 or more points, whereas a jump raise to 3 ♡ would be weak.

2. **If you passed *after* an enemy bid, and partner has made a *direct* overcall,** an invitational cue-bid *usually* (but not always) shows support for partner's suit.

Opp.	Partner	Opp.	You		
				♠	A 8 4 3
				♡	8 6
		1 ♠	P	◇	K J 7
1 NT	2 ◇	P	2 ♠	♣	K 8 6 2

   You are too strong for a raise to 3 ◇, so the 2 ♠ cue-bid neatly solves the problem.

When the enemy has bid *two* suits, an invitational cue-bid can be made only in their *last*-bid suit. This reserves a bid in their first-bid suit (the suit you passed over) as a *natural*, nonforcing bid. Although this agreement is not universally accepted, it is completely logical. For example:

Opp.	Partner	Opp.	You		
				♠	A J 5
				♡	9 8
		1 ◇	P	◇	A 10 8 7
1 ♡	1 ♠	P	2 ♡	♣	Q 9 5 3

   You must cue-bid 2 ♡, not 2 ◇. A bid of 2 ◇ should show a long diamond suit, as you could not have bid diamonds naturally at your last turn.

3. **If you passed *after* an enemy bid, and partner has made a *balancing* overcall,** the situation is *identical* to application (2), except that we invoke the *"queen"* rule (see page *118*). In other words, partner has already overbid by two points, so you must *underbid* by two points to compensate.

Opp.	Partner	Opp.	You		
				♠	9 3
				♡	K 9 6
		1 ♣	P	◇	A Q 5 4
P	1 ♡	P	2 ♣	♣	A 7 5 3

   Your cue-bid suggests 13 or more points (instead of 11), since partner's overcall has a weaker range.

Opp.	Partner	Opp.	You		
				♠	K 9 7 5
				♡	A 9 7 4
1 NT	P	2 ♡	P	◇	3
P	2 ♠	P	3 ♡	♣	Q J 9 8

   Your 3 ♡ cue-bid strongly invites game, but still leaves partner an "out" in 3 ♠. Notice that a raise to 3 ♠ would be a milder invitation.

4. **Other opportunities** for the invitational cue-bid and weak jump raise occur in responding to "weak jump overcalls," the "unusual notrump overcall," and the "Michaels cue-bid." The details are explained under their respective headings.

Responsive Doubles ★ ★

Originated by Dr. F. Fielding-Reid of Dania, Florida

The "responsive double" is an extension of the takeout double that is employed *after* partner has already doubled for takeout. It is based on the principle that it is rarely desirable to double the opponents for penalty below game when they have established a trump fit. Here is the basic rule:

If partner has made a takeout double of an opening bid of one of a suit, and right-hand opponent has raised opener's suit (through 4 ◇), a double is for takeout, showing the unbid suits. This is a responsive double.

The strength required for a responsive double varies according to the level at which it is made. A reasonable minimum might be 6 points at the two-level, 8 points at the three-level, and 10 points at the four-level. In any event, there is no upper limit. Here are some examples:

Opp.	Partner	Opp.	You		
				♠	K 8 4 3
				♡	J 9 5 4
1 ♣	DBL	2 ♣	DBL	◇	Q 7 4
				♣	8 4

Your double suggests equal lengths in the majors, as you would bid a suit yourself with a clear preference.

Opp.	Partner	Opp.	You		
				♠	A Q 7
				♡	K 9 6
1 ◇	DBL	3 ◇	DBL	◇	8 4 2
				♣	J 7 5 4

You have the strength to compete, but where? The responsive double is the only sensible action.

Opp.	Partner	Opp.	You		
				♠	A J 4
				♡	Q 9 8 5
1 ◇	DBL	2 ◇	2 ♡	◇	8 7 5
				♣	J 9 2

There is no point in doubling here; you clearly prefer hearts, so bid your suit.

If there is just *one* unbid major, it is customary to *bid* that suit yourself whenever holding four or more cards; therefore, the responsive double becomes a *minor*-suit takeout. For example:

Opp.	Partner	Opp.	You		
				♠	5 4
				♡	A 6 2
1 ♡	DBL	2 ♡	DBL	◇	Q J 7 5
				♣	10 9 8 3

You would bid spades if you had them, so you are asking partner to choose a minor suit.

Opp.	Partner	Opp.	You		
				♠	9 5
				♡	K 8
1 ♠	DBL	3 ♠	DBL	◇	J 9 8 5 4
				♣	A 10 9 7

Here too, you show both minors. Holding four hearts, you must grit your teeth and bid 4 ♡.

BIDDING AFTER A RESPONSIVE DOUBLE

Bidding after a responsive double follows familiar practice. Most experts would adhere to this agreement:

If partner has made a responsive double (after your takeout double), the principles of limit bidding apply. That is: (a) minimum suit bids show minimum values; (b) jump bids (or 2 NT) show extra values and are invitational if below game; and (c) a cue-bid of the enemy suit is the only force.

Opp.	Partner	Opp.	You		
				♠	9 7
				♡	A K 9 8
		1 ♠	DBL	◇	A 9 8 2
2 ♠	DBL	P	3 ◇	♣	Q 10 7

With a minimum takeout double, just make a minimum bid. Observe that partner's double asks for a minor, not hearts.

Opp.	Partner	Opp.	You		
				♠	A J 7
				♡	K J 10 8
		1 ♣	DBL	◇	A Q 9 8
2 ♣	DBL	P	3 ♡	♣	3 2

Your jump to 3 ♡ shows slightly extra values, but is not forcing. Partner should pass with a minimum responsive double.

Passing a responsive double (for penalty) is rare, but can be done, especially at the higher levels, when your hand contains good defensive potential and poor offensive prospects. For example:

Opp.	Partner	Opp.	You		
				♠	A 8 5
				♡	A K 9 2
		1 ♠	DBL	◇	10 6 5
3 ♠	DBL	P	P	♣	K J 3

Passing 3 ♠ doubled is the only logical action, since partner has denied interest in hearts.

RESPONSIVE DOUBLES AFTER OVERCALLS

Most experts also employ the responsive double after partner has overcalled. Thus, we have another rule:

If partner has made a simple suit overcall of an opening bid of one of a suit, and right-hand opponent has raised opener's suit (through 4 ◇), a double is for takeout, showing the two unbid suits. This is a responsive double.

The minimum strength for this kind of responsive double is slightly higher. Generally, at least 8 high-card points are required, but as usual there is no upper limit. Here are some examples:

Opp.	Partner	Opp.	You		
				♠	10 2
				♡	K Q 10 7
1 ♣	1 ♠	2 ♣	DBL	◇	Q J 9 8 3
				♣	7 6

Your double shows hearts and diamonds, and denies normal spade support. Hopefully, partner will bid a red suit, but no great tragedy should befall you if he rebids 2 ♠.

Opp.	Partner	Opp.	You	♠ K J 10 8
				♡ J 9 7 6 5
1 ◇	2 ♣	2 ◇	DBL	◇ 8
				♣ K 9 4

It is permissible to conceal support for partner's minor *suit, in the hope that a major-suit fit may be found.*

Opp.	Partner	Opp.	You	♠ 6
				♡ Q J 9 8 3
1 ♠	2 ♣	3 ♠	DBL	◇ A K 9 6 2
				♣ 10 2

It is quite common to have five-five shape, as in this high-level situation.

After this kind of responsive double, overcaller should always strain to bid an *unbid* suit, even with just three cards, rather than repeat a five-card suit. The same "limit" style of bidding applies. For example:

Opp.	Partner	Opp.	You	♠ A Q 9 7 5
				♡ K J 6
		1 ◇	1 ♠	◇ 10 4 3
2 ◇	DBL	P	2 ♡	♣ 9 8

Partner has at least four hearts, and often five, so 2 ♡ will be a good spot. Rebidding 2 ♠ (poor) may lead to a terrible contract if partner is very short.

DON'T BE FOOLED

Responsive doubles tend to cause more than their share of partnership mix-ups. Other than simply forgetting the convention, this is probably due to the fact that many players like to invent opportunities at the table, just because it "looks right" at the time. The following auctions illustrate *penalty* doubles that are frequently misused (or mistaken) as responsive doubles. Of course, you wouldn't be fooled—or would you?

Opp.	Partner	Opp.	You
1 ♣	DBL	1 ♠	DBL

For penalty; no suit has been raised.

Opp.	Partner	Opp.	You
1 ♣	2 ♠	3 ♣	DBL

For penalty; responsive doubles do not apply after jump overcalls.

Opp.	Partner	Opp.	You
2 ♡*	DBL	3 ♡	DBL

*Weak two-bid

For penalty; responsive doubles do not apply after enemy preemptive openings.

Opp.	Partner	Opp.	You
1 ◇	1 NT	2 ◇	DBL

For penalty; responsive doubles do not apply after notrump overcalls.

S-O-S Redouble ★ ★

Introduced by Rudolph Kock and Einar Werner of Stockholm, Sweden,
leading international players of the 1940s and '50s

It is a well-known fact that making a doubled contract is practically always a good result, whether the form of scoring is matchpoints, IMPs, board-a-match, or whatever. Thus, if you expect to *make* a low-level contract, it is usually foolhardy to redouble just to increase the score. After all, why give the opponents a chance to run? Why jeopardize a favorable result?

Consequently, the redouble of a low-level penalty double can be put to much better use. The so-called "S-O-S redouble" is a handy rescue maneuver, which says, in effect, "Let's get the hell out of here!" Here is a more formal definition:

After a penalty double of a *natural* suit bid (below game), or a penalty pass of a takeout double, a redouble is a rescue attempt, provided there are at least two unbid suits.

Opp.	Partner	Opp.	You		
				♠	Q 9 8 6 5
				♡	10 8 6 4 3
1 ◇	2 ♣	DBL	RDBL	◇	6 5 4
				♣	—

Your redouble is for rescue, demanding that partner choose a major suit.

Opp.	Partner	Opp.	You		
				♠	Q J 9 5
				♡	3
1 ♣	1 ♡	P	P	◇	Q 10 9 6 3
DBL	P	P	RDBL	♣	7 6 3

The penalty pass suggests that partner is running into a terrible heart stack. You hope to improve matters.

The overcaller himself may use this gadget:

Opp.	Partner	Opp.	You		
				♠	A J 5 4 3
				♡	3
	2 ♡*	2 ♠		◇	K Q 10 7
DBL	P	P	RDBL	♣	Q J 9

*Weak two-bid

Apparently, you have run into a spade stack. Your redouble asks partner to bid his (hoped-for) minor.

The S-O-S redouble may also be employed by the side that has opened the bidding, as these two examples illustrate:

Opp.	Partner	Opp.	You		
				♠	A J 9 5
				♡	K 10 3
			1 ♣	◇	Q 7 2
DBl	P	P	RDBL	♣	A 3 2

You do not relish the prospect of playing in 1 ♣ doubled, so redouble for rescue.

Opp.	Partner	Opp.	You		
				♠	J 9 8 5
				♡	10 7 5 4
	1 ◇	P	P	◇	3
DBL	P	P	RDBL	♣	J 8 7 4

Surely, there is a better contract than 1 ◇ doubled.

BIDDING AFTER AN S-O-S REDOUBLE

The responsibilities of bidding after an S-O-S redouble should be apparent; just don't pass! That is:

If partner has made an S-O-S redouble, every effort must be made to *remove* it to an unbid suit. This often involves bidding a *three*-card suit (conceivably, even a doubleton).

Opp.	Partner	Opp.	You	
		1 ♠	2 ◇	♠ A 10 8
P	P	DBL	P	♡ 8 6 3
P	RDBL	P	<u>2 ♡</u>	◇ A K J 8 6 5
				♣ 5

Your 2 ♡ bid merely cooperates with partner. Indeed, be happy you have three hearts.

AVOIDING MISUSE

Although every convention is occasionally misused, the S-O-S redouble may be at the head of the list. Do not forget that partner's bid must be a *natural suit,* and the enemy double must be for *penalty.* Observe these two predicaments:

Opp.	Partner	Opp.	You	
				♠ 9 4
				♡ 7 5 4
1 ♠	1 NT	DBL	?	◇ 10 5 4 3
				♣ J 7 4 3

Do not *redouble; that would be for business. You should pass.*

Opp.	Partner	Opp.	You	
				♠ J 9 7 6 4
				♡ 9 8 7
1 ♡	2 ♣	DBL*	?	◇ Q 10 7 6 3
				♣ —

*Negative

Do not *redouble; that would show a good hand over a negative double. Just pass and hope opener bids.*

Another form of misuse might be called the "Mighty Mouse syndrome," or "Here I come to save the day . . ." Just because partner gets doubled, it does *not* mean that you must rescue him. Discretion is required. For example:

Opp.	Partner	Opp.	You	
				♠ 9 7
				♡ 7
1 ♠	2 ♡	DBL	?	◇ J 9 8 5 4
				♣ K 9 7 5 2

Do not *redouble. Your chances for improvement are too doubtful, especially when the level must be increased.*

Astro

Co-invented by Paul <u>A</u>llinger, Roger <u>St</u>ern, and Lawrence <u>Ro</u>sler, all prominent American players. The name was derived by combining the beginning letters of their last names (as underlined).

Entering the bidding after an opponent's 1 NT opening is an awkward practice. If you overcall in a suit in which partner is very short, you may find yourself in serious trouble, especially if you get doubled. Then again, if you pass, you may find yourself talked out of a part-score, or even a game! This may seem like the old cliche, "Heads they win, tails you lose," but your chances can be considerably improved with the "Astro" convention.

Overcalling with a two-suited hand is more promising than with a one-suited hand. Not only is it safer (two chances to find a fit instead of one), but the prospects of bidding a makable game are improved. These are the principles behind Astro. An overcall in either minor suit is used artificially to show a two-suited hand, as described below:

1. **Two clubs (over 1 NT)** shows at least five-four shape with *hearts* plus one of the minor suits. The strength required is about 9 to 14 high-card points, or slightly less with extreme shape.

Opp.	You		
		♠	7
		♡	K J 10 9 4
1 NT	2 ♣	♢	A Q J 9
		♣	9 4 2

You promise at least four hearts, but your minor suit is not yet known.

Opp.	You		
		♠	9 2
		♡	A Q 10 7
1 NT	2 ♣	♢	A 5
		♣	Q J 9 8 4

    Notice that your five-four shape may be "either way," i.e., at least nine cards in your two suits.

2. **Two diamonds (over 1 NT)** shows at least five-four shape with *spades* plus another suit (which could be hearts). The strength is identical to 2 ♣.

Opp.	You		
		♠	Q 10 9 8 3
		♡	5
1 NT	2 ♢	♢	9 3
		♣	A K 10 6 2

You promise at least four spades, but your second suit is completely unknown.

Opp.	You		
		♠	K Q J 6
		♡	A J 10 6 3
1 NT	2 ♢	♢	8
		♣	10 9 3

    This is the way to bid with both majors.

NOTE: Our suggested point range of 9 to 14 high-card points is approximate, of course, and serves only as a helpful guideline. As any experienced player knows, various factors (especially vulnerability) must be considered to determine whether an aggressive or conservative course of action is better.

RESPONSES

Now that we have established the meanings of the basic two-suited overcalls, let us see what responder (partner of Astro bidder) is supposed to do. Observe that one of Astro bidder's suits will always be known; i.e., 2 ♣ guarantees hearts and 2 ♢ guarantees spades. This suit shall be referred to as the "known major." Most of the time, responder will make one of these two bids:

1. **Two of the known major** shows at least *three* cards. This is not forcing and usually ends the bidding, unless Astro bidder is strong enough to try for game.

Opp.	Partner	Opp.	You
1 NT	2 ♣	P	2 ♡

♠ A J 6 4 3
♡ J 6 3
♢ 7
♣ 9 8 7 6

   Do not bid your spades! Partner has shown a heart suit, so 2 ♡ will be a reasonable contract.

2. **Cheapest step response** *denies* three cards in the known major, and is called the "relay" response. This does *not* indicate a real suit, although responder usually has at least three cards in the suit bid.

Opp.	Partner	Opp.	You
1 NT	2 ♢	P	2 ♡

♠ 6 2
♡ 10 8 2
♢ K 7 6 5
♣ J 9 8 2

   Your 2 ♡ response simply denies spade support. (Astro bidder's rebids are covered later.)

The remaining responses to the Astro overcall occur much less frequently. Their meanings are as follows:

3. **Two spades (over 2 ♣) or three clubs (over 2 ♢)** shows at least a six-card suit and denies support for the known major. This, of course, is not forcing.

Opp.	Partner	Opp.	You
1 NT	2 ♣	P	2 ♠

♠ J 10 9 7 6 5
♡ 2
♢ 8 4 2
♣ A 9 6

   Even opposite a singleton, 2 ♠ may be your best contract, so bid it.

4. **Two notrump** is the only *forcing* response to Astro. This asks Astro bidder to show his second suit, and usually requires about 11 or more points.

Opp.	Partner	Opp.	You
1 NT	2 ♢	P	2 NT

♠ K 3
♡ A J 9 4
♢ A 5 4
♣ 10 8 7 4

   You have definite game interest and would like to find out what partner's other suit is.

5. **Raise of the Astro overcall** (rare) shows at least a good six-card suit, and is mildly invitational to game. Obviously, this denies support for the known major. NOTE: With a weaker, but similar hand, responder may actually *pass* the Astro overcall if he feels that no better contract can be reached.

Opp.	Partner	Opp.	You
1 NT	2 ♣	P	3 ♣

♠ 9 3 2
♡ 3
♢ A J 8
♣ K Q J 9 8 7

   Your "raise" to 3 ♣ shows a self-sufficient suit. If your ace of diamonds was a small diamond, you should pass partner's 2 ♣ bid!

6. **Jump in any suit** is natural and invitational to game. This includes a jump to three in the known major.

Opp.	Partner	Opp.	You
1 NT	2 ◇	P	3 ♠

♠ K J 8 5
♡ A J 7 3
◇ 3 2
♣ J 10 4

You are inviting game in spades. Partner should pass 3 ♠ with a minimum, or bid 4 ♠ with a maximum.

7. **Any game bid** is obviously a sign-off.

IN COMPETITION: If the Astro overcall is doubled, responder may (a) pass to show at least four cards in the suit doubled; or (b) make his normal response. Also, if right-hand opponent *bids* over the Astro overcall, the preceding responses would have the same meanings, insofar as possible.

AUCTIONS AFTER THE RELAY RESPONSE

When the Astro bidder receives the "relay" response (cheapest step) over his 2 ♣ or 2 ◇ overcall, the partnership must still scramble to a playable trump suit. Here are the options available to Astro bidder:

1. **Pass** indicates that your second suit is the "relay" suit.

Opp.	Partner	Opp.	You
		1 NT	2 ◇
P	2 ♡	P	P

♠ A K 9 6 5
♡ K J 10 3
◇ 9 8 2
♣ 6

Partner has denied three spades, so he rates to have heart support. If he doesn't, then the hand is a misfit, and you wouldn't want to bid any higher anyway.

2. **Two of the known major** shows at least five cards. This implies that your second suit did not coincide with the "relay" response.

Opp.	Partner	Opp.	You
		1 NT	2 ◇
P	2 ♡	P	2 ♠

♠ K Q 9 8 7
♡ 7
◇ A Q J 7
♣ 8 7 2

Your 2 ♠ bid shows five spades; partner should then pass with a doubleton.

If responder still cannot tolerate the known major, he may bid 2 NT (forcing) to request Astro bidder's second suit. For example:

Opp.	Partner	Opp.	You
1 NT	2 ◇	P	2 ♡
P	2 ♠	P	2 NT

♠ 2
♡ Q 9 8 2
◇ 10 9 8 5
♣ A 9 6 5

Your 2 NT bid asks partner to bid his other suit, which is obviously a minor since he did not pass 2 ♡.

3. **Three of a suit** shows at least five cards.

Opp.	Partner	Opp.	You		
				♠	7
				♡	A J 8 7
		1 NT	2 ♣	◇	K 5 3
P	2 ◇	P	3 ♣	♣	K Q 10 9 7

Partner has denied three hearts, so 3 ♣ appears to be your only remaining hope.

If Astro bidder's rebid of three of a suit is a *raise* or a *jump* bid, then he is, obviously, inviting game. For example:

Opp.	Partner	Opp.	You		
				♠	K Q 10 8 7
				♡	A K Q 6 5
		1 NT	2 ◇	◇	6 5
P	2 ♡	P	3 ♡	♣	3

You would pass 2 ♡ in order to sign off, so this is definitely a game try.

Finally, one cute little twist should be mentioned:

4. **Two spades when Astro bidder has denied spades** shows exactly *three* cards. This gives responder the opportunity to pass if, by chance, he happens to hold four or five spades.

Opp.	Partner	Opp.	You		
				♠	K J 9
				♡	A Q 9 8
		1 NT	2 ♣	◇	5
P	2 ◇	P	2 ♠!	♣	Q J 8 7 6

Your 2 ♠ bid allows all avenues to be explored. If partner has fewer than four spades, he should bid 2 NT to ask for your minor.

OTHER OVERCALLS OF ONE NOTRUMP

Thus far, we have discussed only the 2 ♣ and 2 ◇ overcalls, which are the essence of the Astro convention. Nevertheless, the use of Astro sheds some different light on the meanings of other overcalls. The remaining overcalls are approximately equal in strength to the Astro overcalls (roughly, 9 to 14 high-card points). The following interpretations apply:

1. **Two of a major** shows at least a six-card suit.

Opp.	You		
		♠	A Q J 9 7 6
		♡	A 3
1 NT	2 ♠	◇	9 5 2
		♣	10 4

You show at least six spades. With only five spades and no second suit, it is poor tactics to overcall.

2. **Two notrump** shows at least five-five shape in the *minor* suits. This is just another application of the "unusual notrump overcall" (see page *136*).

3. **Three of a minor** shows at least a *seven*-card suit, or a very good six-card suit. When playing Astro, it is necessary to jump to 3 ♣ or 3 ◇ to show a minor one-suiter. *Never* overcall 2 ♣ or 2 ◇ with just a one-suited hand!

	Opp.	You	
			♠ 5
			♡ K 3
1 NT	3 ♣		♢ A 9 2
			♣ K J 9 8 7 6 4

Your 3 ♣ bid is not a weak jump overcall; it is the proper way to show clubs. Because of the increased level, avoid this bid on doubtful hands.

4. **Higher suit overcalls** show at least a *seven*-card suit, and within *one* playing trick (or 1½, in a pinch) of your actual bid (see page *135*).

BALANCING POSITION

As with any convention, the partnership must agree on its use and limitations. We recommend the use of Astro also in the balancing position. That is:

If the 1 NT opening is followed by two passes, the Astro convention and other overcalls still apply. However, the requirements may be shaded slightly.

Opp.	Partner	Opp.	You	
				♠ A 6
				♡ J 10 9 7 6
1 NT	P	P	2 ♣	♢ Q J 9 8
				♣ 8 2

Your 2 ♣ bid shows hearts and a minor, but notice that your hand is too weak for a direct overcall.

Opp.	Partner	Opp.	You	
				♠ K J 10 8
				♡ Q J 9 6
1 NT	P	P	2 ♢	♢ A 7 6 2
				♣ 5

Despite having only four-four shape, it is reasonable to gamble that partner can support one of the majors. But in direct position, such a bid would be inviting trouble.

Opp.	Partner	Opp.	You	
				♠ 10 9 7
				♡ Q J 8 7 6 5
1 NT	P	P	2 ♡	♢ A 3
				♣ 6 2

Your 2 ♡ bid is justifiable in passout seat.

Opp.	Partner	Opp.	You	
				♠ 9
				♡ Q 9 6
1 NT	P	P	P	♢ Q J 9 6 5 4
				♣ A 4 2

You must draw the line somewhere. Even in balancing seat, it would be injudicious to bid 3 ♢ with such a poor suit. Also, do not make the mistake of bidding 2 ♢!

ASTRO OVER TWO NOTRUMP

Although it is indeed rare to bid over an enemy 2 NT opening, the possession of extreme distribution would seem to be the more opportune moment, especially at favorable vulnerability when a profitable sacrifice is most likely. In order to describe both one- and two-suited hands, the principles of Astro should still apply, in both direct and balancing position. Therefore:

1. **Three clubs** shows *hearts* and a minor suit. Respond accordingly.

Opp.	You	♠	9 8
		♡	K J 10 9 8
2 NT	3 ♣	◇	Q J 10 9 7 5
		♣	—

(favorable)

> *Your 3 ♣ bid implies freakish shape. Lacking three hearts, partner should bid 3 ◇ (relay response), which you will pass, of course.*

2. **Three diamonds** shows *spades* and another suit. Respond accordingly.

3. **All other suit bids** are natural.

4. **Three notrump** shows both *minor* suits.

NOTE: The Astro convention may also be used in defending against an enemy "gambling 3 NT opening" (see page *177*).

Jump Cue-Bid Overcall   ★ ★ ★

To introduce this section, let's assume you pick up either of the following two hands after your right-hand opponent opens the bidding with 1 ♡:

A.	♠	A 3		B.	♠	A Q J 9 8 7 6 5
	♡	8 2			♡	—
	◇	A K Q 10 8 7 6			◇	9 4
	♣	K 3			♣	A K 8

Admit it. You wouldn't be happy with any action. With hand A, you might be lay-down for 3 NT if partner has a heart stopper, but how do you get there? If you double 1 ♡, partner is likely to bid spades, not notrump. With hand B, it is easy enough to jump to 4 ♠, but what if partner has the right cards for slam? To double is no solution either; you might find yourself on lead against 1 ♡ doubled!

NOTE: If you are suggesting a "strong cue-bid" (2 ♡) for either of the above two hands, your methods are antiquated. Most experts have given this up, and rightly so, for the "Michaels cue-bid" (see page *143*) or one of its variations.

The point is this. There is a definite need for some sort of convention to handle strong one-suited hands. As you may have guessed, there just happens to be one . . . the "jump cue-bid overcall." Here is how it works:

Three-level jump cue-bid shows a strong one-suited hand (in an unbid suit) of about 8½ or more playing tricks. Suit must be of at least six (usually seven) cards, and solid or semi-solid. If a *minor* suit is held, overcaller is usually trying for 3 NT (asking for a stopper). If a *major* suit is held, overcaller confirms a singleton or void in the enemy suit.

Observe that hands A and B at the beginning of this section would be perfect for a 3 ♡ overcall of the 1 ♡ opening bid. Some more examples follow:

Opp.	You		
		♠	9
		♡	K 9
1 ♠	3 ♠	♢	A Q 6
		♣	A K J 10 9 6 5

You wish to chance 3 NT if partner has a spade stopper. If the opening bid had been 1 ♢ or 1 ♡, you should jump to 3 NT yourself.

Opp.	You		
		♠	A 5
		♡	K Q J 10 9 5 4
1 ♢	3 ♢	♢	2
		♣	A K 4

When your suit is a major, you promise shortness in the enemy suit. If the opening bid had been 1 ♣ or 1 ♠, you should double.

The jump cue-bid overcall applies any time that you *jump* to the *three*-level in a suit bid by the enemy, provided, of course, you have not previously passed and partner has never acted. Witness this example:

Opp.	Partner	Opp.	You		
				♠	A 9
				♡	A Q 7
1 ♣	P	1 ♡	3 ♣	♢	A K Q J 9 3
				♣	4 3

If partner has a club stopper, you intend to play 3 NT. With your club and heart holdings reversed, you would bid 3 ♡.

RESPONSES

As should be apparent, the jump cue-bid overcall cannot be passed! Responder's primary concern is whether or not his hand contains a *stopper* in the enemy suit. Here are the possible responses:

1. **Three notrump** shows a stopper in the enemy suit. This does *not* indicate a balanced hand, nor even the desire to play notrump. Remember, if partner's long suit is a minor, he can provide the tricks; all you need is the stopper.

Opp.	Partner	Opp.	You		
				♠	K J 7 6 4 3
				♡	6 3
1 ♢	3 ♢	P	3 NT	♢	K 8 5
				♣	3 2

Your 3 NT bid shows a diamond stopper, which is more important than your broken spade suit.

2. **Cheaper minor** (3 ♢ over 3 ♣; or 4 ♣ over any other bid) is an artificial "weakness" response. This denies a stopper in the enemy suit, and denies as much as an ace and a king (or three kings).

Opp.	Partner	Opp.	You		
				♠	9 5 3 2
				♡	K 10 6 3
1 ♠	3 ♠	P	4 ♣	♢	J 4 2
				♣	8 3

Your 4 ♣ bid has no relation to clubs, but just shows a weak hand with no spade stopper.

3. **Higher minor** (4 ♣ over 3 ♣; or 4 ♢ over any other bid) is an artificial "constructive" response. This denies a stopper in the enemy suit, but promises at least an *ace* and a *king* (or three kings).

Opp.	Partner	Opp.	You		
				♠	A 9 7 5
				♡	8 7 4 3
1 ♡	3 ♡	P	4 ◇	◇	K J 9
				♣	10 8

You show a useful hand for partner, but nothing about diamonds, of course.

4. **Any major suit** is natural and shows at least a good six-card suit. This is forcing if below game.

Opp.	Partner	Opp.	You		
				♠	K Q 10 9 7 5
				♡	3 2
1 ♣	3 ♣	P	3 ♠	◇	9 8 2
				♣	J 7

You cannot bid 3 NT, so you may as well show your good spade suit.

5. **Higher notrump bids** (rare) show a stopper in the enemy suit plus at least an outside *ace* and a *king* (or three kings). For practical purposes, 4 NT (not forcing) should show a "non-control" stopper (e.g., Q-X-X or J-10-X-X); whereas 5 NT (forcing) should show a "control" stopper (e.g., A or K-X).

IN COMPETITION: If responder's right-hand opponent *bids* or *doubles* after the jump cue-bid overcall, a "common sense" approach is dictated. Responder may (a) pass with a weak hand; (b) bid the cheaper minor (or redouble) to indicate a "constructive" response; (c) bid notrump, if sensible, to show a stopper; (d) bid a major suit naturally; or (e) double for penalty. For example:

Opp.	Partner	Opp.	You		
				♠	K 9 7 5 3
				♡	A J 7
1 ♣	3 ♣	4 ♣	4 ◇	◇	7 4
				♣	6 5 2

Your 4 ◇ bid is artificial, showing at least an ace and a king (or three kings). You would pass, of course, with a weak hand.

REBIDS BY JUMP CUE-BIDDER

The rebids by the jump cue-bidder are completely natural and logical. Here are the available options:

1. **Pass** if you feel the proper contract has been reached. This occurs in two common situations: if responder bids 3 NT and your long suit is a minor, or if responder's "weakness" response coincides with your long minor.

Opp.	Partner	Opp.	You		
				♠	A 8
				♡	A J
		1 ♣	3 ♣	◇	A K Q 9 8 7 3
P	3 NT	P	P	♣	6 2

Partner's 3 NT bid was just what you wanted to hear.

Opp.	Partner	Opp.	You		
				♠	8 5
				♡	A
		1 ♠	3 ♠	◇	K 5 2
P	4 ♣	P	P	♣	A K Q J 8 4 2

Partner has no spade stopper and a weak hand, so pass; indeed, you may already be too high.

2. **Any suit bid** is natural and shows your real suit. This is not forcing, but **partner may bid again** with appropriate values.

Opp.	Partner	Opp.	You		
				♠	A 8
				♡	5 3
		1 ♡	3 ♡	◇	A Q J 10 9 7 5
P	4 ♣	P	4 ◇	♣	A J

You show a diamond suit. Partner will usually pass, but may raise to 5 ◇ with a useful dummy.

Opp.	Partner	Opp.	You		
				♠	10 8
				♡	A K Q J 10 4 3
		1 ♣	3 ♣	◇	A J 9
P	4 ♣	P	4 ♡	♣	3

Partner's 4 ♣ bid is "constructive" (3 ◇ would show a weak hand), but an ace and a king is not enough for slam. With extra values, partner should bid again.

Opp.	Partner	Opp.	You		
				♠	A K Q 10 8 7 6 5
				♡	K 2
		1 ◇	3 ◇	◇	—
P	4 ◇	5 ◇	6 ♠	♣	Q J 3

Partner shows at least an ace and a king outside of diamonds, so you can confidently bid a slam, despite the enemy barrage.

3. **Four notrump** is ordinary Blackwood (even over a 3 NT response).

Opp.	Partner	Opp.	You		
				♠	J
				♡	Q 8
		1 ♠	3 ♠	◇	A K Q J 10 7 6 5
P	4 ◇	P	4 NT	♣	K Q

You will make partner declarer in 5 ◇ or 6 ◇, according to whether he has one or two aces.

Defense to One-Club Forcing ★ ★ ★

A modification of the method devised by Alan Truscott of New York City, a leading expert, and bridge editor of the New York Times

Some systems today employ the "1 ♣ forcing" concept (see Glossary), which prescribes a 1 ♣ opening as the strong, artificial, forcing bid. It cannot be denied that this gives them greater freedom in the bidding of strong hands . . . if you roll over and play dead, that is. Unquestionably, the best defense to this opening is a quick offense. Obstructing the flow of the enemy auction is the chief goal.

Therefore, all immediate actions should suggest *weak* hands (less than opening-bid strength). To emphasize the aggressive tendencies of such actions, we have deliberately chosen borderline hands in most of the examples that follow. As always, however, an eye must be kept on the vulnerability when deciding just what liberties may be taken.

We recommend a structured system of intervention to allow both one-suited and two-suited hands to be shown. WARNING: These methods are intended for use only over *strong*, artificial, forcing 1 ♣ bids; they do *not* apply against the so-called "short club" bid (see Glossary). *One-suited* hands are shown as follows:

1. **Double** shows clubs.

Opp.	You		
		♠	7 2
		♡	9 4 3
1 ♣*	DBL	♢	9 8 2
		♣	K Q 10 8 5

*Artificial

> Since 1 ♣ is artificial, your double shows that suit. Hence, partner will know what to lead.

2. **One of a suit** shows that suit.

Opp.	You		
		♠	9 3
		♡	Q 10 8 7 3
1 ♣*	1 ♡	♢	A 6 2
		♣	5 4 3

*Artificial

> Your 1 ♡ overcall is weaker than usual, although at unfavorable vulnerability, you should pass.

3. **Three of a suit** (or higher) shows that suit. This is just a "weak jump overcall" (see page *132*).

TWO-SUITED OVERCALLS

The remaining overcalls of the 1 ♣ opening are put to special use. Any of the six combinations of *two-suited* hands may be specifically shown with one bid. Here is how:

1. **Two of a suit** shows the *bid* suit plus the *next higher* suit.

Opp.	You		
		♠	4
		♡	J 10 9 6 4
1 ♣*	2 ♢	♢	K 10 9 7 3
		♣	9 6

*Artificial

> You show diamonds and hearts. Observe that all "touching" combinations of two-suiters can be described with an appropriate two-level suit overcall.

2. **One notrump** shows the *pointed* suits.

Opp.	You		
		♠	K J 7 4 3
		♡	3
1 ♣*	1 NT	♢	Q J 9 5 4
		♣	5 2

*Artificial

> You show diamonds and spades.

3. **Two notrump** shows the *rounded* suits.

Opp.	You		
		♠	7
		♡	K 10 9 7 5
1 ♣*	2 NT	♢	3
		♣	Q 9 8 5 3 2

*Artificial

> You show clubs and hearts.

HINT: To avoid confusing the 1 NT and 2 NT overcalls, a helpful memory aid is the fact that the numeral "1" is *pointed*, whereas "2" is *rounded.*

DEFENSE TO ONE-DIAMOND RESPONSE

All systems that employ the strong, artificial 1 ♣ opening also employ an artificial 1 ◇ response. We recommend this agreement:

After a 1 ◇ response to the artificial 1 ♣ opening, the *identical* principles apply as over the 1 ♣ opening.

Opp.	Partner	Opp.	You		
				♠	6
				♡	6 4 3 2
1 ♣*	P	1 ◇*	DBL	◇	A J 10 8 3
				♣	5 4 2

*Artificial

Your double now shows diamonds, since the 1 ◇ bid is artificial.

Opp.	Partner	Opp.	You		
				♠	7 5
				♡	5
1 ♣*	P	1 ◇*	2 ♣	◇	Q 10 8 5 3
				♣	Q J 10 4 2

*Artificial

You show both minors. Observe that you must bid 3 ♣ on this auction to show only clubs.

RESPONSES

The methods of responding to immediate actions are similarly geared toward obstruction. In most cases, responder should bid as high as he dares to compete in *one* bid. We suggest these agreements:

1. **All suit bids** are natural and not forcing.

Opp.	Partner	Opp.	You		
				♠	6 2
				♡	9 8 3
1 ♣*	1 ♠	P	2 ♣	◇	J 3
				♣	K J 10 8 6 3

*Artificial

You show a club suit. Observe that this is not a "cue-bid," as clubs have never been shown.

Opp.	Partner	Opp.	You		
				♠	7 3
				♡	Q 10 4
1 ♣*	1 ♡	P	2 ♡	◇	J 8 7 4
				♣	8 7 6 2

*Artificial

Your raise to 2 ♡ is purely obstructive.

2. **All jump suit bids** are natural and preemptive.

Opp.	Partner	Opp.	You
1 ♣*	2 ◇	P	3 ♡

♠ 8 7 4 2
♡ J 9 7 3
◇ 7 6
♣ A 9 5

*Artificial

Your 3 ♡ bid is not strength-showing; you are just bidding your "all," based on partner's red two-suiter.

Opp.	Partner	Opp.	You
		1 ♣*	P
1 ◇*	DBL	1 ♡	3 ◇

♠ K 8
♡ 9 8 5 3
◇ K J 7 4
♣ Q 5 3

*Artificial

Partner has shown diamonds, so you wish to obstruct the enemy by raising to 3 ◇.

3. **One or two notrump** (whichever is cheaper) is equivalent to an "invitational cue-bid" (see page *149*) when the enemy has *not* shown a real suit. This becomes a one-round *force*, and serves as a game try.

Opp.	Partner	Opp.	You
1 ♣*	1 ♠	P	1 NT

♠ A K 9 6
♡ A J 9 3
◇ J 10 3
♣ 8 4

*Artificial

Your 1 NT response is forcing and shows legitimate game interest.

Opp.	Partner	Opp.	You
		1 ♣*	P
1 ◇*	2 ♡	P	2 NT

♠ A K 7
♡ J 10 7
◇ 8 5 4
♣ A 9 8 6

*Artificial

Partner has shown both majors and you are definitely worth a game try.

After the "notrump cue-bid," overcaller rebids in the same manner as after an "invitational cue-bid." That is: (a) returning to his cheapest known suit confirms a minimum; (b) bidding below that level is ambiguous; and (c) bidding beyond that level confirms a maximum. Remember, though, that overcaller *already* has shown a weakish hand, so the terms "minimum" and "maximum" are relative to that fact. For example:

Opp.	Partner	Opp.	You
		1 ♣*	2 ♠
P	2 NT	P	3 ♣

♠ K 10 9 6 3
♡ 7 4
◇ 5
♣ J 10 8 3 2

*Artificial

By returning to 3 ♣ (your cheapest known suit), you indicate that your overcall was "really bad." With a better hand, you could make any other rebid.

CONSTRUCTIVE INTERFERENCE

Because all immediate actions over the strong, artificial 1 ♣ opening (or the 1 ◇ response) show *weak* hands, the natural question that comes to mind is, "How do you show a good hand?" Actually, the situation is easily handled, as the nature of the enemy system *assures* you of two opportunities to bid! We recommend this agreement:

Any action at your *second* opportunity (assuming neither you nor partner acted previously) shows a good hand (at least opening-bid strength), and its meaning is established by *ignoring* all previous artificial bids.

Opp.	Partner	Opp.	You		
				♠	A 4 3
				♡	K 2
		1 ♣*	P	◇	A Q 10 9 7 3
1 ◇*	P	1 ♠	2 ◇	♣	7 4

*Artificial

You show a sound overcall in diamonds, just as if the bidding had been opened with 1 ♠.

Opp.	Partner	Opp.	You		
				♠	A J 9 7
				♡	K J 10 5
1 ♣*	P	1 ◇*	P	◇	K 10 9 2
2 ♣	P	P	DBL	♣	3

*Artificial

You show a full-valued takeout double of clubs. With a weak hand, you must bid early, or never.

Opp.	Partner	Opp.	You		
				♠	A K J 9 7
				♡	K Q 10 8
		1 ♣*	P	◇	3
1 ◇*	P	1 NT	2 ◇!	♣	10 8 2

*Artificial

Assuming you play "Astro" (see page 160), your 2 ◇ overcall shows spades and another suit. It is just as if 1 NT were the opening bid.

The possession of a good hand does not mean that you *must* enter the bidding, but only that you *may*. On many occasions, especially with balanced hands, it pays to keep quiet throughout. For example:

Opp.	Partner	Opp.	You		
				♠	A J 7
				♡	A Q 8
		1 ♣*	P	◇	K 10 8 5
1 ◇*	P	1 ♠	P	♣	Q 9 8

*Artificial

You could overcall 1 NT as a natural strong bid, but what is the future? Not only is such a bid dangerous, but it will tip off the enemy to where the missing strength is.

Defenses to Two-Level and
Higher Conventional Openings ★ ★ ★

Previously in this book, we have discussed several countermeasures to enemy-conventions. The use of "lead-directing doubles" (see page *128*) can be applied to a variety of artificial enemy bids. In addition, certain specific defenses were covered, such as "Lebensohl" (page *24*), "invisible cue-bids" (page *83*), and our recommended defense to "1 ♣ forcing" (page *169*).

In the following few pages, we will discuss specific defenses to conventional opening bids at the *two*-level and higher. These methods fall into six different categories, for *defending* against these kinds of openings:

1. Strong artificial 2 ♣ opening.
2. Flannery.
3. Three-suited openings.
4. Unusual 2 NT opening.
5. Gambling 3 NT opening.
6. Transfer preempts.

DEFENSE TO STRONG ARTIFICIAL TWO-CLUB OPENING

The very popular "strong artificial 2 ♣ opening" (see page *93*) and the also-ran "two clubs 19 to 21" (see Glossary) both use an artificial opening bid of 2 ♣ to show a strong hand. Since it is very unlikely that your side can *constructively* outbid the enemy, defensive tactics should be aimed to (a) obstruct their bidding; (b) suggest a sacrifice; or (c) direct a lead. Successful interference is characterized by "good" distribution and a watchful eye on the vulnerability. The following agreements are accepted as standard:

1. **Double** (of 2 ♣) shows a club suit. This follows the basic theory of doubling an artificial bid to show that suit. NOTE: Similarly, the double of an artificial 2 ◊ response to the 2 ♣ opening would show a diamond suit.

2. **All suit overcalls** (at any level) are natural.

Opp.	You		
		♠	6
		♡	K Q 10 9 7
2 ♣*	2 ♡	◊	J 8 7 6 5
		♣	5 4

*Artificial

Your 2 ♡ overcall directs a lead, and also could lead to a sacrifice if the vulnerability is "right."

Opp.	You		
		♠	5 4
		♡	6
2 ♣*	4 ♣	◊	J 6 3
		♣	K Q 10 9 8 7 4

*Artificial
(favorable)

You could also double or bid 3 ♣ to show a club suit, but it pays to preempt as high as sensible.

3. **Two notrump** shows both *minor* suits. This is just another application of the "unusual notrump overcall" (see page *136*).

DEFENSE TO FLANNERY

The popular "Flannery 2 ◇ opening" (see Glossary) shows a minimum-range opening bid with *five* hearts and *four* spades. We recommend this defense:

1. **Double** shows diamonds. This indicates a normal 2 ◇ overcall.

Opp.	You		
		♠	4 3
		♡	10 8
2 ◇*	DBL	◇	A Q J 8 5 4
		♣	A J 2

*Flannery

You show a diamond suit. Partner should continue as if you had bid 2 ◇ over 1 ♡.

2. **Two hearts** is a three-suit takeout. You would have doubled 1 ♡.

Opp.	You		
		♠	A J 8 5
		♡	3
2 ◇*	2 ♡	◇	K Q 7 5
		♣	Q J 9 7

*Flannery

Your "cue-bid" shows support for the other three suits.

3. **Two spades** is a *minor*-suit takeout. NOTE: With a spade suit, you are best advised to pass, then bid later if you must. Likewise, with hearts.

Opp.	You		
		♠	7
		♡	A 3
2 ◇*	2 ♠	◇	K J 8 7 5
		♣	Q J 10 9 3

*Flannery

You show both minor suits.

4. **Two notrump** is natural. You would have overcalled 1 NT over 1 ♡.

5. **All other bids** are natural in meaning.

NOTE: Against players who use the variation of opening 2 ♡ (instead of 2 ◇) as Flannery, the above defense may still be used, except a *double* is for takeout, replacing the 2 ♡ cue-bid.

DEFENSE TO THREE-SUITED OPENINGS

The "Roman 2 ◇," "mini-Roman 2 ◇," "Precision 2 ◇," and "Roman 2 ♣" are among the variations of three-suited opening bids (see Glossary for individual descriptions). Also, the "multicolored 2 ◇" (see Glossary) should be included in this group, although it does not necessarily show a three-suiter. We recommend this defense:

1. **Double** shows at least 15 high-card points. This suggests a balanced hand with good defensive prospects; hence, all further doubles are for penalty.

Opp.	You	
		♠ K J 9 7
		♡ A 6 4
2 ◇*	DBL	◇ K Q 10
		♣ A 8 3

   *Mini-Roman

   Your double shows all-around strength, and alerts partner that the opponents may be in trouble.

2. **Suit bids** (including a "cue-bid") are natural and show *good* suits.

3. **Two notrump** is natural and invitational to 3 NT. This implies an offensive hand (otherwise double), typically with a five- or six-card minor suit.

   WARNING: Do not enter the bidding on doubtful hands. It is usually wise to pass and await developments, rather than step into a potential misfit. For example:

Opp.	You	
		♠ A Q 7 6 3
		♡ 5
2 ◇*	P	◇ K 7 6
		♣ K 10 7 2

   *Roman

   Lay low for a while. Your spade suit is not sturdy enough to venture 2 ♠.

DEFENSE TO UNUSUAL TWO-NOTRUMP OPENING

A few systems, most notably "Schenken," employ the "unusual 2 NT opening" (see Glossary). This shows both *minor* suits, much like the "unusual notrump overcall." We recommend this defense:

1. **Double** shows a good defensive hand. This implies the ability to double one (or both) of the minor suits for penalty.

2. **Three clubs** shows a *weak* major two-suiter.

Opp.	You	
		♠ K J 7 6 5
		♡ A J 6 4 2
2 NT*	3 ♣	◇ 8
		♣ 9 2

   *Unusual

   You show both majors, but skimpy values.

3. **Three diamonds** shows an *intermediate* (or better) major two-suiter.

Opp.	You	
		♠ K Q 10 8
		♡ A J 10 9 4
2 NT*	3 ◇	◇ A 8 2
		♣ 4

   *Unusual

   Here you promise sound values.

4. **All other bids** are natural in meaning.

DEFENSE TO GAMBLING THREE-NOTRUMP OPENING

The "gambling 3 NT opening" (see Glossary) and related bids, such as the Acol 3 NT opening (see page *107*) and the "3 NT minor-suit preempt" (see Glossary), all show a long minor suit, with or without outside strength. Against any of these bids, we recommend the following defense, which applies in either direct or balancing position:

1. **Double is** for penalty.

2. **Four clubs** shows *hearts* and a minor suit. NOTE: This is another application of the "Astro" convention (see page *160*).

Opp.	You	
		♠ A 3
		♡ K J 10 9 7
3 NT*	4 ♣	◇ —
		♣ Q J 10 9 7 4

*Gambling

Your 4 ♣ bid confirms hearts. If partner responds 4 ◇ (denying three hearts), you will bid 5 ♣.

3. **Four diamonds** shows *spades* and another suit (which could be hearts).

Opp.	You	
		♠ A Q J 8 7
		♡ K Q 10 9 5
3 NT*	4 ◇	◇ 3
		♣ 6 5

*Gambling

Here you show spades. Partner should respond 4 ♡ with better hearts than spades, which you will pass.

4. **All other suit bids** are natural in meaning.

When a gambling 3 NT opening becomes the final contract, the opening leader should try to lead a winning card. The purpose is to retain the lead, so as to see the dummy and partner's signal. This way, the best attack can be found. For example:

Opp.	Partner	Opp.	You	
				♠ K 9 7 5 4
				♡ A J 8 3
		3 NT*	P	◇ 9 7
P	P			♣ 10 2

*Gambling

Lead your ace of hearts! You will then be able to shift (probably to spades) if hearts are stopped by the enemy. Notice that a spade lead, if wrong, gives you no second chance.

DEFENSE TO TRANSFER PREEMPTS

"Transfer preempts" (see Glossary), also known as "Namyats," are opening bids of 4 ♣ to show *hearts* and 4 ◇ to show *spades*. The purpose is to distinguish them from opening bids of 4 ♡ and 4 ♠, which usually show weaker hands. We recommend this defense:

1. **Double** is a "takeout double" of the major *shown,* but may be of very moderate strength. With a stronger takeout double, simply double *again* when they arrive in four of their major.

Opp.	You
4 ◇*	DBL

♠ 3
♡ K J 9 6
◇ Q J 7 3
♣ A 10 6 2

*Shows spades

The enemy system allows you to make this "no risk" takeout double, just in case partner can compete.

2. **Pass, then double four of their major** is an "optional double" (see page *123*).

3. **Cue-bid of their major** shows a two-suiter in the *other major* and either *minor.*

Opp.	You
4 ♣*	4 ♡

♠ A Q J 9 7
♡ 3
◇ 6
♣ K Q 10 8 6 4

*Shows hearts

You show spades and an unknown minor. This is nothing more than a high-level "Michaels cue-bid."

4. **Four notrump** is a takeout for the *minor* suits.

5. **All other bids** are natural in meaning.

NOTE: Passing the opening bid, then bidding later, has the same meaning as a direct bid, but shows a *weaker* hand.

6

Slam Bidding

♣　　♦　　♥　　♠　　♣　　♦　　♥　　♠

Slam bidding is perhaps the most challenging aspect of the game of bridge. Nothing is more satisfying than a well bid, and successful slam. But just as important as bidding a *good* slam, is staying out of a *bad* one, which is sometimes more easily said than done.

Natural bidding alone is inadequate when it comes to accurate slam bidding. Certain facts just cannot be determined without the use of conventional methods. Consequently, in this chapter, we will discuss the various slam conventions that can enrich your bidding.

In this chapter:

Control-Showing Bid
Blackwood
Gerber

Voluntary Bid of Five in a Major
Grand Slam Force

Extended Splinter Bids
Mathe Asking Bid
Control Asking Bid

Control-Showing Bid ★

The "control-showing bid," or "cue-bid" as it is usually called, is the most valuable of all slam exploring devices. The best partnerships use this bid over and over in their slam bidding ventures; it is truly indispensable.

Unfortunately, the control-showing bid is subject to a great deal of confusion, even among experienced players. Haven't you ever wondered, in trying to decipher one of partner's bids, "Is it natural, or is it a cue-bid?" Indeed, you probably have, as we all have from time to time. Clearly, this emphasizes the need for greater partnership understanding in this area. As the first step toward reaching this goal, we recommend the following rule:

1. **After a trump suit is agreed, a non-jump bid in an unbid suit (not shown by your side)** *beyond* **three of the trump suit** is a control-showing bid.

Let us now examine a few typical auctions to illustrate *when* this control-showing bid may be used. Remember, we are concerned only with the *application* of this bid; its specific meaning will be covered later. For example:

You	Partner
1 ♠	3 ♠
4 ♦	

Control-showing

Partner	You
1 ♠	2 ♡
3 ♡	4 ♣

Control-showing

You	Partner
1 ♣	1 ♦
1 ♡	3 ♡
3 ♠	

Control-showing

Partner	You
1 ♠	2 ♣
2 ♦	3 ♠
4 ♣	4 ♡

Control-showing

Recognizing a control-showing bid is one thing, but it is equally important to recognize when a bid is *not* control-showing. Observe that your last bid in each of the following auctions, for one reason or another, does not fit the rule:

Partner	You
1 ♠	2 ♡
3 ♦	4 ♣

Natural bid
(no agreed suit)

Partner	You
1 ♡	1 ♠
3 ♠	4 ♡

Natural bid
(heart raise)

You	Partner
1 ♠	2 ♠
3 ♣	

Game-trial bid
(below 3 ♠)

Partner	You
1 ♡	1 ♠
2 ♠	4 ♦

Splinter bid
(jump bid)

NOTE: The above "game-trial bid" (see page *54*) and "splinter bid" (see page *201*) are our recommendations, but other interpretations are possible.

You may have noticed that all of our previous examples of control-showing contained an agreed *major* suit. This was deliberate. When only a *minor* suit is agreed, we must make this amendment to our previous rule:

2. **If only a *minor* suit is agreed, and there are two or three unbid suits, the bid of an unbid suit *below* 3 NT may not be control-showing. Such a bid shows either a natural suit or a *stopper* for notrump.**

You	Partner		Partner	You
1 ♦	3 ♦		1 ♡	2 ♣
<u>3 ♡</u>			3 ♣	<u>3 ♠</u>

Natural bid, or heart stopper   *Natural bid, or spade stopper*

This amendment does not eliminate, but merely restricts or postpones, the use of control-showing after minor-suit agreement. It is still very possible, as illustrated by the following two examples:

Partner	You		You	Partner
			1 ♡	2 ♣
1 ♠	2 ♦		2 ♦	3 ♦
3 ♦	<u>4 ♣</u>		<u>3 ♠</u>	

Control-showing (beyond 3 NT)   *Control-showing (only unbid suit)*

THE INITIAL CONTROL-SHOWING BID

Now that we have established the conditions for its use, let us define the meaning of the control-showing bid when it first occurs. The following agreement is generally accepted:

Initial control-showing bid is a slam try, and usually shows *first*-round control of the suit bid. Most often, this shows the *ace*.

♠ A K J 7 5	You	Partner
♡ 4 3		
♦ A K 9 8	1 ♠	3 ♠*
♣ K J	<u>4 ♦</u>	

*Limit raise

You show slam interest and indicate the ace of diamonds along the way.

♠ K J 10 9 6	You	Partner
♡ A 8 3	1 ♠	2 ♣
♦ A K J 5	2 ♦	3 ♦
♣ 3	3 ♡	

You show the heart ace. Observe that your bid does not just show a stopper, as hearts is the only unbid suit.

Partner	You		♠ 7
1 ♠	2 ♦		♡ K J 9
3 ♦	3 ♡		♦ A Q J 7 5 3
3 ♠	<u>4 ♣</u>		♣ A 8 3

Your previous 3 ♡ bid merely promised a stopper, but now you confirm true slam interest and show the ace of clubs.

Partner	You
1 ♠	2 ♡
3 ♡	4 ♣

♠ K 4
♡ A Q J 9 6 5 4
♢ 9 8 5 3
♣ —

Here your first-round control happens to be a void, but the message is the same.

On rare occasions, the initial control-showing bid may be made with only *second-round* control (king or singleton). This is generally dictated by the lack of alternatives. For example:

♠ 9 3
♡ A K Q 10 6 5
♢ K 8
♣ K Q 10

You	Partner
1 ♡	3 ♡*
4 ♣	

*Limit raise

You wish to try for slam, but there is no ace to cue-bid; thus, you have to improvise.

BIDDING AFTER THE INITIAL CONTROL-SHOWING BID

If partner has made a control-showing bid, he has expressed interest in slam. It is now your duty to decide whether or not you have a suitable hand, which, of course, depends on the quality of your hand with respect to your previous bidding. Good judgment is often the key in making the right decision. The available options are listed below:

1. **Return to the agreed trump suit** (or rarely, 3 NT) is the most discouraging response. In effect, this says *"no"* to partner's slam try.

Partner	You
1 ♠	3 ♠*
4 ♢	4 ♠

♠ 10 9 8 4
♡ Q J 8 6
♢ Q 4
♣ A Q 10

*Limit raise

You have a poor limit raise, including several doubtful values, so warn partner by bidding 4 ♠.

♠ A Q 10 8 5
♡ Q 10 3
♢ K J 9
♣ 7 5

You	Partner
1 ♠	2 ♢
3 ♢	4 ♣
4 ♢	

Your bare minimum opening and dubious heart queen suggest conservatism, so return to 4 ♢.

2. **Any non-agreed suit bid** encourages slam, and is simply another control-showing bid. NOTE: This is true even in a suit previously bid (but not agreed) by your side. In other words, after the initial control-showing bid has been made, only a previously *agreed* suit may be bid naturally.

Partner	You		♠	Q 9 8 5
			♡	A K 3
1 ♠	3 ♠*		◇	5 4
4 ♣	4 ♡		♣	Q 8 7 5

*Limit raise

You are not unhappy with your hand, so show your heart ace.

♠	A J 9 7 5		You	Partner
♡	K Q 10 8		1 ♠	2 ♡
◇	K J		3 ♡	4 ◇
♣	7 5		4 ♠	

With a good solid opening, cue-bid 4 ♠, which shows the ace (not extra length), since only hearts are agreed.

3. **Other options** include (a) Blackwood; (b) a "voluntary bid of five in a major"; or (c) the "grand slam force," each of which is covered under its respective heading. Also, it is possible to (d) jump directly to slam if you have all the information needed to place the final contract.

CONTROL-SHOWING GUIDELINES

Once a control-showing auction has begun, the bidding may end only in an *agreed* suit (or possibly in a notrump contract) at game or higher. All non-agreed suit bids are, of course, control-showing. Listed here are some useful guidelines to improve your effectiveness in this area:

1. **It is never mandatory to make a control-showing bid;** however, when partner initiates the control-showing, you do not need extra strength to cooperate *below* the game level.

♠	K J 10 7 5		You	Partner
♡	K J 5		1 ♠	2 ♡
◇	A 9 3		3 ♡	4 ♣
♣	5 3		4 ◇	

Despite your minimum, you are not embarrassed with your hand, so cue-bid 4 ◇.

2. **When faced with a choice of control-showing bids,** generally prefer to cue-bid *unbid* suits before bid suits, and *aces* before voids.

♠	A 6 3		You	Partner
♡	A Q 10 8 5		1 ♡	2 ◇
◇	K J 10		3 ◇	4 ♣
♣	9 8		4 ♠	

Your spade control is far more important to show than your heart control.

Partner	You		♠	Q 4
			♡	A J 10 9 5 4 3
1 ♠	2 ♡		◇	A 8 6 3
3 ♡	4 ◇		♣	—

Partner will upgrade the king of the suit you cue-bid, so show your ace first, not your void.

3. **Try to be economical in your control-showing,** subject, of course, to the preceding guideline. This does *not* necessarily mean showing the cheapest control first; you must *plan* your bidding to allow the maximum exchange of information.

	♠ A K Q 9 8	*You*	*Partner*
	♡ A J 10 7		
	◇ 6 5	1 ♠	3 ♠*
	♣ A 9	<u>4 ♣</u>	

*Limit raise

Cue-bidding 4 ♣ instead of 4 ♡ leaves room for partner to bid 4 ◇ if he can. Then you can bid 4 ♡.

Partner	*You*	♠ A 7 6
		♡ K Q 10 9 7
1 ◇	1 ♡	◇ 6 3
3 ♡	<u>4 ♣</u>	♣ A 7 6

It might seem cheaper to cue-bid 3 ♠, but that is shortsighted. You plan to show both aces, so 4 ♣ followed by 4 ♠ (over the expected 4 ◇ or 4 ♡) is more economical than 3 ♠ followed by 5 ♣.

4. **The second control-showing bid in the *same* suit** shows *second*-round control (king or singleton) of that suit.

Partner	*You*	♠ 8 5
1 ♠	2 ◇	♡ 5 3
3 ◇	4 ♣	◇ A K J 9 8
4 ♡	<u>5 ♣</u>	♣ A K 6 3

Your 5 ♣ bid shows second-round control, since you already showed first-round control.

Partner	*You*	♠ 9 6 5 4
2 ♣*	2 ◇**	♡ Q 8 6 5
2 ♡	3 ♡	◇ K 8
4 ◇	<u>5 ◇</u>	♣ 10 4 3

*Artificial force
**Negative response

Partner is trying for slam despite your weakness, so show your diamond king, which rates to be valuable.

5. **A control-showing bid in a suit naturally bid by partner** may be made with the *king*, as well as the ace. We do *not* advocate making this bid with a singleton or void, as such values are dubious.

Partner	*You*	♠ K 5
1 ♠	2 ♡	♡ A Q J 8 5
3 ♡	4 ♣	◇ 5 4 3
4 ◇	<u>4 ♠</u>	♣ A Q 8

Your 4 ♠ bid (forcing) shows the ace or king, but does not suggest normal support.

6. **If partner's control-showing bid is *doubled,*** you should be grateful! In addition to the normal options, you may (a) redouble to show second-round control; or (b) pass to encourage slam but deny second-round control. NOTE: If you elect to pass, then partner may redouble to show second-round control.

		You	*Opp.*	*Partner*	*Opp.*
♠	A Q 9 8 5	1 ♠	P	2 ◇	P
♡	6 5 4	3 ◇	P	4 ♣	DBL
◇	A Q 7 3	RDBL			
♣	4				

You show second-round club control. Lacking any club control, you should pass with sound values, or bid 4 ◇ to discourage slam.

7. **Every bid made is *relative* to all previous bids made.** Inferences can often be drawn, not only from the bids made (and not made) but also from the order in which they were made.

		You	*Partner*
♠	A K Q 10 6	1 ♠	3 ♠*
♡	10 2	4 ♣	4 ◇
◇	K J 9	4 ♠	
♣	A J 10		

*Limit raise

Your 4 ♠ bid (not forcing) implies two things: Your slam try was mild, and you do not have the ace of hearts (you would surely bid 4 ♡ with that card).

		You	*Partner*
♠	K Q 10 7 5	1 ♠	2 ♡
♡	J 9 4	3 ♡	4 ◇
◇	9 3	4 ♡	4 ♠
♣	A Q 9	5 ♣	

Your 5 ♣ bid shows the ace, but your previous sign-off in 4 ♡ warns partner of minimum values. With a better hand, you would have bid 5 ♣ over 4 ◇.

8. **Any control-showing bid *beyond* five of the agreed suit is a *grand*-slam try.** This should be apparent as it forces your side to at least a small slam. Also, observe that a control-showing bid *cannot* be made beyond six of the agreed suit for obvious reasons.

		You	*Partner*
♠	K 5	1 ♡	3 ♡*
♡	A K 7 6 4 3	4 ♣	4 ♠
◇	–	5 ◇	5 ♡
♣	A Q 7 3 2	5 ♠	

*Limit raise

Your 5 ♠ cue-bid is a grand-slam try, since it commits your side to at least 6 ♡. If partner can cue-bid 6 ♣, you will bid 7 ♡.

THE ADVANCE CUE-BID

The most basic requirement of the control-showing bid is the agreement on a trump suit. Indeed, you cannot just start cue-bidding if you don't know where you are headed. Traditionally, the trump suit is *explicitly* agreed prior to any control-showing.

The so-called "advance cue-bid" is a normal control-showing bid, except that it is made before a trump suit has been explicitly agreed. This does *not* mean, however, that trumps are unknown. The advance cue-bid *implicitly* agrees the suit last bid by partner, and simultaneously initiates a control-showing auction.

The opportunities for making an advance cue-bid generally occur at the four-level, when a particular suit bid is impossible in a natural sense. Although occasions do arise where this device may be employed at the three-level, they are too uncommon, not to mention, ambiguous. Consequently, to avoid headaches, we recommend the use of the advance cue-bid *only* at the four-level and higher. The principal opportunities are:

1. **New-suit bid by a balanced hand** (beyond 3 NT) is an advance cue-bid.

Partner	You	♠ A 6
		♡ K Q 9 5
1 ♠	2 NT*	◇ Q 9 5
3 ♡	4 ♣	♣ A Q 8 2

*Unlimited (13+ points)

Your 4 ♣ bid shows the ace of clubs, extra strength, and agrees hearts *by inference.*

♠ A Q 10		You	Partner
♡ K 5		1 NT	2 ♣*
◇ A K J 6		2 ◇	3 ♠
♣ 9 8 6 5		4 ◇	

*Stayman

A raise to 4 ♠ would not do justice to your hand, so cue-bid 4 ◇ along the way.

Partner	You	♠ K 8
		♡ A K 6
1 ◇	2 NT	◇ K J 9 4
3 ♠	4 ♡	♣ J 9 7 5

Here your cue-bid agrees diamonds *(instead of partner's last bid suit), since your first bid denied four spades.*

2. **Fourth-suit bid at your third bid** (beyond 3 NT) is an advance cue-bid.

♠ K 4		You	Partner
♡ A K 9 7 5		1 ♡	1 ♠
◇ Q 10 9 8		2 ◇	3 ♠
♣ A 3		4 ♣	

You show a good raise to 4 ♠ with club control.

Partner	You	♠ A K 8 6 5
1 ♡	1 ♠	♡ J 9
2 ♡	3 ♣	◇ A
3 ♡	4 ◇	♣ Q J 10 5 2

Your 4 ◇ bid is an advance cue-bid agreeing hearts.

3. **Cue-bid of the enemy suit** (beyond 3 NT) is an advance cue-bid. However, this is commonly made with *second*-round, as well as first-round, control.

Opp.	Partner	Opp.	You	♠ A K 8 6
				♡ 4
3 ♡	4 ◇	P	4 ♡	◇ Q J 10 6
				♣ 9 8 5 2

You show at least second-round heart control, and imply a diamond fit.

Opp.	Partner	Opp.	You
	1 ♡	2 ♣	2 ♠
P	3 ♡	P	4 ♣

♠ A K 9 5 4 3
♡ Q 10 3
◇ 4 3
♣ A 2

Your 4 ♣ bid shows a good raise to 4 ♡ with club control.

Blackwood ★

Invented and popularized by Easley Blackwood of Indianapolis, Indiana, a leading American expert and bridge writer

Just about everyone plays Blackwood in some form or other, from the rankest novice to the greatest expert. Next to the takeout double, it is the most widely used of all conventions. A bid of 4 NT is used to ask partner how many aces he holds. As you undoubtedly know, the responses are:

1. **Five clubs** shows *zero* (or all four) aces.

2. **Five diamonds** shows *one* ace.

3. **Five hearts** shows *two* aces.

4. **Five spades** shows *three* aces.

NOTE: Many modern players have adopted variations of Blackwood, the most popular being "Roman key-card Blackwood" (see Glossary). Nevertheless, we still recommend the standard responses, because of the occasional confusion over which is the agreed trump suit when any form of "key-card Blackwood" is used.

Blackwood, unfortunately, is also one of the most widely abused conventions. Thus, it is our objective in the following pages, not to acquaint you with Blackwood, but to improve your use and understanding of it.

WHEN IS FOUR NOTRUMP BLACKWOOD?

Deciding just when, and when not, a bid of 4 NT is Blackwood has always been a problem for most players. Indeed, even experts are not in complete agreement regarding this.

We will present our recommended agreements. Although we do not contend that this is the *only* method, or even the *best* method, it is essentially a *good* method that is both effective and uncomplicated. Here are the guidelines:

1. **If partner's last bid was 1 NT, 2 NT, or 3 NT, or if your own last bid was 3 NT,** a bid of 4 NT is *not* Blackwood, unless a *major* suit has been agreed.

Partner	You	Partner	You
	1 ♠	1 ♡	2 ◇
2 NT	4 NT	3 NT	4 NT

Not Blackwood   *Not Blackwood*

Partner	You		Partner	You
1 ♠	2 ♡		1 ♠	2 ♣
3 ◇	3 NT		3 ♣	3 ♠
4 ◇	<u>4 NT</u>		3 NT	<u>4 NT</u>
Not Blackwood			*Blackwood*	

2. **Immediately after Stayman, Jacoby transfer bid, or minor-suit transfer bid,** 4 NT is *not* Blackwood. NOTE: For more information, refer to the respective convention involved.

Partner	You		Partner	You
1 NT	2 ♣		1 NT	2 ♡*
2 ♡	<u>4 NT</u>		2 ♠	<u>4 NT</u>
Not Blackwood			*Not Blackwood*	
*Jacoby				

3. **If partner has never bid or doubled,** 4 NT is *not* Blackwood, except as an opening bid, or over an opponent's 4 ♣ or 4 ◇ bid. NOTE: For more information, refer to the "4 NT overcall" (page *141*).

Opp.	You		Opp.	You
4 ♡	<u>4 NT</u>		4 ♣	<u>4 NT</u>
Not Blackwood			*Blackwood*	

You	Opp.	Partner	Opp.	You
1 ♡	1 ♠	P	4 ♠	<u>4 NT</u>
<u>4 NT</u>				
Not Blackwood				*Blackwood*

4. **In all other situations,** 4 NT should be Blackwood, barring any specific agreement to the contrary.

USING BLACKWOOD WISELY

There is much truth in the statement, "A bridge player's skill is inversely proportional to the frequency in which he uses Blackwood." Inexperienced players often develop the habit of using Blackwood as an all-purpose slam try. Nothing could be farther from the right track. Blackwood should be used *only* if the information obtained (the number of aces held) will allow you *confidently* to place the final contract. Therefore:

1. **If you are unsure in which trump suit (or notrump) to play,** do *not* use Blackwood.

2. **If you are not reasonably sure that your side holds the required strength (point count or playing tricks) to produce twelve tricks,** do *not* use Blackwood.

3. **If your hand contains a void suit,** do *not* use Blackwood.

Partner	You		
		♠	—
		♡	K Q J 9 8 7
1 ♠	2 ♡	◇	K J 9 8 2
3 ♡	?	♣	A 10

If you bid 4 NT, you will be unable to tell which ace (or aces) partner holds. Cue-bid 4 ♣ instead.

4. **If your hand contains *two* fast losers in an unbid suit,** do *not* use Blackwood.

Partner	You		
1 ◇	1 ♠	♠	A K 10 4 3
1 NT	3 ♡	♡	K Q 9 5 2
4 ♡	?	◇	A
		♣	10 7

Blackwood will not help if partner has one ace, since he may or may not have club control. Bid 5 ♡ (see page 194).

5. **If some response by partner will put you overboard,** do *not* use Blackwood. That is, you should have at least *two* aces when clubs will be trump or *one* ace when diamonds will be trump, to avoid any embarrassment. NOTE: In the event you are willing and able to sign off in 5 NT (see next topic), these requirements may be dropped.

SIGNING OFF IN FIVE NOTRUMP

It is rare, but the Blackwood bidder is sometimes able to sign off the bidding in 5 NT. This must be done by a devious route, as follows:

Five of an "unplayable" suit (by Blackwood bidder) is a "transfer" to 5 NT. In other words, this illogical bid forces partner to correct the contract to 5 NT.

Partner	You		
1 ♡	2 ◇	♠	K 6
3 ◇	4 NT	♡	Q 2
5 ◇	5 ♠	◇	A K J 9 7 6 5
		♣	K J

You could pass 5 ◇, but at matchpoint scoring it pays to try for a better result. Over 5 ♠, partner must bid 5 NT, which should be reasonably safe with you as declarer. Had your long suit been clubs, you would bid the hand the same way, but then out of necessity, not luxury.

ASKING FOR KINGS

It should be no mystery to any reader that a 5 NT rebid by Blackwood bidder asks for *kings.* Since the 5 NT bid commits the partnership to at least a small slam, it is necessarily a *grand-slam* try, and Blackwood bidder must *not* abuse it. Therefore:

1. **If an ace is missing,** do *not* bid 5 NT.

2. **If a particular response by partner will put you overboard,** do *not* bid 5 NT.

3. **If you have no interest in a grand slam,** do *not* bid 5 NT.

The responses to 5 NT are almost the same as the responses to 4 NT. Responder shows the number of kings held by straight steps, as follows:

1. **Six clubs** shows *zero* kings.

2. **Six diamonds** shows *one* king.

3. **Six hearts** shows *two* kings.

4. **Six spades** shows *three* kings.

5. **Six notrump** shows all *four* kings.

Furthermore, responder has the following option:

6. **Seven of anything** is natural and indicates an undisclosed source of tricks. In other words, responder thinks he has the "right" hand for a grand slam.

Partner	You		
1 ♠	2 ◇	♠	A 5 4
3 ♣	3 ♠	♡	9 5 2
4 NT	5 ◇	◇	K Q J 10 9 7
5 NT	<u>7 ◇</u>	♣	Q

> *Partner could hardly expect your diamonds to be that strong. Since you know diamonds are solid, and spades may not be, jump to 7 ◇. Incidentally, if partner corrects to 7 ♠, you should bid 7 NT, because if spades are solid, there are thirteen tricks in notrump.*

SHOWING A VOID

Occasionally, a responder to Blackwood will have a *void* suit which he feels may be the key to a slam (or grand slam). It would be nice to be able to show this void to partner, but such is not possible through the normal Blackwood responses. Under *no* circumstances may a void suit be counted as an ace.

Therefore, another opportunity for gadgetry arises. As usual, there are several variations, so we will present the method that we feel is the most effective, with the least complication. Provided a trump suit is *agreed,* a void suit may be shown over Blackwood, as follows:

1. **Six of a suit** (below the trump suit) shows *one* ace and a void in the suit bid. NOTE: If your void suit is higher ranking than the trump suit, then bid six of the trump suit.

Partner	You		
		♠	9 7 3
		♡	A J 9 8 6
1 ♡	4 ♡	◇	Q 9 7 6 5
4 NT	<u>6 ♣</u>	♣	—

> *Your 6 ♣ bid shows one ace and a club void. With a diamond void, you would bid 6 ◇; but with a spade void, you must bid 6 ♡ (not 6 ♠, of course).*

2. **Five notrump** shows *two* aces and a void. If the agreed trump suit is a *major,* Blackwood bidder may continue with 6 ♣ to ask *where* the void is. Then, bid your void suit (below six of the trump suit), or bid six of the trump suit if it cannot be shown.

Partner	You		
1 ♡	2 ♣	♠	A 7 2
2 ♠	3 ♡	♡	A 10 7
4 NT	5 NT	◇	—
6 ♣	<u>6 ◇</u>	♣	K 9 8 7 5 4 2

> *Your 5 NT bid shows two aces and a void, and 6 ♣ asks where. Your 6 ◇ bid shows a diamond void. With a spade void, you would bid 6 ♡.*

A void suit may be shown over Blackwood *only* when accompanied with one or two aces, as described above. Thus:

3. **Make your normal response** with *zero* or *three* aces and a void. With *zero* aces, just bid 5 ♣, then if partner signs off at the five-level, it is permissible to gamble on slam if you feel you have the "right" void. With *three* aces, bid 5 ♠ (which is clearly forcing). Since partner is a strong favorite to hold the missing ace, your void is a doubtful asset, and any attempt to show it would deprive partner of the opportunity to bid 5 NT to ask for kings.

INTERFERENCE BY THE OPPONENTS

Once in a while, an opponent will *bid* over partner's Blackwood 4 NT bid, thus throwing a monkey wrench into your normal responses. This typically occurs when the enemy is sacrificing against you. NOTE: A *double* of the 4 NT bid (however unlikely) should just be ignored, as it poses no problem.

Numerous methods have been devised to cope with interference. As there is little to choose from among them, we will recommend the most popular, which is commonly known by the acronym, "D-O-P-I." If an opponent *bids* over Blackwood, respond as follows:

1. **Double** shows *zero* aces.

2. **Pass** shows *one* ace.

3. **Cheapest bid** shows *two* aces.

4. **Next bid** shows *three* aces, etc.

NOTE: D-O-P-I stands for "Double-zero, pass-one."

Here is an example of D-O-P-I in action:

Opp.	Partner	Opp.	You		
				♠	A Q 9 4
				♡	10 9 2
	1 ♠	2 ♡	3 ♠	◇	6 5
4 ♡	4 NT	5 ♡	**P**	♣	K J 8 2

Your pass shows one ace. With no aces, you would double. With two aces, you would bid 5 ♠, etc.

In the rare event that the enemy interference is *beyond* 5 ♠, it is necessary to modify D-O-P-I slightly. In that case:

1. **Double** shows *zero* or *two* aces.

2. **Pass** shows *one* or *three* aces.

This modification is obviously less accurate. For example, if you double, Blackwood bidder must deduce from your previous bidding (and his own hand) whether you have "zero" or "two" aces. Nonetheless, this policy is dictated by the high level of the interference. Here is an illustration:

Opp.	Partner	Opp.	You		
				♠	A J 7 6
				♡	9 4
			1 ◇	◇	A J 9 8
3 ♡	4 NT	6 ♡!	**DBL**	♣	Q J 10

Over 6 ♡ (gulp), your double shows zero or two aces. With one or three aces, you would pass. Only with all four aces (rare) would you bid.

Gerber ★

Devised by the late John Gerber of Houston, Texas, a leading American expert and bridge personality

The "Gerber" convention is a popular offshoot of Blackwood. Instead of 4 NT, a bid of 4 ♣ is used to ask for aces. Most players use Gerber, not as an alternative, but in conjunction with Blackwood to allow ace asking at times when the latter is not available. The responses to the Gerber 4 ♣ bid are as follows:

1. **Four diamonds** shows *zero* (or all four) aces.

2. **Four hearts** shows *one* ace.

3. **Four spades** shows *two* aces.

4. **Four notrump** shows *three* aces.

NOTE: In the unlikely event that an opponent *bids* over the Gerber 4 ♣ bid, disregard the above responses and use "D-O-P-I," just as you would after Blackwood interference (see page *191*).

WHEN IS FOUR CLUBS GERBER?

There are a great many attitudes regarding the use of Gerber. Indeed, there is the "no Gerber" school all the way to the "everything is Gerber" school. Some middle-of-the-road approach is undoubtedly best. Our recommendation is conveyed by the following simple rule:

If partner's last bid was a natural bid of 1 NT or 2 NT, then a *jump* to 4 ♣ is Gerber.

Partner	*You*		*Partner*	*You*	
1 NT	4 ♣		2 NT	4 ♣	
Gerber			*Gerber*		

You	*Partner*		*Partner*	*Opp.*	*You*
1 ♡	2 NT		1 NT	2 ♠	4 ♣
4 ♣					
Gerber			*Gerber*		

Partner	*You*		*Partner*	*Opp.*	*You*
1 ♠	2 ♡		1 NT	3 ♡	4 ♣
3 NT	4 ♣				
Not Gerber			*Not Gerber*		

As long as the conditions of the rule are met, it matters not whether clubs have been previously bid. For example:

You	*Partner*		*Partner*	*You*
1 ♣	2 NT		1 ♣	1 ♠
4 ♣			1 NT	4 ♣
Gerber			*Gerber*	

Finally, there is one further application of Gerber, *not* specifically covered by the rule. This occurs after a Stayman 2 ♣ response to 1 NT. A jump rebid of 4 ♣ (by Stayman bidder) is Gerber. For example:

Partner	You		Partner	You
1 NT	2 ♣		2 NT	3 ♣
2 ♡	<u>4 ♣</u>		3 ♡	<u>4 ♣</u>
Gerber			*Not Gerber*	

USING GERBER WISELY

Gerber, like Blackwood, is not a miracle solution to slam bidding, but must be used discriminately. Therefore:

If you cannot confidently place the final contract (after asking for aces), do *not* use Gerber. Furthermore, much of the advice under "Using Blackwood Wisely" (see page *188*) applies equally well to Gerber.

Partner	You		
		♠	Q 9 7
		♡	A K 6
1 NT*	?	◇	Q J 7 5
		♣	A 10 2

*15 to 17 points

Gerber will not tell you whether partner has a minimum or a maximum. Bid 4 NT (not forcing) as a quantitative invitation to 6 NT.

Here are two examples illustrating the *proper* use of Gerber:

Partner	You		
		♠	K 9
		♡	10 7 3
2 NT*	4 ♣	◇	K Q J 9 8 5
		♣	J 5

*20 to 22 points

Your diamond suit should provide the tricks needed (for 6 NT), but the obvious danger is that two aces might be missing.

Partner	You		
		♠	A 8
		♡	K Q 10 9 8 5 4
1 ◇	1 ♡	◇	K Q J
1 NT	4 ♣	♣	4

Gerber solves all your problems. If partner has: one ace, you will stop safely in 4 ♡; two aces, you will bid 6 ♡; three aces, you will bid 7 NT!

ASKING FOR KINGS

There is no universal agreement regarding the follow-up methods of Gerber. The most popular variation, which we recommend, is explained as follows:

Five clubs (by Gerber 4 ♣ bidder) is forcing and asks for *kings*. Hence, any other minimum rebid (including 4 NT) is a natural sign-off attempt.

The responses to 5 ♣ follow familiar practice:

1. **Five diamonds** shows *zero* kings.

2. **Five hearts** shows *one* king.

3. **Five spades** shows *two* kings.

4. **Five notrump** shows *three* kings.

5. **Six clubs** shows all *four* kings.

Here is a final example:

Partner	You		
		♠	K 5 4
		♡	K
1 NT	4 ♣	♢	K J 10
4 NT	5 ♣	♣	A Q J 6 5 2

Your 5 ♣ bid asks for kings. You will then bid 6 NT over 5 ♢, or 7 NT over 5 ♡. At worst, the latter will depend on the diamond finesse, but will be laydown if partner has any queen or receives a favorable lead.

Voluntary Bid of Five in a Major ★ ★

Because there is no additional bonus for bidding *five* in a major suit, the following interpretation is apparent:

Voluntary bid of five in a major is a slam try. The key word is "voluntary," i.e., it must have been possible to bid (or pass) *four* of that same major. Compare these auctions:

Partner	You
4 ♠	5 ♠
Slam try	

Partner	Opp.	You
1 ♠	4 ♡	5 ♠
Slam try		

Partner	You
1 ♠	2 ♡
3 ♣	5 ♡
Slam try	

Partner	Opp.	You
1 ♡	4 ♠	5 ♡
Not a slam try		

EXCEPTION: If partner has *preempted* in a *competitive* auction, a raise to five of his major is *not* a slam try, even if voluntary. This is commonly recognized as an "advance sacrifice." For example:

Partner	Opp.	You
3 ♡	3 ♠	5 ♡
Not a slam try		

Opp.	Partner	Opp.	You
1 ♢	3 ♠	P	5 ♠
Not a slam try			

CONTROL INQUIRY

Now that we have determined *when* a bid of five in a major is a slam try, let us see exactly what it inquires about. The most frequent application is to ask for *control* of a specific suit, in the priority listed below:

1. **If the enemy has bid,** five of a major asks for control of their suit, provided you or partner has not previously shown control.

Opp.	Partner	Opp.	You		
				♠	K 10 8
				♡	A K J 9 7 5
	1 ♠	3 ♣	3 ♡	◇	A 7
P	3 ♠	P	<u>5 ♠</u>	♣	5 2

The *danger of two fast club losers is apparent. Your 5 ♠ bid inquires about club control.*

2. **If your side has bid all except one suit,** five of a major asks for control of that suit.

♠	Q 5		You	Partner
♡	A Q J 8 7 6		1 ♡	3 ♡*
◇	K 7		4 ♣	4 ◇
♣	A K 3		<u>5 ♡</u>	

*Limit raise

Your 5 ♡ bid asks about spades, the only unbid suit.

RESPONSES TO THE CONTROL INQUIRY

The method of responding to the control inquiry is very logical. Here are the available options:

1. **Pass with *no* control** (two or more fast losers) in the critical suit.

Partner	You		
1 ♠	3 ♠*	♠	Q J 5 4
4 ♣	4 ♡	♡	A K 6 3
5 ♠	<u>P</u>	◇	J 7 3
		♣	8 2

*Limit raise

You have no diamond control, so you must pass.

2. **Six of the agreed trump suit** shows *second*-round control of the critical suit.

Opp.	Partner	Opp.	You		
				♠	7 6 5
				♡	A Q J 10 7
			1 ♡	◇	K Q 8 6
3 ♣	5 ♡	P	<u>6 ♡</u>	♣	5

The opponents cannot cash two club tricks, so proceed to slam.

3. **Five notrump** (rare) shows the guarded *king* of the critical suit, and suggests 6 NT as the final contract.

Partner	You		
1 ♠	2 ♡	♠	Q 9 8
3 ♣	3 ♠	♡	A K 10 7 5
5 ♠	<u>5 NT</u>	◇	K 9 3
		♣	J 2

You show the king of diamonds. Partner has the option of raising to 6 NT or returning to 6 ♠.

4. **Any suit bid** (except the trump suit) is a *cue-bid,* and guarantees *first-*round control of the critical suit.

Opp.	Partner	Opp.	You
			1 ♠
3 ♡	5 ♠	P	6 ♣

♠ K J 10 8 6
♡ A 3
♢ 7 5
♣ A J 6 4

You show first-round control of both clubs and hearts. With just the heart ace, you would cue-bid 6 ♡.

TRUMP INQUIRY

When the previous use is illogical, the voluntary bid of five in a major suit asks about *trump* quality, as described below:

If a single suit cannot be pinpointed, five of a major expresses the concern of losing *two* trump tricks.

Partner	You
3 ♠	5 ♠

♠ 7 4
♡ A K 8
♢ A 10 8 2
♣ A K Q 3

(none vul)

Obviously, you could not be asking about a particular side suit (which one?), so this asks about the trump suit. You are worried about two trump losers.

♠ A 4
♡ Q 9 8 6 3
♢ A
♣ A K J 7 4

You	Partner
1 ♡	2 ♢
3 ♣	3 ♡
3 ♠	4 ♡
5 ♡	

There is no unbid suit, so your 5 ♡ bid inquires about trumps.

RESPONSES TO THE TRUMP INQUIRY

Responding to the trump inquiry is less rigid, and mostly a matter of using good judgment. Therefore:

After the trump inquiry has been made, responder must carefully appraise his trump holding, then (a) pass if he feels there will be *two* trump losers; (b) bid six of the agreed major if he expects only *one* trump loser; or (c) consider bidding seven with a *solid* trump suit.

♠ K J 9 8 6 5 3
♡ 7 4
♢ 3
♣ J 10 9

You	Partner
3 ♠	5 ♠
P	

(none vul)

Your trumps are not particularly good, so pass. However, with K-Q-J, you would bid 6 ♠.

Partner	You		
1 ♡	2 ♦	♠	Q 8
3 ♣	3 ♡	♡	A J 7 4
3 ♠	4 ♡	♦	K Q 10 7 5
5 ♡	<u>6 ♡</u>	♣	4 3

You are happy to accept, but had your hearts been, say, A-7-4, you should pass.

Grand Slam Force

Devised by the late Ely Culbertson, the foremost authority during the early years of contract bridge, and publicized by his wife, Josephine

The "grand slam force" is a convention to inquire about *trump* honors when the partnership is considering a grand slam. Its name is slightly misleading, as it does *not* "force" the partnership to a grand slam; indeed, a more appropriate name might be "grand slam try," but the actual title has become well accepted. Most players use the grand slam force in its elementary form (if at all), as explained below:

Five notrump (after a trump suit is agreed) asks partner to bid a grand slam if he holds at least *two* of the top three trump honors. Failing that, partner returns to six of the agreed suit. NOTE: This, of course, does not apply after Blackwood, since 5 NT is the normal continuation to ask for kings.

Partner	You		
1 ♠	2 ♡	♠	—
3 ♡	4 ♣	♡	A J 9 7 2
4 ♦	<u>5 NT</u>	♦	K Q 8 7 4
		♣	A K J

Once partner has cue-bid the diamond ace, your only concern is the trump suit. Over your 5 NT bid, partner must bid 7 ♡ with the king-queen of hearts.

If there is no agreed trump suit, the grand slam force may be employed by *jumping* to 5 NT, which inferentially agrees with partner's *last*-bid suit. For example:

Partner	You		
		♠	K
		♡	A K 7 5
3 ♠	<u>5 NT</u>	♦	A 7 6
		♣	A K Q 4 2

Your jump to 5 NT implies that spades will be trumps. With the ace-queen of spades, partner must bid 7 ♠.

IMPROVED RESPONSES

The functioning of the basic grand slam force is not good enough for the serious player. More information is often needed than, "Do you have two of the top three trump honors?" To be sure, many experts have developed highly intricate responses to utilize every possible inch of bidding space. Unfortunately, these responses are generally too taxing on the memory for the relative infrequency with which they occur.

Therefore, we recommend the following "easy to remember" responses to 5 NT, which offer a great improvement over the basic grand slam force:

1. **Six clubs** (if clubs are not agreed) shows the *ace* or *king* of trumps.

		You	Partner
♠	K Q J 6 5	1 ♠	2 ◇
♡	A 7 5	3 ◇	4 ♣
◇	K 10 3	4 ♡	5 NT
♣	6 4	<u>6 ♣</u>	

Your 6 ♣ bid shows the ace or king of diamonds.

2. **Six diamonds** (if a minor is not agreed) shows the *queen* of trumps.

Partner	You		
2 ♣*	2 ◇**	♠	Q 8 5
2 ♠	3 ♠	♡	7 5
4 ♣	4 ◇	◇	A 10 7 2
5 NT	<u>6 ◇</u>	♣	9 8 7 5

    *Artificial force
    **Negative response

You show the queen of spades.

NOTE: It is desirable to treat "excessive" trump length as equivalent to the queen. For instance, if 5 NT bidder held A-K-J-X-X in trumps, he wouldn't care whether you held Q-X-X or X-X-X-X-X; either way, there should be no trump loser.

3. **Six of the agreed trump suit** is the "worst" response. This simply denies the ability to make any other response.

		You	Partner
♠	3		
♡	J 10 9 8 4 3 2	3 ♡	5 NT
◇	4 2	<u>6 ♡</u>	
♣	Q 8 4		

(favorable)

You deny as much as the queen of hearts.

NOTE: Observe that a sign-off in six of the trump suit is less informative when a *minor* suit is agreed. That is, 6 ◇ (with diamonds agreed) might include the *queen* of trumps, and 6 ♣ (with clubs agreed) might include the *ace, king,* or *queen* of trumps.

4. **Seven of the agreed trump suit** shows *two* of the top three honors (as usual).

GRAND SLAM FORCE AFTER BLACKWOOD

> *Invented by the late Walter Malowan of New York City, a leading American player of the pre-World War II period*

Thus far, we have considered the grand slam force in complete isolation from Blackwood; i.e., the two cannot be used together. Insofar as 5 NT is concerned, this will *always* be true, as 5 NT is an integral part of the Blackwood machinery. Nevertheless, Blackwood bidder may employ the grand slam force, as follows:

Six of the cheapest "unplayable" suit below the trump suit (by Blackwood bidder) is the grand slam force. Partner is requested to bid a grand slam if holding any two of the top three trump honors. NOTE: As should be apparent, this cannot occur when the agreed suit is clubs.

♠ A 9 8 6 5	*You*	*Partner*
♡ K	1 ♠	3 ♠*
◇ A K Q 8 7	4 NT	5 ◇
♣ A 3	6 ♣	

*Limit raise

Your 6 ♣ bid is the grand slam force. With the king-queen of spades, partner must bid 7 ♠.

Partner	*You*	♠ K 3
1 ♣	1 ♡	♡ Q 10 8 7 6 4
3 ♡	4 NT	◇ K Q 6 4
5 ♠	6 ◇	♣ A

Here you must bid 6 ◇, since 6 ♣ could logically be natural. With the ace-king of hearts, partner must bid 7 ♡.

NOTE: When the grand slam force is used after Blackwood, some experts require that both the *king* and *queen* of trumps (with or without the ace) are needed to bid seven, since the *ace* of trumps is already known. While this works well on some occasions, it creates additional problems on others (the previous example is a case in point). Thus, for the sake of simplicity, we recommend that *any* two of the top three honors are always sufficient to bid seven.

If a *major* suit is agreed, it may still be possible to indicate lesser trump holdings, i.e., the *king* or *queen,* by utilizing any "idle" steps *below* six of the trump suit. Following previous principles, the cheaper step would show the *king,* and the higher step (if available) would show the *queen.* For example:

Partner	*You*	♠ K 9 5 4
1 ♠	3 ♠*	♡ K 6 4
4 NT	5 ◇	◇ 9 8
6 ♣	6 ◇	♣ A 10 5 3

*Limit raise

You show the spade king. A bid of 6 ♡ would show the queen, and 6 ♠ would deny either.

Extended Splinter Bids ★ ★ ★

The "splinter bid" is one of the most valuable contributions to the theory of slam bidding. Many slams are makable due to the presence of a "perfect fit" that is undetectable in standard methods. The splinter bid can immediately reveal these fitting hands, yet on other occasions warn the partnership about dangerous duplication that will doom a slam.

A splinter bid is defined as an unusual jump in an unbid suit to show a singleton or void in the suit bid, plus excellent trump support for partner's last-bid suit. All splinter bids are forcing to game, and hence, show slam interest.

In its most basic form, the splinter bid was introduced with regard to direct major-suit raises (see page *31*), where a double jump-shift response was explained to show a "forcing raise," as in this example:

Partner	You	
		♠ A K 6 5
		♡ A 9 7
1 ♠	4 ◇	◇ 3
		♣ 9 8 7 4 2

Your 4 ◇ bid shows a game-forcing spade raise with a singleton or void in diamonds.

The above, however, is but one application of this valuable tool. Splinter bids may also be extended to the areas of *rebidding*, by both the opening bidder and responder in non-competitive auctions. In this respect, we recommend the following rule:

If a particular new-suit bid would be forcing, then one level *higher* in that same suit is a splinter bid. The specific applications of this rule are detailed in the next two sections.

APPLICATIONS BY OPENER

Let us first look at the specific occasions on which the opening bidder may make a splinter bid by applying the rule. Here they are:

1. **Double jump-shift rebid after a one-level suit response** is a splinter bid.

♠ 6	You	Partner
♡ A Q 9 7		
◇ A K J 4 3	1 ◇	1 ♡
♣ K 10 2	3 ♠	

Since 2 ♠ would be forcing, 3 ♠ is a splinter bid, showing the strength equivalent to a raise to 4 ♡. If your black-suit holdings were reversed, you would jump to 4 ♣.

2. **Jump-shift rebid after a two-level new-suit response** is a splinter bid.

♠ A Q 7 6 5	You	Partner
♡ 3		
◇ K J 9 4	1 ♠	2 ◇
♣ A 9 8	3 ♡	

A simple 2 ♡ rebid would be forcing, so 3 ♡ is a splinter bid. Observe that about 3 or 4 points less strength is required here, since partner has shown a better hand.

3. **Jump-shift rebid after a single raise** is a splinter bid.

♠ A K 9 8 7 4	You	Partner
♡ K Q 3		
◇ A Q 2	1 ♠	2 ♠
♣ 3	4 ♣	

In this case, partner's "suit" is actually your suit, but the effect is the same. A 3 ♣ rebid would be forcing, so 4 ♣ is a slam try indicating short clubs.

APPLICATIONS BY RESPONDER

Now we will see how the responder may make a splinter bid (at his *rebid*) by applying the rule. Here are the possibilities:

1. **Double jump-shift rebid after an original one-level suit response** is a splinter bid.

Partner	You		
		♠	3
		♡	A Q 9 7
1 ♣	1 ♢	♢	A K 9 5 2
1 ♡	3 ♠	♣	J 4 2

   You show at least the values to raise to 4 ♡, with a singleton or void in spades.

2. **Four-level jump-shift rebid after an original one-level suit response** is a splinter bid.

Partner	You		
		♠	A K J 8 7 4
		♡	K 8 6
1 ♡	1 ♠	♢	9 8 4 2
2 ♡	4 ♣	♣	—

   You show a raise to 4 ♡ with club shortness.

As implied by the preceding two conditions, a three-level single jump-shift rebid (after an original one-level suit response) is *not* a splinter bid. This is generally recognized as a *natural* bid, and constitutes an exception to the rule. For example:

Partner	Opp.		
		♠	6
		♡	A Q J 6 5
1 ♣	1 ♡	♢	A K 10 4 3
1 ♠	3 ♢	♣	9 2

   Your 3 ♢ bid shows a real suit and is game-forcing. Observe that 4 ♢ would be a splinter bid.

3. **Jump-shift rebid after an original two-level new-suit response** is a splinter bid.

Partner	You		
		♠	K 2
		♡	3
1 ♠	2 ♣	♢	K Q 10 7
2 ♢	3 ♡	♣	A J 10 8 7 3

   You show a diamond fit and shortness in hearts.

4. **Jump-shift rebid after your original suit has been raised** is a splinter bid.

Partner	You		
		♠	A Q 10 8 4 3
		♡	K 9 3
1 ♢	1 ♠	♢	A 4 3
2 ♠	4 ♣	♣	5

   Your 4 ♣ bid is a slam try showing a club splinter.

5. **Jump-shift rebid after a "Jacoby transfer bid"** (see page 7) is a splinter bid.

Partner	You		
		♠	A 8 5
		♡	K Q J 9 8 5
1 NT	2 ♢*	♢	3
2 ♡	4 ♢	♣	Q 10 9

   *Jacoby (showing hearts)

   In effect, you are "raising" your own suit, showing slam interest and shortness in diamonds.

6. **Jump-shift rebid after a negative or positive response to a "strong artificial 2 ♣ opening"** (see page *93*) is a splinter bid.

Partner	You
2 ♣*	2 ◇**
2 ♠	<u>4 ♣</u>

♠ K 9 5 4
♡ 9 8 6 3 2
◇ K 5 3
♣ 8

*Artificial force
**Negative response

You show a spade fit and shortness in clubs. Notice the greatly reduced strength, since partner has shown a very strong hand.

SPLINTER BIDS IN COMPETITION

The use of splinter bids in a competitive auction is a controversial matter. To be sure, there are pros and cons either way. It would be nice to say, "Just ignore all enemy interference," but that simply doesn't work. Sooner or later (probably sooner) you would encounter an ambiguous sequence, possibly ending in disaster if a misunderstanding occurs. Therefore, we recommend a limited use of splinter bids in competition, as clarified below:

1. **After an enemy takeout double,** all splinter bids are *on*, provided that neither opponent has *bid*. In other words, a takeout double, in itself, does not alter any of the previous agreements.

♠ 4
♡ A K J 6 3
◇ K Q J 6
♣ J 9 2

You	Opp.	Partner	Opp.
1 ♡	P	2 ◇	DBL
<u>3 ♠</u>			

Your 3 ♠ rebid is a splinter bid, i.e., completely unaffected by the double.

2. **After an enemy bid,** only a *jump cue-bid* in their suit is a splinter bid. Hence, all other splinter bids are *off*.

Partner	Opp.	You
1 ♡	2 ◇	<u>4 ◇</u>

♠ A 8 4
♡ K Q 9 6
◇ 3
♣ K 8 5 4 2

You show a forcing heart raise and a diamond splinter. Observe, however, that 3 ♠ or 4 ♣ would not *be a splinter bid.*

♠ A Q J 6
♡ 4
◇ K Q J 7
♣ A 10 6 2

You	Opp.	Partner	Opp.
1 ◇	P	1 ♠	2 ♡
<u>4 ♡</u>			

Your 4 ♡ bid is obviously a splinter bid, but a 4 ♣ bid would not *be.*

BIDDING AFTER A SPLINTER BID

After a splinter bid has been made, it is the *partner* of splinter bidder who must evaluate the degree of "fit," and accordingly, the chances for slam. The holding in the splinter suit is often the key in making this decision. Observe the following table, which provides some useful guidelines:

HOLDING IN SPLINTER SUIT

Good holdings	Fair holdings	Poor holdings
A-X-X-X	A-Q-X-X	K-J-X-X
X-X-X-X	Q-X-X-X	A-K-X
X-X-X	X-X	X

As suggested above, honors (except the ace) in the splinter suit are dubious values, and may be completely worthless. Also, notice that shortness opposite shortness is *not* an asset, with matching singletons the ultimate misfit. A good rule of thumb for evaluating your hand is the following:

If partner of splinter bidder does *not* count points for the *king, queen, jack,* or *shortness* in the splinter suit, a slam can probably be made with a combined total of about 30 points (instead of the mythical 33).

Partner	You		
		♠	A Q 9 7
		♡	J 5
1 ♡	1 ♠	◇	8 7 5 2
4 ◇	?	♣	K 10 7

Partner shows about 20 points, so with nothing wasted in diamonds, your 10 is enough for slam; bid 4 NT Blackwood. In contrast, had partner bid 4 ♣, you should sign off in 4 ♠.

Any of your normal slam bidding methods may be employed after a splinter bid. If "control-showing" is used, this custom is generally accepted: A cue-bid of the splinter suit shows the *ace* if made by partner of splinter bidder, or a *void* if made by splinter bidder himself. For example:

Partner	You		
1 ◇	1 ♡	♠	A Q 10 8
1 ♠	4 ♣	♡	K J 9 6 5 3
4 ♡	5 ♣	◇	K 7 2
		♣	—

Your 5 ♣ cue-bid shows a void. While it might be contended that you could have a singleton ace, most experts would not subscribe to that practice.

Mathe Asking Bid ★ ★ ★

Devised by Lewis Mathe of Los Angeles, one of America's greatest players and former World Champion

After a jump major raise, successful slam exploration often depends on learning about partner's distribution, or more specifically, his *short* suit. This will enable a more accurate evaluation, just as explained under "Bidding After a Splinter Bid" (see page *203*). Observe this hand:

♠	A K Q 8 5	*You*	*Partner*
♡	K Q 10		
◇	A 7 3	1 ♠	3 ♠*
♣	10 4	?	

*Limit raise

It would be nice to be able to find out partner's short suit, if he has one. For instance, a singleton diamond would indicate a "perfect fit," making slam an odds-on favorite. On the other hand, a singleton heart would be abominable. Also, partner may not even *have* a singleton. Is there any way to learn about all this?

Yes, there is. The "Mathe asking bid" was designed specifically for this purpose. As originally prescribed, the Mathe asking bid was intended for use after direct "limit major raises" only (like the preceding example); however, we recommend an extended application, as defined by this rule:

In an uncontested auction, after a jump raise from one to three of a major by responder at his first response, or by opener at his first rebid, the cheapest step rebid (3 ♠ or 3 NT) is the Mathe asking bid.

Or to put it in simpler terms, the underlined bid in each of the following auctions is the Mathe asking bid. NOTE: "X" = any suit.

	You	*Partner*		*Partner*	*You*
A.	1 ♡	3 ♡	B.	1 X	1 ♡
	3 ♠			3 ♡	3 ♠

	You	*Partner*		*Partner*	*You*
C.	1 ♠	3 ♠	D.	1 X	1 ♠
	3 NT			3 ♠	3 NT

The above sequences are the *only* ones where the Mathe asking bid may be used, although partner could be a passed hand in auctions **A** and **C**, and you could be a passed hand in auctions **B** and **D**. The artificial use of 3 NT, as in auctions **C** and **D**, is possible due to the great improbability of desiring to play in that contract after a jump major raise.

RESPONSES

The Mathe asking bid merely inquires, "Do you have a singleton or void and, if so, where is it?" Here are the replies:

1. **Four of a new suit** shows a splinter in that suit.

Partner	*You*		
		♠	10 9 7 2
		♡	J 8 4 3
1 ♠	3 ♠*	◇	2
3 NT	4 ◇	♣	A K 9 2

*Limit raise

Your 4 ◇ bid shows a singleton or void in diamonds.

2. **Three notrump** (over 3 ♠) shows a *spade* splinter.

		You	Partner
♠	7	1 ♣	1 ♡
♡	A Q 9 4	3 ♡	3 ♠
◇	J 10 3	3 NT	
♣	A K J 9 5		

It would be too dangerous to bid 4 ♠, so 3 NT conveniently shows short spades.

3. **Four of the agreed major** denies a splinter.

Partner	You		
		♠	A 3
		♡	Q J 9 8
1 ♡	3 ♡*	◇	9 7 5
3 ♠	4 ♡	♣	K 10 7 3

*Limit raise

As usual, returning to the trump suit is the discouraging reply.

An interesting bonus is available when the opening bidder is responding to the Mathe asking bid. Let us see:

4. **Four of opener's original suit** shows a good five-card suit, and denies a splinter. In other words, this shows exactly 5-4-2-2 shape.

		You	Partner
♠	K J 8 7	1 ♣	1 ♠
♡	5 4	3 ♠	3 NT
◇	A 3	4 ♣!	
♣	A K 10 7 3		

You could not have a club splinter, of course, so this shows a five-card club suit and two doubletons.

NOTE: Any further bidding (after the reply to the Mathe asking bid) simply follows your normal methods.

Control Asking Bid ★ ★ ★

Based on the concepts originated by the late Albert Morehead and Ely Culbertson

A few systems played today advocate the use of specialized asking bids with great abandon. We are not of that school. Not only do such devices tax the memory considerably, but their superiority over traditional methods is questionable. We much prefer a cooperative approach to slam bidding, with the benefits of "control-showing bids" (see page *180*) and "splinter bids" (see page *199*) as the most frequent tools.

Consequently, our version of the "control asking bid" applies only when it cannot possibly interfere with these other bids. The following rule sets down the conditions:

In an uncontested auction, after partner has bid, a *jump* to the *five*-level in a new suit is a control asking bid. NOTE: This need not be a jump if partner has opened the bidding with *four* in a major suit.

♠ A K 10 7 6 5   *You*   *Partner*
♡ —
♢ A K 9 7 3   1 ♠   2 ♢
♣ 9 3   5 ♣

Your 5 ♣ bid asks about club control, which is your only concern regarding the success of a diamond slam.

Partner   *You*   ♠ A K 4
                          ♡ A K 4 2
3 ♡   5 ♢   ♢ K J 7 6 5 4
                          ♣ —

Your intention is to gamble on 6 ♡, but just maybe partner is void (or has the ace) in diamonds, in which case you will bid a grand slam.

Partner   *You*   ♠ A 10 6
                          ♡ A 9 8 7 5 3
4 ♠   5 ♡   ♢ A J 4
                          ♣ A

Here you need not jump. If partner has a singleton heart (or the king or a void) you will bid 7 ♠. Otherwise, 6 ♠ will be high enough.

RESPONSES

Responding to the control asking bid is no more difficult than responding to Blackwood. Just bid up the line, by steps, to indicate the degree of control held in the asked suit. Here are the responses:

1. **One step** shows *no* first- or second-round control.

   Partner   *You*   ♠ J 4
                             ♡ Q J 10 8 5
   1 ♠   2 ♡   ♢ Q 9
   5 ♢   5 ♡   ♣ A K J 8

   You have no diamond control, so make the cheapest step response of 5 ♡.

2. **Two steps** shows *second*-round control (king or singleton).

3. **Three steps** shows *first*-round control (ace or void).

   ♠ 9 8 4   *You*   *Partner*
   ♡ K J 10 9 8 6 5 4
   ♢ Q 5   4 ♡   5 ♣
   ♣ —   5 ♠

   Your 5 ♠ response shows first-round club control.

7

Summary

♣   ♦   ♥   ♠   ♣   ♦   ♥   ♠

This chapter is unlike the previous ones. Instead of dealing with specific conventions, we will discuss some general topics that relate to the proper use of conventions. Also included are some guidelines about duplicate bridge procedures.

In this chapter:

Organized Bridge
The Alert Procedure
The Convention Card
The Skip-Bid Warning
Ethics and Proprieties
Building a Partnership

Organized Bridge

Since the birth of contract bridge in 1925, the game has been unequaled in its growth in popularity. It soon surpassed all other card games, and now ranks, undisputedly, as the number one card game in the world. This widespread acclaim is undoubtedly due to the multifaceted composition and unending challenge of the game of bridge.

THE AMERICAN CONTRACT BRIDGE LEAGUE

On the North American continent, the American Contract Bridge League is the principal governing authority for organized bridge activities. The A.C.B.L. comprises over 200,000 members and is the largest single bridge organization in the world. One of its main functions is the sanctioning of duplicate bridge tournaments of all shapes and sizes, all over North America. The four basic kinds of tournaments are described below:

CLUB GAMES.   Held in virtually every city, large and small, usually on a weekly basis. Many of the larger cities have bridge clubs running games twice a day, *every* day!

SECTIONAL TOURNAMENTS.   Hundreds of cities across the continent hold annual or semi-annual tournaments to attract the local bridge players. These typically run for three or four consecutive days (over a weekend) and are subdivided into separate events.

REGIONAL TOURNAMENTS.   Many of the larger cities conduct an annual tournament that runs for five or six days. In addition to the local crowds, these larger tournaments draw many out-of-state players. It is not uncommon to find more than 1000 players participating at the same time.

NORTH AMERICAN CHAMPIONSHIPS.   The "Nationals," as they are commonly called, are held in March, July, and November at different large cities each year. These extravaganzas last for ten consecutive days each, and attract thousands of players from all over A.C.B.L. land.

The rewards sought at all of the above bridge tournaments are *Master Points*. These are issued by the A.C.B.L. for winning or placing high in any of its various events. The A.C.B.L. also assumes the massive task (aided by its computer) of recording and tallying the Master Points accumulated by every player. This is done for the purpose of player ranking, as follows:

Rank	*Master Points Required*
Junior Master	1
Master	20
National Master	50
Senior Master	100
Advanced Senior Master	200*
Life Master	300*

  *A certain portion of which must be won in regional or higher tournaments

Membership in the A.C.B.L. also entitles each member to the monthly published *Bulletin.* In addition to providing tournament schedules and other news, this magazine contains many instructive articles to improve your bridge game. The cost of membership is surprisingly low, compared to other organizations. For more information, contact:

> Amer. Contract Bridge League
> 2200 Democrat Road
> Memphis, TN 38116
>
> Phone: (901) 332-5586

THE WORLD BRIDGE FEDERATION

The game of bridge is played world-wide, which is quite an unusual status for a card game! On the international level, the governing authority is the World Bridge Federation, which is made up of representatives from various member countries. Its principal function is to conduct the World Championships, held annually in different locations around the world. The W.B.F. also has a ranking system based on success in their conducted events:

Rank	W.B.F. Points Required
International Master	10
World Master	50*
Grand Master	200*

*Plus some other secondary requirements

The Alert Procedure

Because of the multitude of bridge conventions in use today, it is becoming more and more difficult for the average player to keep up with the game. In the past, it was the responsibility of each player to examine his opponents' convention card in order to understand their bidding. Not only was this time consuming, but it detracted from the enjoyment of the game. Furthermore, many bad results were obtained because a player was unaware that his opponents had used an artificial bid.

The *Alert Procedure* was introduced to alleviate this problem. The A.C.B.L. now places the burden of disclosure upon the *user* of the convention, rather than the "victim." Once again, the average player can sit back and enjoy the game. Here is how it works.

When a conventional, or otherwise non-standard, call is made, it is up to the *partner* of that player to immediately utter the single word, *"Alert." No further explanation should be volunteered.* Either opponent may then, *at his proper turn,* inquire as to the meaning of the alerted call. For example, say the bidding proceeds as follows:

North	East	South	West
1 NT	P	2 ◇	

Immediately after the 2 ◇ bid, the conversation might proceed as follows:
North: "Alert!"
West: "Okay, what is it?"
North: "It is Jacoby, showing at least five hearts."
West: "Thank you. Pass."

However, if West did not desire an explanation, the conversation could go:
North: "Alert!"
West: "Pass."

In either case, the bidding proceeds normally from that point on. Observe that, in the latter case, if *East* wished an explanation of the 2 ◇ bid, he would have to wait until his own turn.

Once an alert is made, it is not necessary to ask for an explanation immediately. Any player has the right, *at his turn,* or after the auction is completed, to inquire about any previously alerted call made by an opponent. In fact, if you do not contemplate entering the bidding, it is to your own best interest to *wait until the end of the auction* before inquiring. In other words, don't ask until you need to know.

ALERTABLE CALLS

Throughout this book, we have used the terms "convention" and "treatment" in their normal liberal sense, i.e., to refer to bridge agreements in general. The A.C.B.L., however, draws a fine distinction between the two for "legal" purposes. Basically, a *convention* is an artificial agreement, whereas a *treatment* is a natural agreement. As an example, the "strong artificial 2 ♣ opening" is a convention, but the "weak two-bid" is a treatment.

All *conventions* have been classified by the A.C.B.L. The most common are designated "Class A" and do *not* require an alert. Below is the current list of *non*-alertable conventions:

"Class A" Conventions

[no alert required]

BLACKWOOD, and conventions to handle interference after it
GERBER
GRAND SLAM FORCE
STAYMAN (club response to notrump)
LIGHTNER DOUBLE
TAKEOUT DOUBLE
UNUSUAL NOTRUMP OVERCALL (must be at the two-level or higher if by an unpassed hand)
S-O-S REDOUBLE
STRONG CUE-BID (for takeout)
STRONG ARTIFICIAL TWO-CLUB OPENING
NEGATIVE TWO-DIAMOND RESPONSE (to above)
TWO-NOTRUMP NEGATIVE RESPONSE (to strong two-bids)

The remaining classifications, "Class B" through "Class F," *must be alerted.* We should also point out that a particular convention must be *approved* for the event participated in. In most tournaments, conventions through "Class D" may be readily used. Conventions of "Class E" and "Class F" are permitted only with advance approval, or in extended team matches. A complete classification chart is generally posted at all tournaments, and may also be obtained by contacting the A.C.B.L.

As far as *treatments* are concerned, the rule is this: If a particular treatment can be *"checked off"* on the convention card in a *"black box,"* it does *not* require an alert. Otherwise, the treatment *must be alerted.* The A.C.B.L. imposes no restrictions on the use of treatments, provided they are properly alerted.

The Convention Card

The A.C.B.L. has designed, and periodically updates, an official convention card for the listing of partnership agreements. The purpose of this card is primarily for the benefit of your opponents, who can view a "nutshell" presentation of your bidding methods. In tournament play, each partnership is required to have *two* identical, properly marked, convention cards, which must be kept on the table in plain sight at all times.

We have included three sample convention cards to illustrate the proper markings for the conventions covered in this book. In addition, each card has an accompanying chart to explain these markings, as well as to designate which conventions, or which parts of a convention, must be *alerted* when used. The three cards are distinguished as follows:

ONE-STAR CONVENTION CARD. Contains conventions of *one* star only.

TWO-STAR CONVENTION CARD. Contains conventions of both *one* and *two* stars.

THREE-STAR CONVENTION CARD. Contains conventions of *one, two,* and *three* stars; i.e., all the conventions recommended in this book.

Each of these convention cards also includes (a) point ranges for 1 NT and 2 NT opening bids; and (b) suit lengths for major- and minor-suit opening bids. These are just recommendations, however, and need not be followed.

NOTE: The sample cards are printed in black only. However, the "Official A.C.B.L. Convention Card" is printed in two colors, red and black, to aid in the alerting process. In general, *red* areas require an alert, but *black* areas do not.

One-Star Conventions

Convention Title	How to Mark on Convention Card	Alert
STAYMAN	Check "Non-Forc." box	No
	Check "Preemptive" box for 3 ♣/3 ◇ response	Yes
JACOBY TRANSFER BID	Check "Jacoby" box	Yes
LIMIT MAJOR RAISES	Check "Limit" and "Limit in Comp." boxes	No
Splinter bids	Check "Splinter" box	Yes
3 NT forcing raise	Check "3 NT" box	Yes
Unlimited 2 NT	Enter "Unlimited 2 NT Resp."	Yes
ONE NOTRUMP FORCING	Check "1 NT Forcing" box	Yes
WEAK JUMP SHIFT RESPONSES	Enter under "Other Conventional Calls"	Yes
	Check "Weak" box under "Over Opp's Takeout Double"	No
NEGATIVE DOUBLES	Enter "Thru 4 ◇" on appropriate line	Yes
STRONG ARTIFICIAL TWO-CLUB OPENING	Check "2 ♣" box (at top of card)	No
	Check "STR" box in red and enter "Artificial"	No
	Check "2 ◇ Neg." box	No
	Enter "Special Jump Responses" (if played)	Yes
	Enter "Cheaper Minor 2nd Neg." (if played)	Yes
WEAK TWO-BIDS	Check "WK" box in black	No
	Enter "5 to 11" and "Natural"	No
	Check "2 NT Force" box	No
	Enter "Feature"	Yes
TAKEOUT DOUBLES	Check "Takeout" boxes under "Vs Opp's Preempts Dbl is"	No
	Enter "Thru 4 ◇" to the left of the lower box	
OPTIONAL DOUBLES	Check "Opt." boxes and enter "4 ♡" and "4 ♠" beside	No
DOUBLE OF ONE-NOTRUMP OPENING	(no markings necessary)	No
LEAD-DIRECTING DOUBLES	(no markings necessary)	No*
WEAK JUMP OVERCALLS	Check "Preempt" box under "Jump Overcall"	No
UNUSUAL NOTRUMP OVERCALL	Check "2 Lower Unbid" box under "Direct NT Overcalls"	No
	Enter "4 NT" on line marked "Conv. takeout"	
CONTROL-SHOWING BID	(no markings necessary)	No
BLACKWOOD	Check "Interference over 4 ♣ or 4 NT" box	No
	Enter "DOPI" after above	
GERBER	Check "Gerber" box and enter "Jump Over NT"	No

*An alert is required in the case of a double of notrump to request the "weaker major" lead.

All conventions marked in gray and all nonstandard partnership agreements must be alerted.

SPECIAL DOUBLES (Describe)
Negative _THRU 4D_
_____
Responsive _____
Other _____
_____

SIMPLE OVERCALL
_____ to _____ HCP (occ. light □)
Responses: New Suit Forcing □
Cuebid Is: One-Round Force □
  Game Force □ Limit Raise □
Other _____

JUMP OVERCALL
Strong □ Interm □ Preempt ☒
Special Responses _____
_____

OPENING PREEMPTS
  Sound Light Solid Minor
3-bids □   □   □
Other _____

PSYCHICS   Systemic □
  Never Rare Occ. Frequent
   □   □   □   □
Describe: _____
Controls _____

SLAM CONVENTIONS
Gerber ☒ _JUMP OVER NT._ 4NT Var. □ _____
Interference over 4♣ or 4NT ☒ [Describe] _DOPI_

DEFENSIVE CARD PLAY
Opening lead vs. SUITS: 3rd best □ 4th best □ 5th best □ Other ____
  Mark card led: x x x **A K x** **K Q x** **Q J x** **J 10 x** **10 9 x**
  K J 10 x **K 10 9 x** **Q 10 9 x** **x x x x x**
Opening lead vs. NT: 3rd best □ 4th best □ Other ____

(Red Dot)
  Mark card led: x x x **A K J x** **A Q J x** **A J 10 9**
  A 1098 **K Q J x** **K Q 109** **K J 109** **K 1098**
  Q J 10 x **Q 1098** **J 109 x** **1098 x** **x x x x x**

Special Carding _____ Frequent Count Signals □

DIRECT NT OVERCALLS
1NT _____ to _____ HCP
Jump to 2NT: ____ to ____ HCP
  Unusual for Minors □
  2 Lower Unbid ☒
Other _____

Vs. Wk.□ Strong□ NT Opening
  Direct □   Balance □

	♣	♦	♥	♠
2♣ shows	♣	♦	♥	♠
2♦ shows	♣	♦	♥	♠
2♡ shows	♣	♦	♥	♠
2♠ shows	♣	♦	♥	♠

Other _____

OVER OPP'S TAKEOUT DOUBLE
New Suit Force 1-level □ 2-level □
Jp. Shift Force□ Good□ Weak☒
  Redouble Implies No Fit □
Other _____

Vs. Opp's Preempts Dbl. Is
        Takeout Opt. Penalty
Wk. 2's   ☒ _4H_ ☒   □
3 Bids _THRU 4D_ ☒ _4S_ ☒   □
Conv. takeout _4NT_

DIRECT CUEBID
Strong Takeout: Minor □ Major □
Natural: ♣ □ ♦ □ Artif. Bids □
Two Suits □ _____

Strong Forcing Opening: 2♣ ☒ 2 bids □ 1♣ □ Other _____

NOTRUMP OPENING BIDS
1NT _15_ to _17_   2NT _20_ to _22_ HCP
1NT _____ to _____   3NT _____ to _____ HCP
2♣ Forc.□ Non-Forc.☒Stayman   Solid Suit □: _____
2♦ Forc.□ Non-Forc.□ Stayman   _____
Transfers: Jacoby☒ Texas□ Other□   _____
1NT-3♣/3♦ Is invitational □   Preemptive ☒   Forcing □
Other _____

MAJOR OPENINGS
1♡-1♠ Opening on 4 Cards

	Often	Seldom	Never/Almost
1st-2nd	□	□	☒
3rd-4th	□	☒	□

RESPONSES
Double Raise Forcing □ Limit ☒
Preemptive □ Limit in Comp. ☒
  Conv. Raise: 3NT ☒
    Swiss □ Splinter ☒
Conv. Responses: 1NT Forcing ☒
Drury □ Single Raise Constr. □
Other _UNLIMITED 2NT RESP._

MINOR OPENINGS
  Length Promised

	4+	3+	Shorter
1♣	□	☒	□
1♦	□	☒	□

RESPONSES
  Double Raise
Forcing □ Limit □ Preempt □
  Single Raise Forcing □
1NT/1♣ _____ to _____ HCP
1♦ Resp. Conv. _____
Other _____

2♣	WK □ □	_____ to _____ HCP. Describe _ARTIFICIAL_	
	INT □ □	Conv. Resp. & Rebids _SPECIAL JUMP RESP._	
	STR □ ☒	_CH. MINOR 2ND NEG._ 2♦ Neg. ☒ 2 NT Neg. □	
2♦	WK ☒ □	_5_ to _11_ HCP. Describe _NATURAL_	
	INT □ □	Conv. Resp. & Rebids	
	STR □ □	_FEATURE_ 2 NT Force ☒ 2 NT Neg. □	
2♡	WK ☒ □	_5_ to _11_ HCP. Describe _NATURAL_	
	INT □ □	Conv. Resp. & Rebids	
	STR □ □	_FEATURE_ 2 NT Force ☒ 2 NT Neg. □	
2♠	WK ☒ □	_5_ to _11_ HCP. Describe _NATURAL_	
	INT □ □	Conv. Resp. & Rebids	
	STR □ □	_FEATURE_ 2 NT Force ☒ 2 NT Neg. □	

OTHER CONVENTIONAL CALLS
WEAK JUMP SHIFT RESPONSES
_____
_____
_____

If in doubt as to the meaning of a conventional call — ASK AT YOUR TURN!

ONE-STAR CONVENTION CARD

Two-Star Conventions

Convention Title	How to Mark on Convention Card	Alert
TEXAS TRANSFER BID	Check "Texas" box Enter "Texas in Comp. thru 3 ♣" (if played)	Yes
MINOR-SUIT STAYMAN	Enter "2 ♠ = Minor Suit Stayman"	Yes
ACOL THREE-NOTRUMP OPENING	Enter "16 to 21" HCP Enter "Acol"	Yes
INVERTED MINOR RAISES	Check "Preempt" and "Single Raise Forcing" boxes Enter "Also in Comp." (if played)	Yes
STRUCTURED REVERSES	Enter "Structured Reverses" on appropriate line Enter "Jump Reverse = Singleton" below (if played)	Yes* Yes
REVERSE DRURY	Check "Drury" box and enter "Reverse" above	Yes
PREEMPTIVE RERAISES	Enter "Preemptive Reraises" on appropriate line	Yes
TRUSCOTT TWO NOTRUMP	Enter "2 NT = Limit Raise" Check "Redouble Implies No Fit" box Check "New Suit Force 1-level" box (if played)	Yes Yes No
LIMIT BIDDING AFTER AN ENEMY OVERCALL	Enter under "Other Conventional Calls"	No
MICHAELS CUE-BID	Check "Two Suits" box and enter "Michaels"	Yes
INVITATIONAL CUE-BID	Check "One-Round Force" box Enter "Weak Jump Raises" on appropriate line Enter "Jump Cue = Mini-Splinter" (if played)	Yes
RESPONSIVE DOUBLES	Enter "Thru 4 ◇" on appropriate line	Yes
S-O-S REDOUBLE	(no markings necessary)	No
ASTRO	Check "Wk.," "Strong," "Direct," and "Balance" boxes Circle suits guaranteed Semi-circle possible suits and connect with "or" Enter "Astro" (for emphasis)	Yes
VOLUNTARY BID OF FIVE IN A MAJOR	(no markings necessary)	No
GRAND SLAM FORCE	(no markings necessary)	No

*Opener's simple-reverse bid requires no alert, but responder's specialized rebids do.

All conventions marked in gray and all nonstandard partnership agreements must be alerted.

SPECIAL DOUBLES (Describe)
Negative **THRU 4D**

Responsive **THRU 4D**

Other _____

DIRECT NT OVERCALLS
1NT _____ to _____ HCP
Jump to 2NT: ____ to ____ HCP
Unusual for Minors ☐
2 Lower Unbid ☒
Other _____

Names _____
General Approach **STANDARD AM.** Pair # _____

Strong Forcing Opening: 2♣ ☒ 2 bids ☐ 1♣ ☐ Other _____

NOTRUMP OPENING BIDS
1NT **15** to **17**   2NT **20** to **22** HCP
1NT ____ to ____   3NT **16** to **21** HCP
2♣ Forc.☐ Non-Forc.☒ Stayman   Solid Suit ☐: **ACOL**
2♦ Forc.☐ Non-Forc.☐ Stayman
Transfers: Jacoby ☒ Texas ☒ Other ☐ **TEXAS IN COMP. THRU 3C**
1NT - 3♣ /3♦   Is Invitational ☐   Preemptive ☒   Forcing ☐
Other **2S = MINOR SUIT STAYMAN**

SIMPLE OVERCALL
____ to ____ HCP (occ. light ☐)

Responses: New Suit Forcing ☐
Cuebid is: One-Round Force ☒
JUMP CUE = MINI-SPLINTER
Game Force ☐
Other **WEAK JUMP RAISES**

Vs. Wk. ☒ Strong ☒ NT Opening
Direct ☒   Balance ☒
2♣ shows ♣ OR ♦ / ♡
2♦ shows ♣ OR ♦ OR ♡ / ♠
2♡ shows ♠   ♦   ♡
2♠ shows ♠   ♦   ♠
Other **(ASTRO)**

JUMP OVERCALL
Strong ☐ Interm ☐ Preempt ☒
Special Responses _____

OVER OPP'S TAKEOUT DOUBLE
New Suit Force 1-level ☒ 2-level ☐
Jp. Shift Force ☐ Good ☐ Weak ☒
Redouble Implies No Fit ☒
Other **2NT = LIMIT RAISE**

MAJOR OPENINGS
1♡ -1♠ Opening on 4 Cards
       Often Seldom **ALMOST Never**
1st-2nd ☐   ☐   ☒
3rd-4th ☐   ☒   ☐

RESPONSES
Double Raise Forcing ☐ Limit ☒
Preemptive ☐ Limit in Comp. ☒
Conv. Raise: 3NT ☒
  Swiss ☐ Splinter ☒
Conv. Responses: 1NT Forcing ☒
REVERSE
Drury ☒ Single Raise Constr. ☐
Other **UNLIMITED 2NT RESP.**
PREEMPTIVE RERAISES

MINOR OPENINGS
       Length Promised
       4+   3+   Shorter
1♣   ☐   ☒   ☐
1♦   ☐   ☒   ☐

RESPONSES
Double Raise
Forcing ☐ Limit ☐ Preempt ☒
(ALSO IN COMP.)
Single Raise Forcing ☒
1NT/1♣ _____ to _____ HCP
1♦ Resp. Conv. _____
Other **STRUCTURED REVERSES**
JUMP REVERSE = SINGLETON

OPENING PREEMPTS
Sound   Light   Solid Minor
3-bids ☐   ☐   ☐
Other _____

Vs. Opp's Preempts Dbl. Is
         Takeout Opt. Penalty
Wk. 2's   ☒   4H ☒   ☐
3 Bids **THRU 4D** ☒ 4S ☒   ☐
Conv. takeout **4NT**

PSYCHICS   Systemic ☐
Never Rare Occ. Frequent
 ☐   ☐   ☐   ☐
Describe: _____
Controls: _____

DIRECT CUEBID
Strong Takeout: Minor ☐ Major ☐
Natural: ♣ ☐ ♦ ☐ Artif. Bids ☐
Two Suits ☒ **MICHAELS**

		WK		____ to ____ HCP. Describe **ARTIFICIAL**
2♣	INT	☐ ☐	Conv. Resp. & Rebids **SPECIAL JUMP RESP.**
	STR	☐ ☒	**CH. MINOR 2ND NEG.** 2♦ Neg. ☒ 2 NT Neg. ☐

		WK	☒ ☐	**5** to **11** HCP. Describe **NATURAL**
2♦	INT	☐ ☐	Conv. Resp. & Rebids _____
	STR	☐ ☐	**FEATURE** 2 NT Force ☒ 2 NT Neg. ☐

		WK	☒ ☐	**5** to **11** HCP. Describe **NATURAL**
2♡	INT	☐ ☐	Conv. Resp. & Rebids _____
	STR	☐ ☐	**FEATURE** 2 NT Force ☒ 2 NT Neg. ☐

		WK	☒ ☐	**5** to **11** HCP. Describe **NATURAL**
2♠	INT	☐ ☐	Conv. Resp. & Rebids _____
	STR	☐ ☐	**FEATURE** 2 NT Force ☒ 2 NT Neg. ☐

SLAM CONVENTIONS
Gerber ☒ **JUMP OVER NT.** 4NT Var. ☐
Interference over 4♣ or 4NT ☒ [Describe] **DOPI**

OTHER CONVENTIONAL CALLS
WEAK JUMP SHIFT RESPONSES
LIMIT BIDDING AFTER AN ENEMY OVERCALL

DEFENSIVE CARD PLAY
Opening lead vs. SUITS: 3rd best ☐ 4th best ☐ 5th best ☐ Other _____
Mark card led: xxx A K x K Q x Q J x J 10 x 10 9 x
  K J 10 x K 10 9 x Q 10 9 x x x x x x
Opening lead vs. NT: 3rd best ☐ 4th best ☐ Other _____

(Red Dot)

Mark card led: xxx A K J x A Q J x A J 109
A 1098 K Q J x K Q 109 K J 109 K 1098
Q J 10 x Q 1098 J 109 x 1098 x x x x x x

Special Carding _____ Frequent Count Signals ☐

If in doubt as to the meaning of a conventional call — ASK AT YOUR TURN!

TWO-STAR CONVENTION CARD

(Also includes ONE-STAR conventions)

Three-Star Conventions

Convention Title	How to Mark on Convention Card	Alert
MINOR-SUIT TRANSFER BIDS	Check "Other" box and enter "2 NT = ♣, 3 ♣ = ◇" NOTE: Observe that no check is now placed in the "Preemptive" box for a 3 ♣/3 ◇ response.	Yes
SPLINTER RESPONSES (To One Notrump)	Enter "3 ◇, 3 ♡, 3 ♠ = Splinter"	Yes
LEBENSOHL	Enter "Lebensohl" Enter "Neg. Dbl. After Jump Overcall" (if played)	Yes
FOURTH SUIT FORCING	Enter under "Other Conventional Calls"	Yes
NEW MINOR FORCING	Enter under "Other Conventional Calls"	Yes
EASTERN CUE-BID	Enter under "Other Conventional Calls"	Yes
INVISIBLE CUE-BIDS	Enter under "Other Conventional Calls"	Yes
COMPETITIVE DOUBLES	Enter under "Special Doubles"	Yes
MAXIMAL OVERCALL DOUBLE	Enter under "Special Doubles"	Yes
JUMP CUE-BID OVERCALL	Enter "Jump Cue = Strong 1-Suiter" under "Direct Cue-bid"	Yes
DEFENSE TO ONE-CLUB FORCING	Enter under "Other Conventional Calls"	Yes*
DEFENSES TO TWO-LEVEL AND HIGHER CONVENTIONAL OPENINGS	Enter "Spec. Def. to Enemy Conv." under "Other Conventional Calls"	Yes*
EXTENDED SPLINTER BIDS	Check "Splinter" box Enter "Extended" immediately above	Yes
MATHE ASKING BID	Enter under "Slam Conventions"	Yes
CONTROL ASKING BID	Enter under "Slam Conventions"	Yes

*Natural overcalls do not require an alert.

All conventions marked in gray and all nonstandard partnership agreements must be alerted.

SPECIAL DOUBLES (Describe)

Negative _THRU 4D_

_____

Responsive _THRU 4D_
Other _COMPETITIVE DBL._
MAXIMAL OVERCALL DBL.

SIMPLE OVERCALL

____ to ____ HCP (occ. llght □)

Responses: New Suit Forcing □
Cuebid is: One-Round Force ☒
JUMP CUE = MINI-SPLINTER
Game Force □ Limit Raise □
Other _WEAK JUMP RAISES_

JUMP OVERCALL

Strong □ Interm □ Preempt ☒
Special Responses _____

_____

OPENING PREEMPTS

Sound Light Solid Minor

3-bids □ □ □
Other_____

PSYCHICS   Systemic □

Never Rare Occ. Frequent
□ □ □ □
Describe: _____
Controls _____

SLAM CONVENTIONS   _MATHE A.B._
CONTROL A.B.
Gerber ☒ _JUMP OVER NT._ 4NT Var. □
Interference over 4♣ or 4NT ☒ [Describe] _DOPI_

DEFENSIVE CARD PLAY

Opening lead vs. SUITS: 3rd best □ 4th best □ 5th best □ Other ____
Mark card led: x x x   A K x   K Q x   Q J x   109 x
K J 10 x   K 109 x   Q 109 x   x x x x x

Opening lead vs. NT: 3rd best □ 4th best □ Other ____

(Red Dot)

Mark card led: x x x   A K J x   A Q J x   A J 109
A 1098   K Q J x   K Q 109   K J 109   K 1098
Q J 10 x   Q 1098   J 109 x   1098 x   x x x x x

Special Carding _____ Frequent Count Signals □

DIRECT NT OVERCALLS

1NT ____ to ____ HCP
Jump to 2NT: ____ to ____ HCP
Unusual for Minors □
2 Lower Unbld ☒
Other _____

Vs. Wk.☒Strong☒ NT Opening

Direct ☒   Balance ☒

	shows		
2♣	♣ OR ♦ ♡	♠
2♦	♣ OR ♦ ♦	♡♠
2♡	♦	♡
2♠	♠ ♦	♡

Other _____ (ASTRO)

OVER OPP'S TAKEOUT DOUBLE

New Suit Force 1-level ☒ 2-level □
Jp. Shift Force□ Good☒ Weak☒
Redouble Implies No Fit ☒
Other _2NT = LIMIT RAISE_

Vs. Opp's Preempts Dbl. Is

	Takeout	Opt.	Penalty
Wk. 2's	☒	4H ☒	□
3 Bids	THRU 4D	4S ☒	□
Conv. takeout		4NT	

DIRECT CUEBID

Strong Takeout: Minor □ Major □
Natural: ♣ □ ♦ □ Artif. Bids □
Two Suits ☒ _MICHAELS_
JUMP CUE = STRONG 1-SUITER

Names _____
General Approach _STANDARD AM._ Pair # ____
Strong Forcing Opening: 2♣ ☒ 2 bids □ 1♣ □ Other_____

NOTRUMP OPENING BIDS

1NT _15_ to _17_   2NT _20_ to _22_ HCP
1NT ____ to ____   3NT _16_ to _21_ HCP
2♣ Forc.□ Non-Forc.☒Stayman   Solid Suit □: _ACOL_
2♦ Forc.□ Non-Forc.□ Stayman   _TEXAS IN COMP. THRU 3C_
Transfers: Jacoby☒ Texas☒ Other☒ _2NT = C, 3C = D_
1NT-3♣/3♦ Is Invitational □   Preemptive □   Forcing □
Other _2S = MINOR SUIT STAYMAN / 3D, 3H, 3S = SPLINTER_
LEBENSOHL / NEG. DBL. AFTER JUMP OVERCALL

MAJOR OPENINGS

1♡-1♠ Opening on 4 Cards

	Often	Seldom	ALMOST Never
1st-2nd	□	□	☒
3rd-4th	□	☒	□

RESPONSES

Double Raise Forcing □ Limit ☒
Preemptive □ Limit in Comp. ☒
Conv. Raise: 2NT □ 3NT ☒
Swiss □ Splinter ☒ _EXTENDED_
Conv. Responses: 1NT Forcing ☒
Drury ☒ _REVERSE_ Single Raise Constr. □
Other _UNLIMITED 2NT RESP._
PREEMPTIVE RERAISES

MINOR OPENINGS

Length Promised

	4+	3+	Shorter
1♣	□	☒	□
1♦	□	☒	□

RESPONSES

Double Raise
Forcing □ Limit □ Preempt ☒
(ALSO IN COMP.)
Single Raise Forcing ☒
1NT/1♣ ____ to ____ HCP
1♦ Resp. Conv. _____
Other _STRUCTURED REVERSES_
JUMP REVERSE = SINGLETON

	WK			HCP. Describe	
2♣	□ □		to	_ARTIFICIAL_	
	INT □ □	Conv. Resp. & Rebids	_SPECIAL JUMP RESP._	
	STR □ ☒	_CH. MINOR 2ND NEG._ 2♦ Neg. ☒ 2 NT Neg. □		

	WK ☒ □	_5_ to _11_ HCP. Describe _NATURAL_	
2♦	INT □ □	Conv. Resp. & Rebids _____	
	STR □ □	_FEATURE_ 2 NT Force ☒ 2 NT Neg. □	

	WK ☒ □	_5_ to _11_ HCP. Describe _NATURAL_	
2♡	INT □ □	Conv. Resp. & Rebids _____	
	STR □ □	_FEATURE_ 2 NT Force ☒ 2 NT Neg. □	

	WK ☒ □	_5_ to _11_ HCP. Describe _NATURAL_	
2♠	INT □ □	Conv. Resp. & Rebids _____	
	STR □ □	_FEATURE_ 2 NT Force ☒ 2 NT Neg. □	

OTHER CONVENTIONAL CALLS

WEAK JUMP SHIFT RESPONSES / INVISIBLE CUE-BIDS
LIMIT BIDDING AFTER ENEMY OVERCALL / EASTERN CUE-BID
FOURTH SUIT FORCING / NEW MINOR FORCING
DEF. TO 1C FORCING / SPEC. DEF. TO ENEMY CONV.

If in doubt as to the meaning of a conventional call — ASK AT YOUR TURN!

THREE-STAR CONVENTION CARD

(Also includes ONE and TWO-STAR conventions)

The Skip-Bid Warning

It would be ideal if every bridge player were to make all of his calls in the same tempo, in the same tone of voice, more or less like a robot. To be sure, an ethical player can approximate this for most routine bidding. A problem arises, however, when one is faced with the unexpected. For example, say the bidding proceeds as follows:

North	East	South	West
3 ♠	?		

The 3 ♠ opening bid has come as a shock. Naturally, East may require a little extra time to consider his options when he contemplates entering the bidding. On the other hand, if East is holding a Yarborough or the like, he has absolutely no problem and will pass without further ado.

See the problem? West is able to deduce (illegally, mind you) something about East's hand from the *amount of time* it takes East to make a call. For instance, a *fast* pass suggests nothing, while a *slow* pass implies some values. Similarly, a *fast* bid indicates confidence, whereas a *slow* bid portrays doubt. Of course, West is not supposed to take advantage of such information (see Ethics and Proprieties), but the information is there, nonetheless.

The *skip-bid warning* is a measure to alleviate this problem. Originated in 1938 by Sam Fry, Jr., it was adopted by the A.C.B.L. in 1957, and works something like this: A player about to make any *jump* bid may announce, *"Skip-bid,"* followed, of course, by the intended bid. After such a warning, it is the duty of the next player to pause approximately *ten seconds* before making his call, even when he has no problem at all. Thus, the conversation in our previous example might proceed as follows:

North: "Skip-bid. Three spades."
East: (ten-second pause) "Pass."

Assuming this procedure is followed, West can no longer deduce anything from the amount of time taken by East. With or without a problem, East must wait ten seconds.

IMPROPER USAGES

Considering how long the skip-bid warning has been in effect, it is amazing the amount of abuse it receives. Some players still do not understand it, yet others seem to violate it willfully. Listed below are a few important points, which might clear up some misconceptions about this rule:

1. The skip-bid warning is *not* intended to alert partner to the fact you are making a jump bid. Its purpose is to inform the *opponents,* so as to protect your side from damage that might have resulted had the opponents not been forewarned.

2. The skip-bid warning is *not* just for preemptive bids, but for *all* jump bids. The announcement is still regarded as optional by the A.C.B.L., but if you *ever* use it, you must *always* use it any time you jump the bidding. For example:

Partner	Opp.	You
1 ♠	P	2 NT

   It is just as proper to announce "skip-bid" before your 2 NT response, as it was in our previous example.

3. The player to bid after the skip-bid warning should study his hand *quietly* (even if

only for show) during the approximate ten-second pause. Nothing is more contemptuous than something like:

North: "Skip-bid. Three spades."

East: "1, 2, 3, 4, 5, 6, 7, 8, 9, 10 . . . Pass."

In effect East is saying, "I have no problem, partner, but I am waiting ten seconds for the record." When this particular East *does* have a problem, the pause is *silent,* which brings us right back to square one.

Ethics and Proprieties

The intent of the game of bridge is that information be exchanged between partners only through the legally available means, i.e., the calls actually made (or the carding signals used on defense). The manner in which calls are made, inflection of voice, physical mannerisms, tempo, etc., should have *no effect whatever* on the interpretation of partner's call or play.

Nevertheless, we are all human beings and do not live in a Utopian environment. It is impossible on occasion not to detect some problem, or dilemma, or slight nuance on partner's part. The human mind is so well trained that it notices the slightest clues, no matter how subtle. These are the facts of life. Does this then mean we are all unethical? Are we all a bit larcenous?

Not necessarily. *Receiving* illegal information is one thing; at times it is unavoidable. *Using* such information is another. The ethical player will "bend over backwards" not to take advantage of improperly obtained information. He will base his actions solely on his own hand (and any properly obtained information). He will search his conscience to monitor his own actions. Here is a relevant example from tournament play:

♠	K 2		*You*	*Partner*
♡	A K Q J 10 8		1 ♡	1 ♠
◇	K 8 7 5		3 ♡	4 NT
♣	3		5 ◇	5 ♡*
			?	

*After a huddle

Partner's problem is easy to surmise; he is concerned about a trump loser, and finally decided to sign off in 5 ♡ even though only one ace is missing. Certainly, if *two* aces were missing, he would have signed off promptly. Therefore, you know it must be "right" to bid the slam, since your hand contains just what partner needs—solid trumps. Nevertheless, you must *pass.* Partner's sign-off after Blackwood normally indicates the absence of two aces, which is the only *proper* information you have received. The fact that partner had a problem is *improper* information, and must not be used. To be sure, partner's choice of Blackwood was probably ill-advised, but that is neither here nor there; you must not be unethical to make up for partner's bad bidding.

The fact that partner hesitates, or otherwise gives improper information, does *not* necessarily mean you must pass at your next turn. What it *does* mean is that you must act in a fashion that could not be influenced by the hesitation. In other words, the action you take must be clear-cut. For example:

Opp.	*Partner*	*Opp.*	*You*			
				♠	A Q 10 9 5 4	
				♡	K 5 3	
1 NT	P*	P	?	◇	4	
				♣	8 5 4	

*After hesitating

You should bid 2 ♠. Of course, you cannot guarantee making 2 ♠ in your own hand, but the calculated risk is routine, and virtually every expert would make that same bid. However, change your hand to:

♠ A Q 9 6 3
♡ K 5 4
◇ 3 2
♣ 7 5 4

Now you must pass. Although *some* experts might venture a bid with this hand, it is by no means clear-cut. Partner's hesitation has clearly made a bid more attractive, and thus, must be rejected for that reason.

The game of bridge would run smoother, and be a lot more pleasant, if *everyone* would adhere to these "unwritten" laws. Let your conscience be your guide, and you will surely develop a reputation as an ethical player.

Building a Partnership

Success at bridge involves more than just learning all of the latest conventions and mastering the techniques of card play. The most skillful player in the world would be helpless without a suitable partner who understands his bidding. The key to good bridge is *partnership,* rather than individual, skills.

The formula for a successful partnership cannot be expressed by any exact criteria. Obviously, no two people are alike, so the ties that bind successful partnerships are probably also not alike. Nevertheless, we feel the following tips will be helpful:

1. Building a good partnership does not necessarily mean limiting your play to one specific partner. On the contrary, it is better to have a handful of "regular" partners, with each of whom you feel *comfortable* at the bridge table. Obviously, this group of players may change from time to time.

2. Avoid partnership discussions *at the bridge table.* This is probably the single most destructive factor to the morale and confidence of a partnership. All discussions should be held in private. It is much easier to receive (or give) constructive criticism, and analyze your poor results, *without* the "ears" of the bridge community listening in. This also leads to a more pleasant bridge game, for *all* concerned.

3. Set aside some time *away* from the bridge table for the discussion of your conventions, system agreements, etc. To minimize the chances of a misunderstanding, it is desirable to have these methods in *writing.* Simply agreeing to play a particular convention does *not* mean you will be on the same wavelength, as most conventions have more than one version. HINT: To avoid the writing, just make sure that each of your regular partners has a copy of this book!

4. It is helpful to practice bidding hands. Two players can do this simply enough by dealing out thirteen cards each, then bidding as partners. After you have reached a final contract, examine both hands to judge the efficiency of your bidding. HINT: To practice game and slam bidding, remove about twelve "spot" cards from the deck before dealing.

5. Be a pleasant partner *yourself.* Remember, *winning* is great, but the *enjoyment* of the game is even greater. The only *bad* game is a game without either.

GLOSSARY

Popular Bidding Conventions, Treatments, and Systems

In this Glossary of popular bidding conventions, treatments, and systems, we have carefully tried to present a *current* cross section of the tournament player's repertoire. To achieve this goal, we have eliminated some of the obsolete, or less popular, conventions. Despite this editing, the list is quite extensive.

The intended purpose of this Glossary is to provide a source of reference. In most cases, our explanation is adequate to become familiar with the topic, but *not* complete enough actually to learn and adopt it. Thus, it is an ideal means of obtaining the preexposure necessary to cope successfully with the enemy conventions you may have to face at the bridge table.

The Glossary also serves as an alphabetical *Index* to this book. Two forms of cross references are provided: When a subject is covered in the main text of the book, a specific page reference is given. When a subject can be found elsewhere in the Glossary, the appropriate cross-reference heading is shown in small capital letters.

ACE-SHOWING RESPONSES. A method of responding to show specific aces, typically employed over STRONG TWO-BIDS or the STRONG ARTIFICIAL TWO-CLUB OPENING. One popular version (over the artificial 2 ♣ opening) is described below:

2 ◇ shows no aces.

2 ♡, 2 ♠, 3 ♣, or 3 ◇ shows that ace.

2 NT shows no aces, but at least 8 high-card points.

3 NT shows two aces.

Some players also incorporate king-showing, by using a more complex set of responses. *See also* STEP RESPONSES.

ACES OVER TWO-BIDS. *See* ACE-SHOWING RESPONSES.

ACES SCIENTIFIC. A bidding system developed in the 1970's by Ira Corn's internationally famous Dallas Aces Team, which Robert Goldman was most influential in publicizing. Principal features include STRONG NOTRUMPS with JACOBY TRANSFER BIDS, FIVE-CARD MAJORS with ONE NOTRUMP FORCING, TWO-OVER-ONE GAME FORCE, and the STRONG ARTIFICIAL TWO-CLUB OPENING. The system is highlighted by many modern bidding gadgets.

ACOL. A bidding system that is considered "standard" in Great Britain, and widely used throughout the world. Principal features include VARIABLE NOTRUMPS (strong vulnerable, weak non-vulnerable), FOUR-CARD MAJORS, LIMIT RAISES, LIMIT TWO-NOTRUMP REOPONOD, and "light" two-over-one responses. The system is characterized by very few forcing bids. Other features are listed separately below.

ACOL FOUR-NOTRUMP OPENING. An opening bid of 4 NT to ask for specific aces. The responses are:

5 ♣ shows no aces.

5 ◇, 5 ♡, 5 ♠, or 6 ♣ shows that ace.

5 NT shows two aces.

ACOL THREE-NOTRUMP OPENING. A strong version of the GAMBLING THREE-NO-TRUMP OPENING, based on a long running minor suit with at least two outside stoppers. *See page 107* for a complete description.

[Defense to]

See page 177 for our recommended defense.

ACOL TWO-BIDS. Opening bids of two in a suit to show eight or more playing tricks and forcing for one round. The suit bid is generally six cards or longer, but may be just five cards when a two-suiter is held. The TWO-NOTRUMP NEGATIVE RESPONSE is customarily played, after which the bidding may die at the three-level.

ALLEN OVER NOTRUMP. A means of locating a four-four minor-suit fit after a 1 NT opening bid, as devised by Larry Allen of Summerville, S.C., for use in conjunction with STAYMAN and JACOBY TRANSFER BIDS. After a Stayman 2 ♣ response, and opener's major-suit rebid, a bid in the other major asks opener to show a four-card minor suit. For example:

Partner	You		
		♠	A 9 7 4
		♡	8 6
1 NT	2 ♣	◇	A K 6 5
2 ♡	2 ♠	♣	A 8 3

Your 2 ♠ bid is artificial and asks for a minor suit. A superior slam may be reached if partner has diamonds.

Also, after a 2 ◇ reply to Stayman, a bid of 3 ♣ is used to initiate a minor-suit inquiry.

ALL-PURPOSE CUE-BID. The very popular use of a cue-bid in the enemy suit as a general strength-showing bid, with no specific relation to one's holding in the enemy suit. This is most often used at the two- or three-level to create a game-forcing auction. For example:

Opp.	Partner	Opp.	You
	1 ♣	P	1 ♡
1 ♠	P	P	2 ♠

♠	8 6 5	
♡	A K 10 5 4	
◇	A 7 3	
♣	K 8	

Your 2 ♠ cue-bid has no precise meaning, but forces partner to keep bidding until game is reached.

We recommend the all-purpose cue-bid in a variety of situations, e.g., refer to pages *70, 77,* and *113.* Alternative treatments include the WESTERN CUE-BID (asking for a stopper), EASTERN CUE-BID (showing a stopper), and the DIRECTIONAL ASKING BID (showing a partial stopper).

APPROACH-FORCING. A bidding concept inherent in virtually every successful bidding system, based on the need for careful low-level suit exploration through minimum forcing bids. In STANDARD bidding, the one-over-one and two-over-one new-suit responses to an opening bid are prime examples.

ASKING BIDS. Any of a variety of bids that ask partner about controls, aces, high cards, trump honors, etc., but in themselves offer no description of asker's hand. Hundreds of variations have been devised over the years, mostly for the purpose of aiding slam investigation. We recommend the following asking bids, which are covered in detail on the pages indicated: BLACKWOOD (page *187*), GERBER (page *192*), VOLUNTARY BID OF FIVE IN A MAJOR (page *194*), GRAND SLAM FORCE (page *197*), MATHE ASKING BID (page *203*), and CONTROL ASKING BID (page *205*).

ASTRO. An effective method of competing against an opponent's 1 NT opening bid, invented by Paul Allinger, Roger Stern, and Lawrence Rosler. An overcall of 2 ♣ shows hearts and a minor suit, and 2 ◇ shows spades and any other suit. *See page 160 for a complete description.*

[Defense to]
See page 27 for our recommended defense.

ASTRO CUE-BID. A method of describing certain kinds of two-suited hands after an enemy opening bid of one of a suit, as devised by the inventors of the ASTRO convention. A direct cue-bid of opener's suit shows a long minor suit (usually six cards) and a shorter major suit (usually four cards), as indicated below:

2 ♣ over 1 ♣ shows diamonds and hearts.
2 ◇ over 1 ◇ shows clubs and hearts.
2 ♡ over 1 ♡ shows clubs and spades.
2 ♠ over 1 ♠ shows clubs and hearts.

[Defense to]
See page 83 for our recommended defense.

AUGUST TWO DIAMONDS. A variation of TWO-WAY STAYMAN invented by William August of Springfield, Mass., which permits responder to bid with many weak two-suited hands. The 2 ◇ response to partner's 1 NT opening bid demands his longer major, after which any further suit bid by responder is a sign-off. Also, a response of 2 ♣ (STAYMAN), followed by 3 ♣, is used to show a weak minor two-suiter. Compare with MURRAY TWO DIAMONDS.

BABY BLACKWOOD. The use of 3 NT (instead of 4 NT) to ask for aces after a major-suit fit has firmly been established. The responses are identical to regular BLACKWOOD, except one level lower, thus allowing the partnership to stop safely at the four-level when two aces are missing. This treatment has attracted very little expert following.

BALANCING TWO CLUBS FOR TAKE-OUT. The use of 2 ♣ as an artificial weak takeout bid after an enemy suit opening bid is followed by two passes. Some players extend this to include all balancing 2 ♣ bids for takeout (regardless of the enemy bidding). *See also* TWO CLUBS GENERAL TAKEOUT.

BARON NOTRUMP OVERCALL. The use of a direct overcall of 1 NT to show a weak hand containing support for the unbid suits, i.e., as a weak TAKEOUT DOUBLE.

BARON TWO-NOTRUMP RESPONSE. A response of 2 NT to partner's opening bid of one of a suit to show 16 to 18 points. As an obvious corollary, a 3 NT response then shows 13 to 15 points. In other words, the STANDARD meanings are reversed.

BECKER. *See* REVISED LANDY.

BIG CLUB. *See* SCHENKEN.

BLACKWOOD. The ever-popular use of 4 NT and 5 NT to ask for aces and kings, respectively, as invented by Easley Blackwood of Indianapolis, Ind. *See* page *187* for a complete coverage.

BLUE TEAM CLUB. One of the more current ITALIAN TEAM SYSTEMS, developed primarily by Benito Garozzo and based on the original Neapolitan system. Principal features include ONE CLUB FORCING (17+ high-card points) with STEP RESPONSES to show controls, FOUR-CARD MAJORS, CANAPE tendencies, 13-to 17-point 1 NT opening, and WEAK TWO-BIDS in the major suits.

BRIDGE WORLD STANDARD. A consensus bidding system based on polls conducted by *The Bridge World* magazine, under the direction of Edgar Kaplan. The purpose was to ascertain the current bidding trends among experts. Principal features include STRONG NOTRUMPS, FIVE-CARD MAJORS (exceptionally, a strong four-card major may be opened with a convenient rebid), LIMIT RAISES, STRONG ARTIFICIAL TWO-CLUB OPENING, and WEAK TWO-BIDS were voted in. Also, various conventions, such as NEGATIVE DOUBLES, RESPONSIVE DOUBLES, PREEMPTIVE RERAISES, and TRUSCOTT TWO NOTRUMP were voted in.

BROZEL. A method of competing against an opponent's 1 NT opening, as devised by Bernard Zeller of West Orange, N.J. A double is used to show a one-suited hand. If partner does not wish to defend, he removes the double to 2 ♣, then doubler can pass (with clubs) or bid his real suit. The overcalls of 1 NT are described below:

2 ♣ shows clubs and hearts.
2 ◊ shows diamonds and hearts.
2 ♡ shows hearts and spades.
2 ♠ shows spades and a minor suit (partner may respond 2 NT to ask for the minor).
2 NT shows clubs and diamonds.
3 ♣, 3 ◊, 3 ♡, or 3 ♠ shows a three-suited hand with a singleton or void in the suit bid. NOTE: Some players prefer to play this as a natural bid instead.

[Defense to]
See page *27* for our recommended defense.

CANAPE. A bidding treatment whereby one's longest suit is typically bid on the second round. For example, an opening bid of 1 ♡, followed by a rebid of 2 ◊, would suggest at least five diamonds and a shorter heart suit. Canape was invented by Pierre Albarran of France and was adopted by many of the ITALIAN TEAM SYSTEMS. On the American continent, however, it has found little following.

CHEAPER MINOR FOR TAKEOUT. A modification of the FISHBEIN defense to preemptive opening bids of two and three of a suit. A bid in the cheaper minor suit is equivalent to a TAKEOUT DOUBLE of opener's suit. A double is for penalty. For example, over a 3 ♡ opening bid, an overcall of 4 ♣ is artificial, asking partner to choose from among the three unbid suits. *See also* SMITH.

CHEAPER MINOR SECOND NEGATIVE. *See* SECOND NEGATIVE.

CHECKBACK STAYMAN. The use of a 2 ♣ bid, after opener's rebid of 1 NT, as a delayed form of STAYMAN. Essentially, this asks opener to show a four-card major or three-card support for responder's bid major. For example:

Partner	You		
		♠	A K 9 3 2
		♡	8 6
1 ♣	1 ♠	◇	A 10 4
1 NT	2 ♣	♣	7 4 3

Your 2 ♣ bid is completely artificial, and asks partner to show a four-card heart suit or three-card spade support. Having neither, partner should rebid 2 ◇.

See NEW MINOR FORCING for a more popular treatment.

COLORFUL CUE-BID. A variation of the MICHAELS CUE-BID, invented by Dorothy Hayden Truscott of New York City, in which a direct cue-bid of an enemy opening bid of one of a suit is used to show a two-suiter of the opposite color. That is:

2 ♣ over 1 ♣ shows both red suits.
2 ◇ over 1 ◇ shows both black suits.
2 ♡ over 1 ♡ shows both black suits.
2 ♠ over 1 ♠ shows both red suits.

[Defense to]
See page 83 for our recommended defense.

COMPETITIVE DOUBLES. Doubles of low-level suit contracts, after partner has already bid or doubled, to show the values necessary to compete but no clear-cut bid. Generally, the bidding is at the two-level and the enemy has raised a suit. *See page 87 for a complete description.*

CONSTRUCTIVE MAJOR RAISES. The use of a single raise of partner's major-suit opening bid to show about 10 to 12 points. This treatment is characteristic of the ROTH-STONE system, in which weaker raises are shown by first bidding ONE NOTRUMP FORCING.

CONTROL ASKING BID. A form of ASKING BID to inquire about control of a specific suit, usually the suit bid by asker. *See page 205 for our recommended version.*

CONTROL-SHOWING BID. A method of probing for slam by bidding a suit in which a control (ace, king, singleton, or void) is held. Commonly called a "cue-bid," this technique

is the cornerstone of accurate slam bidding. *See page 180 for complete coverage.*

CONTROL SWISS. *See* SWISS.

CONTROLLED PSYCHICS. The systemic use of PSYCHIC BIDS, as advocated in the original KAPLAN-SHEINWOLD and ROTH-STONE systems. An opening bid of one of a suit may be made on a hand of about 3 to 6 high-card points (mostly concentrated in the suit bid). Certain responses are unconditionally forcing, after which opener reveals his "psych" by making a designated rebid.

CONVENIENT MINORS. The popular practice of opening the bidding in a three-card minor suit when the hand contains no "biddable" major suit. This is especially common by the practitioners of FIVE-CARD MAJORS. *See also* SHORT CLUB.

COOPERATIVE DOUBLES. *See* COMPETITIVE DOUBLES.

CUE-BID LIMIT RAISE. A method of indicating support for opener's suit after an enemy suit overcall. A cue-bid of the enemy suit shows the equivalent of a LIMIT RAISE (or better) in opener's suit. This allows WEAK JUMP RAISES to be used. For example:

Partner	Opp.	You
1 ♠	2 ◇	3 ◇

♠ K 9 5 4
♡ A 7 5
◇ 8 2
♣ K 8 7 3

Your 3 ◇ cue-bid promises the values to jump to 3 ♠. Had you bid 3 ♠ yourself, that would be weak.

Some players also employ this strategy after partner has made an overcall. That is, a cue-bid of opener's suit is used to show a LIMIT RAISE of overcaller's suit. For a more popular treatment, *see* INVITATIONAL CUE-BID.

CUE-BID ONE-ROUND FORCE. *See* INVITATIONAL CUE-BID.

CUE-BID STAYMAN. A method of employing the STAYMAN convention after partner has made a 1 NT overcall. A cue-bid in the enemy suit asks partner to bid an unbid four-card major suit. For example:

Opp.	Partner	Opp.	You
1 ◇	1 NT	P	2 ◇

♠ Q J 9 8
♡ A 10 8 3
◇ 4 3
♣ J 10 2

Your 2 ◇ bid is "Stayman." Without a major suit, partner should rebid 2 NT with a minimum, or 3 NT with a maximum.

Cue-bid Stayman may also be applied after partner has opened the bidding with 1 NT, and right-hand opponent has overcalled. *See* page *4* for a description of this method.

CULBERTSON. A bidding system developed by the late Ely Culbertson that was the forerunner of GOREN and STANDARD AMERICAN. Principal features include "honor trick" evaluation, standards for "biddable" suits, APPROACH-FORCING, STRONG NOTRUMPS, and STRONG TWO-BIDS. The system is rarely played in its entirety today, although many of its ideas still remain popular.

CULBERTSON FOUR-FIVE NOTRUMP. A slam convention originated by Ely Culbertson to show, as well as ask for, aces and kings. A bid of 4 NT promises three aces, or two aces and the king of a suit genuinely bid by the partnership. The responses are:

5 of the lowest bid suit shows no aces.
5 of any other suit shows that ace.
5 NT shows two aces, or one ace and all the kings of suits genuinely bid.
6 of the lowest bid suit shows that ace.

This convention has dwindled in popularity since the invention of BLACKWOOD.

DECLARATIVE-INTERROGATIVE FOUR NOTRUMP. The use of a non-jump bid of 4 NT as a general slam try, rather than a request for aces. Over the "D.I." 4 NT, partner is invited to show some undisclosed feature, such as a first- or second-round control, or even a key queen. With nothing to show, partner simply returns to the agreed trump suit at the five-level.

DEFENSE TO BLACKWOOD INTERFERENCE. Any of a variety of methods to cope with enemy interference over BLACKWOOD (or GERBER). Each is commonly known by its acronym, e.g., D-O-P-I, P-O-D-I, D-E-P-O, etc. *See* page *191* for our recommended methods.

DEFENSE TO SPECIFIC CONVENTIONS. *See* appropriate convention, [Defense to].

DELAYED STAYMAN. *See* CHECKBACK STAYMAN.

DIRECTIONAL ASKING BID. The use of a low-level cue-bid in the enemy suit, after partner has already bid, to ask for a partial stopper, such as: K, Q-X; or J-X-X. This might allow a successful notrump contract to be reached when neither partner holds a true stopper, but in combination they do (e.g., Q-X opposite J-X-X). Compare with ALL-PURPOSE CUE-BID, WESTERN CUE-BID, and EASTERN CUE-BID.

DOUBLE-BARRELLED STAYMAN. A popular form of TWO-WAY STAYMAN, invented by David Carter of St. Louis, Mo., that utilizes both 2 ♣ and 2 ◇ to request a four-card major suit after partner's 1 NT opening bid. Two clubs is used on all hands that cannot guarantee game, and 2 ◇ creates a game force. After 2 ◇ Stayman, opener rebids in the following specialized manner:

2 ♡ or 2 ♠ shows that four-card suit.
2 NT shows four cards in each minor suit.
3 ♣, 3 ◇, 3 ♡, or 3 ♠ shows that five-card suit.
3 NT shows 4-3-3-3 shape (four-card suit being a minor).

DOUBLE FOR SACRIFICE. The use of a double of an enemy slam contract to suggest a sacrifice, or aid in that decision. *See* NEGATIVE SLAM DOUBLE and POSITIVE SLAM DOUBLE for the two principal variations.

DOUBLE NEGATIVE. *See* SECOND NEGATIVE.

DOUBLE OF ONE-NOTRUMP OPENING. As played by most partnerships, the double of a 1 NT opening bid is primarily for penalty, but partner may exercise his judgment to remove the double with a hand unsuitable for defense. *See* page *125* for a complete description.

[Defense to]

Some players, especially those who use WEAK NOTRUMPS, have certain rescue bids, or "runout" bids, available when their opening

1 NT bid is doubled by the enemy. Below is one such method:

Redouble shows a one-suited hand. No-trump bidder must bid 2 ♣, then responder can pass (with clubs) or correct to his real suit.

2 ♣ shows clubs and another suit.

2 ◇ shows diamonds and a major suit.

2 ♡ shows both major suits.

DRURY. A convention invented by the late Douglas Drury for responding to third- and fourth-seat major-suit opening bids. A response of 2 ♣ is unconditionally forcing. With a subminimum opening bid, opener must rebid 2 ◇ (artificial), after which responder can sign off at a low level. With a full opening bid, opener may make any other rebid. We recommend the variation known as REVERSE DRURY.

EASTERN CUE-BID. The use of a low-level cue-bid in the enemy suit, after partner has already bid, to show (rather than ask for) a stopper in the enemy suit. We have christened it with this name because it is the exact opposite of the WESTERN CUE-BID. *See* page 79 for our recommended use of this bid. *See also* ALL-PURPOSE CUE-BID and DIRECTIONAL ASKING BID.

EASTERN SCIENTIFIC. A bidding system very similar to ACES SCIENTIFIC that evolved primarily around the Philadelphia area. Robert Goldman and William Eisenberg were very instrumental in its development.

EXTREMES CUE-BID. *See* TOP-AND-BOTTOM CUE-BID.

FAST ARRIVAL. A principle whereby jump bids to a particular contract are weaker than gradual forcing bids to that same contract. This is self-evident in the theory of preemptive bidding, and the use of APPROACH-FORCING methods on good hands. Many experts employ this strategy whenever possible.

FEATURE-SHOWING. An extremely popular method of rebidding after a forcing 2 NT response to a WEAK TWO-BID. With a good weak two-bid, opener bids a side suit in which he holds a "feature" (ace, king, or

queen). With a poor weak two-bid, opener simply rebids his original suit, which suggests no "feature." *See* page *103* for a complete description. *See also* OGUST.

FISHBEIN. A defense to preemptive opening bids of two and three of a suit, as devised by the late Harry Fishbein. In direct position, a double is for penalty, and the cheapest possible suit overcall is equivalent to a TAKEOUT DOUBLE of opener's suit. For example, over a 3 ◇ opening bid, an overcall of 3 ♡ requests partner to choose from among hearts, spades, and clubs. Quite understandably, this convention never found much favor. A modification known as CHEAPER MINOR FOR TAKEOUT has acquired a little following. *See also* SMITH.

FISHER DOUBLE. A form of LEAD-DIRECTING DOUBLE of a final notrump contract, as invented by Dr. John Fisher of Dallas, Tex. When no natural suits have been bid, a double asks for a club lead except if a STAYMAN inquiry has been made; then it calls for a diamond lead.

FIVE-CARD MAJORS. A bidding treatment in which an opening bid of one of a major suit shows at least five cards. Many systems, such as KAPLAN-SHEINWOLD, ROTH-STONE, and EASTERN SCIENTIFIC, are founded on this principle. Without a five-card major, it is customary to open the bidding in a CONVENIENT MINOR, often three cards in length. *See also* FOUR-CARD MAJORS.

FLANNERY. An opening bid of 2 ◇ to show five hearts and four spades in a hand of about 11 to 15 high-card points, as invented by William Flannery of McKees Rocks, Pa. Responder may then sign off in two of a major, jump to three of a major to invite game, or bid 2 NT as a forcing inquiry. Over 2 NT, opener rebids in the following manner:

3 ♣ or 3 ◇ shows three cards in that suit.

3 ♡ shows a minimum hand with two-two in the minors.

3 ♠ shows a maximum hand with two-two in the minors.

3 NT shows a maximum hand with two-two in the minors, but with an honor in each minor suit.

4 ♣ or 4 ◇ shows four cards in that suit.

Flannery has found considerable popularity in the U.S., as an alternative to the

WEAK TWO-BID in diamonds. A few players have adopted the variation of opening 2 ♡ as Flannery, thus reserving 2 ◇ for some other purpose. The responses are identical, except responder just passes to sign off in hearts.

[Defense to]

Several methods have been devised for defending against Flannery. *See* page *175* for our recommendations.

FLINT. A response of 3 ◇ to an opening bid of 2 NT, devised by Jeremy Flint of England, to allow the partnership to stop below game when responder is very weak. Opener is obliged to rebid 3 ♡, after which responder may pass (with hearts) or sign off by bidding his real suit. For example:

Partner	You		
		♠	J 10 7 6 5
		♡	4
2 NT	3 ◇	◇	5 4 3
		♣	9 8 5 2

Partner must rebid 3 ♡; then you will correct to 3 ♠ to end the bidding.

A variation, known as "reverse Flint," or "Gladiator," employs a 3 ♣ response to initiate the sign-off (opener is forced to rebid 3 ◇). In that variation, it is customary to use a 3 ◇ response as STAYMAN.

FORCING RAISES. The use of a jump raise (from one to three) in opener's suit as a game-forcing bid, typically showing 13 to 16 points. This treatment is still considered to be STANDARD; however, LIMIT RAISES are gaining in popularity.

FORCING STAYMAN. *See* STAYMAN.

FORCING STYLE. A bidding philosophy that treats jump bids in notrump or previously bid suits as forcing. Compare with LIMIT STYLE. *See also* LIMIT BIDDING AFTER AN ENEMY OVERCALL.

FOUR-CARD MAJORS. A bidding treatment in which an opening bid of one of a major suit is often made with a four-card suit. As practiced in GOREN, STANDARD AMERICAN, JACOBY MODERN, and SCHENKEN, it is customary to have a "good" suit when opening a four-card major. *See also* FIVE-CARD MAJORS.

FOURTH SUIT FORCING. The use of a bid in the fourth suit by responder at his second turn, as an artificial convenient forcing bid. *See* page 56 for a complete description.

FRAGMENT BID. An unusual jump on the second round of bidding to show a "fragment" (typically three cards) in the suit bid, as invented by Monroe Ingberman of White Plains, N.Y. By inference, this shows a singleton or void in the fourth suit, and excellent trump support for partner's suit. For example:

♠	A Q 10 3	*You*	*Partner*
♡	7		
◇	A K 9 6 4	1 ◇	1 ♠
♣	A 10 3	4 ♣	

Your jump to 4 ♣ shows the values to raise to 4 ♠ and promises a singleton or void in hearts.

The fragment bid has been superseded in popularity by the SPLINTER BID, where the unusual jump is made in the short suit itself.

GAMBLING THREE-NOTRUMP OPENING. An opening bid of 3 NT to indicate a long minor suit, usually solid, as the main source of tricks. The number of outside stoppers required (if any) depends on partnership preference. We recommend the variation known as the ACOL THREE-NOTRUMP OPENING.

[Defense to]

See page *177* for our recommended defense.

GAME-TRIAL BIDS. *See* TRIAL BIDS.

GERBER. The popular use of a 4 ♣ bid to ask for aces, as invented by the late John Gerber of Houston, Tex. *See* page *192* for our recommended uses.

GLADIATOR. *See* FLINT.

GOREN. The bidding system developed by Charles Goren and publicized in his books since 1944. This has been the basis of STANDARD AMERICAN bidding for many years. Principal features include point-count evaluation, APPROACH-FORCING, STRONG NOTRUMPS, FOUR-CARD MAJORS on "biddable" suits, FORCING RAISES, and STRONG TWO-BIDS.

GRAND SLAM FORCE. A bid of 5 NT (not following BLACKWOOD) as an inquiry about trump honors, originated by the late Ely Culbertson. Partner is requested to bid a grand slam if holding any two of the three top honors. Most experts have other responses to show lesser trump holdings. *See page 197* for our recommended methods.

GRAND SLAM FORCE AFTER BLACK-WOOD. A method of employing the GRAND SLAM FORCE after a BLACKWOOD inquiry has been made, as invented by the late Walter Malowan. If Blackwood bidder bids six of the cheapest "unplayable" suit (usually 6 ♣), that becomes the grand slam force. *See page 198* for a complete description.

HELP-SUIT GAME TRY. A very slight variation of the LONG-SUIT GAME TRY, in which opener makes his TRIAL BID in a side suit needing help. *See also* WEAK-SUIT GAME TRY.

HERBERT NEGATIVE. The use of the cheapest possible suit bid as a NEGATIVE RESPONSE to partner's forcing bid. Developed by Walter Herbert of Austria, this idea can be applied to a variety of bidding situations. *See also* ONE-DIAMOND NEGATIVE RESPONSE, TWO-DIAMOND RESPONSE TO STRONG ARTIFICIAL TWO-CLUB OPENING, and SECOND NEGATIVE.

HIGHER-SUITS CUE-BID. A variation of the MICHAELS CUE-BID in which a direct cue-bid of an enemy opening bid of one of a suit shows the two higher unbid suits. That is:

2 ♣ over 1 ♣ shows hearts and spades.
2 ◇ over 1 ◇ shows hearts and spades.
2 ♡ over 1 ♡ shows diamonds and spades.
2 ♠ over 1 ♠ shows diamonds and hearts.
[Defense to]

See page 83 for our recommended defense.

IMPOSSIBLE NEGATIVE. A highlight of the PRECISION system which allows responder to describe a POSITIVE RESPONSE with 4-4-4-1 shape after the ONE CLUB FORCING opening bid. Responder first gives the ONE-DIAMOND NEGATIVE RESPONSE; then, at his next turn, he jumps the bidding in his singleton. This strange turn of events indicates that responder "lied" with his first bid, hence the term "impossible."

INTERMEDIATE JUMP OVERCALLS. The use of a jump overcall in a suit to show a hand approximately equivalent to a minimum opening bid, with at least a good six-card suit. For example:

Opp.	You		♠ A Q J 10 5 4
			♡ A 7 3
1 ◇	2 ♠		◇ 7
			♣ Q 7 4

Compare with STRONG JUMP OVERCALLS and WEAK JUMP OVERCALLS.

INTERMEDIATE TWO-BIDS. *See* ACOL TWO-BIDS.

INVERTED MINOR RAISES. A treatment in which a single minor raise is forcing and a jump minor raise is weak, as practiced in the KAPLAN-SHEINWOLD system. This "inverts" the STANDARD meanings of the two bids. *See page 41* for a complete description.

INVISIBLE CUE-BIDS. A general defense to all varieties of two-suited overcalls after partner has opened the bidding with one of a suit. We coined this title, since it involves "cue-bidding" an enemy suit that has been implied rather than truly bid. That is, the base on which the cue-bid is founded is "invisible." *See page 83* for a complete description.

INVITATIONAL CUE-BID. A cue-bid in the enemy suit, after partner has overcalled, used as a one-round force instead of the traditional game force. As developed by Lawrence Rosler of Murray Hill, N.J. and Roger Stern of New York City, this is usually played in conjunction with WEAK JUMP RAISES, and is very popular in expert circles. *See page 149* for a complete description.

IRREGULAR REDOUBLE. *See* REDOUBLE IMPLIES NO FIT.

ITALIAN TEAM SYSTEMS. Any of the various bidding methods of the highly successful Italian Blue Team. All are based on the ONE CLUB FORCING concept. Those with the most current following (and listed separately) are: BLUE TEAM CLUB, ROMAN CLUB, and SUPER PRECISION.

JACOBY MODERN. A bidding system developed by Oswald and James Jacoby of Dallas, Tex. in the early 1970's. Principal features include FOUR-CARD MAJORS on "good" suits, STRONG NOTRUMPS with JACOBY TRANSFER BIDS, LIMIT RAISES, JACOBY TWO NOTRUMP, STRONG ARTIFICIAL TWO-CLUB OPENING with STEP RESPONSES to show point count, and WEAK TWO-BIDS.

JACOBY TRANSFER BIDS. A very popular method of responding to notrump opening bids, as invented by Oswald Jacoby of Dallas, Tex. Over partner's 1 NT opening bid, a response of 2 ◇ shows hearts, and 2 ♡ shows spades. Notrump bidder then completes the transfer by bidding two of responder's major suit. *See* page 7 for complete coverage.

JACOBY TWO NOTRUMP. The use of a 2 NT response as an artificial "FORCING RAISE" of partner's major-suit opening bid, developed by Oswald Jacoby of Dallas, Tex. Over 2 NT, opener must describe his hand as follows:

3 of a new suit shows that singleton or void.
3 of agreed major shows 16 or more points.
3 NT shows 14 or 15 points.
4 of a new suit shows five cards in that suit.
4 of agreed major shows a bare minimum opening bid.

This method has found considerable popularity in the U.S.

JORDAN. *See* TRUSCOTT TWO NOTRUMP.

JUMP CUE-BID LIMIT RAISE. A method of responding to partner's overcall, which utilizes a jump cue-bid in the enemy suit to show a LIMIT RAISE of partner's suit. As a consequence, WEAK JUMP RAISES apply. For example:

Opp.	Partner	Opp.	You
1 ◇	1 ♠	P	<u>3 ◇</u>

♠ Q 10 7 5
♡ A J 5 4
◇ 8 7 3
♣ A 9

Your jump to 3 ◇ shows the equivalent of a raise to 3 ♠. Had you jumped to 3 ♠ yourself, that would be weak.

See also INVITATIONAL CUE-BID *and* CUE-BID LIMIT RAISE.

JUMP CUE-BID OVERCALL. The use of a jump cue-bid in the enemy suit to show a strong one-suited hand (not in the opposing suit). For example, over a 1 ♡ opening bid, an immediate jump overcall of 3 ♡ shows a strong hand containing any suit but hearts. Partner's first duty is to respond 3 NT if holding a stopper in the enemy suit. *See* page 166 for a complete description.

JUMP REVERSE SHOWS SINGLETON. The artificial use of a jump-reverse rebid by opener to show a singleton. This is possible because most modern experts treat a simple-reverse rebid as 100% forcing. *See* page 50 for our recommended use.

JUMP SHIFT SHOWS FIT. The use of a jump-shift response to show both a real suit and a fit for partner's suit. The most popular application is by a passed hand. For example:

♠ K Q 7 3	*You*	*Partner*
♡ 5 4		
◇ 8 3	P	1 ♠
♣ A J 9 8 4	<u>3 ♣</u>	

You show a club suit and a spade fit.

Another application having some following is the jump-shift response to partner's overcall.

KAMIKAZE NOTRUMP. A super-weak 1 NT opening bid to show a balanced hand of 10 to 12 points, as developed by John Kierein. As its name implies, this bid is intended to stir up action, and creates some anxious moments for both sides. Nevertheless, the fact that few experts have adopted it suggests it may be but a passing fad.

[Defense to]

It is probably best to treat the Kamikaze notrump as you would a normal WEAK NO-TRUMP opening. *See* pages 126 and 160 for our recommended methods.

KANTAR CUE-BID. A specialized cue-bid proposed by Edwin Kantar of Los Angeles. After partner's opening bid of one of a suit, a direct cue-bid of an opposing overcall shows a three-suited hand (4-4-4-1 or 5-4-4-0 shape) with shortness in the enemy suit. The strength may be as little as 8 or 9 high-card points, but there is no upper limit. For example:

Partner	*Opp.*	*You*
1 ◇	1 ♠	<u>2 ♠</u>

♠ 5
♡ A 10 8 5
◇ A J 9 4
♣ 8 7 6 4

You show a singleton or void in spades, and at least four cards in every other suit.

KANTAR TWO CLUBS ONLY FORCE.
See CHECKBACK STAYMAN.

KAPLAN-SHEINWOLD. A bidding system developed by Edgar Kaplan of New York City and Alfred Sheinwold of Los Angeles that has withstood the test of time. It is still widely played both in full and in part. Principal features include WEAK NOTRUMPS, SOUND OPENING BIDS in the minor suits, FIVE-CARD MAJORS with ONE NOTRUMP FORCING, LIMIT MAJOR RAISES, INVERTED MINOR RAISES, STRONG ARTIFICIAL TWO-CLUB OPENING, and WEAK TWO-BIDS.

KEY-CARD BLACKWOOD. A method of responding to BLACKWOOD in which the king of the agreed trump suit is counted as an ace. Thus, there are five "key cards," and the responses are:

> 5 ♣ shows 0 or 4 key cards.
> 5 ♢ shows 1 or 5 key cards.
> 5 ♡ shows 2 key cards.
> 5 ♠ shows 3 key cards.

A more popular version is ROMAN KEY-CARD BLACKWOOD.

KEY-CARD GERBER. An adaptation of the responses to GERBER, based on the identical principles of KEY-CARD BLACKWOOD. *See also* ROMAN KEY-CARD GERBER.

LANDY. A popular defense to an opponent's 1 NT opening bid, originated by the late Alvin Landy. An overcall of 2 ♣ is an artificial takeout for the major suits. All other overcalls are natural. The simplicity of this device is most attractive. *See also* REVISED LANDY.

[Defense to]
See page 27 for our recommended defense.

LEAD-DIRECTING DOUBLE. Any of a variety of doubles whose basic purpose is to request a particular lead from partner, such as the LIGHTNER DOUBLE or the FISHER DOUBLE. *See page 128 for complete coverage.*

LEBENSOHL. A method of contending with an enemy suit overcall of partner's 1 NT opening bid, as invented by George Boehm of New York City. Essentially, it involves an artificial response of 2 NT which demands that opener bid 3 ♣ as a "relay" bid. Responder may then pass (with clubs) or sign off in his real suit. *See page 24 for a complete description.*

LEBENSOHL AFTER DOUBLE OF WEAK TWO-BID. A further application of the LEBENSOHL principle used after partner has made a TAKEOUT DOUBLE of an enemy WEAK TWO-BID. A response of 2 NT requires doubler to bid 3 ♣ (except with a very strong hand), then responder may pass (with clubs) or sign off. For example:

Opp.	Partner	Opp.	You
2 ♠	DBL	P	2 NT

> ♠ 9 4
> ♡ 7 6 3
> ♢ Q 9 7 6 3
> ♣ J 8 5

Your 2 NT bid is artificial, requesting partner to bid 3 ♣, after which you will bid 3 ♢ to show a weak hand.

Quite obviously, the failure to engage the Lebensohl 2 NT bid gives a constructive meaning to three-level suit responses to partner's takeout double.

LIGHT OPENING BIDS. A bidding philosophy that lowers the requirements for opening bids of one of a suit. As most commonly practiced, this involves reducing the STANDARD AMERICAN requirements by about one point; rarely, two points. Compare with SOUND OPENING BIDS.

LIGHT PREEMPTS. A liberal philosophy of preemptive opening bids, as practiced by many tournament players. The vulnerability, of course, is the prime consideration. The following table illustrates the most popular strategy:

Vulnerability	Overbid by
Unfavorable	2 tricks
Equal	3 tricks
Favorable	3 to 5 tricks

Compare with SOUND PREEMPTS.

LIGHTNER DOUBLE. A form of LEAD-DIRECTING DOUBLE made of a voluntarily bid slam contract, as originated by Theodore Lightner of New York City. Its purpose is to request an unusual lead, often the dummy's first-bid side suit. *See page 131 for a complete description.*

LIMIT BIDDING AFTER AN ENEMY OVERCALL. An effective bidding agreement that dictates switching from a FORCING STYLE to a LIMIT STYLE only after an enemy overcall. *See* page 76 for a complete description.

LIMIT MAJOR RAISES. The popular practice of using LIMIT RAISES in the major suits only. *See* page 31 for a complete description.

LIMIT RAISES. The use of a jump raise (from one to three) in opener's suit as an invitation to game, rather than the traditional game force. Typically, this bid shows about 10 to 12 points. *See also* LIMIT MAJOR RAISES.

LIMIT STYLE. A bidding philosophy that treats jump bids in notrump and previously bid suits as invitational to game, rather than forcing. This is the opposite of a FORCING STYLE. *See also* LIMIT BIDDING AFTER AN ENEMY OVERCALL.

LIMIT TWO-NOTRUMP RESPONSE. The use of a 2 NT response to partner's opening bid of one of a suit as an invitation to game, instead of a game force. This bid shows about 11 or 12 points. Advocates of this treatment typically employ a 3 NT response to show 13 to 15 points.

LONG-SUIT GAME TRY. The most common form of TRIAL BID. After a single major raise, a bid is made in a side suit containing length (at least three cards) as a means of inviting game. This additional information may help responder evaluate his hand. *See* page 54 for a complete description.

MALOWAN. *See* GRAND SLAM FORCE AFTER BLACKWOOD.

MATCH-POINT PRECISION. A modified version of the PRECISION system developed by C.C. Wei and Ron Andersen of New York City. The most significant difference (from regular Precision) is the catch-all 1 ◇ opening bid, made on a variety of hands, with or without a diamond suit. The system also includes some new specialized gadgetry.

MATHE ASKING BID. A device to inquire about a singleton or void after a LIMIT MAJOR RAISE to the three-level, as invented by Lewis Mathe of Los Angeles. The cheapest possible rebid (3 ♠ or 3 NT) is completely artificial, and asks partner to bid the suit of his singleton or void. *See* page 203 for a complete description.

MAXIMAL OVERCALL DOUBLE. The use of a double as a game try, when the enemy interference precludes the use of any TRIAL BID after partner has made a single raise of your suit. *See* page 91 for a complete description.

MEXICAN TWO DIAMONDS. An opening bid of 2 ◇ to show a balanced hand of 19 to 21 points, as invented by Dr. George Rosenkranz of Mexico City and used in his "Romex" system. The responses are mostly artificial, involving numerous transfer bids.

MICHAELS CUE-BID. An extremely popular use of the direct cue-bid of an enemy opening bid of one of a suit, as invented by the late Mike Michaels. Cue-bidder promises a two-suited hand, as described below:

2 ♣ over 1 ♣ shows hearts and spades.
2 ◇ over 1 ◇ shows hearts and spades.
2 ♡ over 1 ♡ shows spades and either minor suit.
2 ♠ over 1 ♠ shows hearts and either minor suit.

Partner of cue-bidder simply chooses between the suits shown. In the latter two cases above, a response of 2 NT is used to ask for the unknown minor suit. *See* page 143 for complete coverage.

[Defense to]
See page 83 for our recommended defense.

MINI-ROMAN TWO DIAMONDS. A weaker variation of the ROMAN TWO DIAMONDS opening. An opening bid of 2 ◇ shows about 11 to 15 high-card points, and an undisclosed three-suited hand. The responses are similar to those to the Roman 2 ◇.

[Defense to]
See page 175 for our recommended defense.

MINI-SPLINTER BID. A variation of the SPLINTER BID, with the difference being that the strength promised is merely invitational to game, rather than forcing to game. Some players give this meaning to a jump-shift response by a passed hand. For example:

♠ A 6 5	*You*	*Partner*
♡ K J 9 7		
◇ 5	P	1 ♡
♣ 10 7 5 4 3	3 ◇	

Your jump to 3 ◇ shows a LIMIT RAISE *in hearts, with a singleton or void in diamonds.*

Another application of the mini-splinter bid is a jump cue-bid in the enemy suit after partner has overcalled. *See page 153* for an explanation.

MINOR-SUIT STAYMAN. A method of asking for a four-card minor suit after partner's opening bid of 1 NT. When JACOBY TRANSFER BIDS are used, a response of 2 ♠ often is used for this purpose. *See* page *15* for our recommended methods.

MINOR-SUIT TRANSFER BIDS. Any of several methods of transferring to the minor suits after partner's opening bid of 1 NT, very much as JACOBY TRANSFER BIDS work for the major suits. *See* page *20* for our recommended methods.

MULTICOLORED TWO DIAMONDS. An opening bid of 2 ◇, originated in England, that contains multiple possible meanings. One variation allows for three different kinds of hands, as described below:

1. WEAK TWO-BID in hearts.
2. WEAK TWO-BID in spades.
3. ROMAN TWO DIAMONDS (strong three-suiter).

A response of 2 ♡ is customarily played as a NEGATIVE RESPONSE, after which opener will pass with hand (1); correct to 2 ♠ with hand (2); or make some other rebid with hand (3).

[Defense to]
See page *175* for our recommended defense.

MURRAY TWO DIAMONDS. A variation of TWO-WAY STAYMAN developed by Eric Murray of Toronto, Canada. A response of 2 ◇ to partner's 1 NT opening bid requests opener to bid his longer major suit. Responder may then pass (with a weak major two-suiter) or continue with 2 NT (game-forcing) to ask for four-card suits up the line. Compare with AUGUST TWO DIAMONDS.

NAMYATS. "Stayman" spelled backwards. *See* TRANSFER PREEMPTS.

NATURAL CUE-BID. The use of an overcall in the enemy suit to show a real suit, rather than as an artificial takeout bid. This treatment has found some popularity in the minor suits, since a 1 ♣ or 1 ◇ opening is often made on a non-existent suit. Also, many players apply this strategy when the enemy has bid two suits. For example:

Opp.	Partner	Opp.	You
1 ◇	P	1 ♡	<u>2 ♡</u>

> ♠ 7 5
> ♡ A K J 10 7 5
> ◇ 7 3
> ♣ K 8 2

Your 2 ♡ bid may be used to show a real suit. Similarly, some players would treat a 2 ◇ overcall the same way.

NATURAL TWO-CLUB OPENING. An opening bid of 2 ♣ to show a real club suit, typically in a hand of about 11 to 16 high-card points. This is the popular treatment in virtually every ONE CLUB FORCING system, since the 1 ♣ opening is artificial. A response of 2 ◇ is usually played as some form of artificial inquiry.

NEGATIVE DOUBLES. The use of a double by responder as a TAKEOUT DOUBLE after partner's opening bid of one of a suit has been overcalled by an opponent. This was invented by Alvin Roth of New York City, and originally christened "Sputnik." The negative double normally shows four cards in an unbid major suit, to facilitate the search for a four-four fit. *See* page *68* for complete coverage.

NEGATIVE FREE BIDS. The use of a new-suit response to partner's opening bid of one of a suit, after an opposing overcall, as a nonforcing limited bid. Stronger hands are shown by first making a NEGATIVE DOUBLE, then bidding your suit at your next turn. This is the exact opposite of STANDARD practice. For example:

Partner	Opp.	You
1 ♠	2 ♣	<u>2 ♡</u>

> ♠ 6 2
> ♡ A Q J 9 7
> ◇ 9 8 2
> ♣ 7 6 3

Your 2 ♡ response shows less than 10 points and is not forcing. To force the bidding, you must double 2 ♣, then bid your hearts later.

NEGATIVE RESPONSE. Any response to partner's forcing bid that, by agreement, is artificial and promises no real values. *See* TWO-DIAMOND RESPONSE TO STRONG ARTIFICIAL

TWO-CLUB OPENING, TWO-NOTRUMP NEGA-
TIVE RESPONSE, ONE-DIAMOND NEGATIVE RE-
SPONSE, HERBERT NEGATIVE, and SECOND
NEGATIVE. Compare with POSITIVE RESPONSE.

NEGATIVE SLAM DOUBLE. The double
of an enemy slam contract, after doubler's
side has bid and raised a suit preemptively, to
suggest a sacrifice. As developed by Ira Rubin
of Paramus, N.J., the double (direct or balancing position) shows zero defensive tricks!
Partner must then sacrifice, unless he can defeat the slam. A pass of a slam bid, by inference, always shows one or more defensive
tricks. Compare with the POSITIVE SLAM DOU-
BLE.

NEW MINOR FORCING. The use of a bid
in an unbid minor suit by responder as an
artificial convenient forcing bid after a 1 NT
rebid by the opening bidder. *See page 61* for
a complete description.

**NEW SUIT FORCING AT THE ONE-
LEVEL.** A popular treatment after an enemy
TAKEOUT DOUBLE of partner's opening bid of
one of a suit. A new-suit response at the one-
level is unlimited and forcing, just as if the
double had not occurred. *See page 74* for a
complete description.

NONFORCING STAYMAN. *See* STAYMAN.

OGUST. A very popular method of rebidding after a forcing 2 NT response to a WEAK
TWO-BID, as invented by the late Harold
Ogust. Weak two-bidder describes both his
suit quality and relative strength in the following manner:

3 ♣ shows a poor suit and minimum
    strength.
3 ♢ shows a poor suit and maximum
    strength.
3 ♡ shows a good suit and minimum
    strength.
3 ♠ shows a good suit and maximum
    strength.

All of the above rebids are completely artificial and have nothing to do with opener's
holding in the suit actually bid. Some players
prefer to reverse the meanings of the 3 ♢ and
3 ♡ rebids. *See also* FEATURE-SHOWING.

ONE CLUB FORCING. The use of 1 ♣ as
the strong, artificial, forcing opening bid

(usually at least 16 or 17 high-card points), as
originated in the VANDERBILT CLUB system.
The underlying principle is to allow the maximum possible room for the bidding of strong
hands, as well as to limit the strength of other
one-bids. Virtually all such systems also employ the ONE-DIAMOND NEGATIVE RESPONSE
and the NATURAL TWO-CLUB OPENING. *See
also* PRECISION, SCHENKEN, MATCH-POINT PRE-
CISION, and the ITALIAN TEAM SYSTEMS.

[Defense to]
Many varieties of defensive strategy have
been invented for use over ONE CLUB FORC-
ING. Two of the most popular are described
below. NOTE: Each of these devices also applies after the ONE-DIAMOND NEGATIVE RE-
SPONSE.

Simplified. A double shows both major
suits, and 1 NT shows both minor suits. This
has been adopted by many players for the
sake of simplicity.

Truscott Defense. Invented by Alan Truscott of New York City, this method is more
complicated, but allows all one-suiters and
two-suiters to be shown. One-suited hands
are shown by making a jump overcall. Two-
suited hands can then be described as follows:

Non-jump suit bids show the suit bid plus
    the next higher suit.
Double shows the suit doubled plus the
    non-touching suit.
1 NT shows the remaining two non-touch-
    ing suits.

We recommend an "inverted" form of the
Truscott defense, which is described in detail
on *page 169*.

ONE-DIAMOND NEGATIVE RESPONSE.
The use of 1 ♢ as an artificial weakness-
showing response to a strong, artificial, forcing 1 ♣ opening, as advocated in virtually
every ONE CLUB FORCING system.

[Defense to]
See ONE CLUB FORCING, [Defense to].

ONE NOTRUMP FORCING. The use of a
1 NT response to partner's major-suit opening bid as a one-round force, as introduced in
the KAPLAN-SHEINWOLD and ROTH-STONE systems. The purpose is to allow a more thorough investigation by assuring responder of a

second opportunity to bid. *See* page *33* for a complete description.

ONE-TWO-THREE STOP. *See* PREEMPTIVE RERAISES.

OPTIONAL DOUBLE. A double that is neither for penalty nor takeout, but leaves the decision on whether to bid or defend up to doubler's partner. The most practical use of this kind of double is after an enemy preemptive bid of four in a major suit. *See* page *123* for a complete description.

PINPOINT ASTRO. A variation of the ASTRO convention, attempting to "pinpoint" the suits actually held. After an enemy 1 NT opening bid, all two-level overcalls show two-suiters, as follows:

2 ♣ shows clubs and hearts.
2 ◇ shows diamonds and hearts.
2 ♡ shows hearts and spades.
2 ♠ shows spades and a minor suit (partner may respond 2 NT to ask for the minor).

Insofar as the above overcalls are concerned, this convention is identical to BROZEL.

[Defense to]
See page *27* for our recommended defense.

POSITIVE DOUBLE. The use of a double of an enemy overcall to show a POSITIVE RESPONSE. This treatment is popular in SCHENKEN and other ONE CLUB FORCING systems when the 1 ♣ opening bid meets with interference.

POSITIVE RESPONSE. Any response to partner's forcing bid that, by agreement, promises specific high-card values. This is associated primarily with responding to ONE CLUB FORCING or the STRONG ARTIFICIAL TWO-CLUB OPENING. *See* page *94* for our recommended use with regard to the latter. Compare with NEGATIVE RESPONSE.

POSITIVE SLAM DOUBLE. The double of an enemy slam contract, after doubler's side has bid and raised a suit preemptively, to aid in the decision whether or not to sacrifice. A direct double indicates you can defeat the slam (normal interpretation), but a balancing double shows exactly one defensive trick, leaving the final decision up to partner. Compare with the NEGATIVE SLAM DOUBLE.

PRECISION. A bidding system invented by C.C. Wei of New York City (formerly of Nationalist China) that has gained considerable popularity in the U.S. Principal features include ONE CLUB FORCING (16+ high-card points), WEAK NOTRUMPS (13 to 15 points), FIVE-CARD MAJORS with ONE NOTRUMP FORCING, and WEAK TWO-BIDS in the majors only. The system also introduced a variety of ASKING BIDS to inquire about trump quality, controls, and aces. *See also* MATCH-POINT PRECISION, SUPER PRECISION, PRECISION TWO DIAMONDS, IMPOSSIBLE NEGATIVE, and UNUSUAL POSITIVE.

PRECISION TWO DIAMONDS. An opening bid of 2 ◇ to indicate a three-suited hand of 11 to 15 high-card points, specifically with shortness in diamonds, as advocated in the PRECISION system. As originally developed, a response of 3 ◇ was used as an artificial force for further clarification, although many players now employ 2 NT for that purpose.

[Defense to]
See page *175* for our recommended defense.

PREEMPTIVE RERAISES. The use of a reraise to the three-level, after a single raise, as a preemptive or competitive bid, rather than the traditional invitation to game. This treatment applies with or without interference. *See* page *54* for a complete description.

PSYCHIC BIDS [*never, rare, occasional,* or *frequent*]. The relative frequency in which a partnership employs "psychic" bids. A psychic bid is a bid that, by intention, grossly misrepresents one's hand with regard to high-card strength or suit length. Most players "rarely" use such bids, as the danger that partner will be the victim generally outweighs the chances of fooling the enemy. *See also* CONTROLLED PSYCHICS.

PSYCHIC CONTROLS. *See* CONTROLLED PSYCHICS.

PUPPET STAYMAN. A unique variation of STAYMAN, invented by Kit Woolsey of Arlington, Va. The 2 ♣ response to partner's opening bid of 1 NT forces opener to rebid 2 ◇ (except to show a five-card major suit), then responder continues in the following manner.

2 ♡ shows a four-card *spade* suit.
2 ♠ shows a four-card *heart* suit.

2 NT shows both four-card majors and invitational strength.

3 NT shows both four-card majors and game-going strength.

The main advantage of this procedure is to allow opener to become declarer without divulging any information about opener's hand. The defenders' tasks are thus more difficult. A similar treatment may be used over a 2 NT opening bid.

RAISE ONLY NON-FORCE [R-O-N-F]. A method of responding to WEAK TWO-BIDS which utilizes both 2 NT and a new suit as forcing responses. Hence, a raise of opener's suit is the only nonforcing response below game.

REDOUBLE IMPLIES NO FIT. The use of a redouble of an enemy TAKEOUT DOUBLE of partner's opening bid of one of a suit to show a defensively oriented hand, i.e., usually containing no fit for opener's suit. This is used primarily in conjunction with the TRUSCOTT TWO NOTRUMP bid. *See* page 75 for a complete description.

RESCUE BIDS. *See* DOUBLE OF ONE-NO-TRUMP OPENING, [Defense to].

RESPONSIVE DOUBLE. The use of a double for takeout, after partner has made a TAKEOUT DOUBLE or suit overcall, and right-hand opponent has raised the suit bid by opener. This was invented by Dr. F. Fielding-Reid of Dania, Fla. *See* page *156* for complete coverage.

REVERSE-BIDDING STRUCTURE. *See* STRUCTURED REVERSES.

REVERSE DRURY. An improved variation of the DRURY convention that "reverses" the meanings of opener's rebids. After the 2 ♣ response to a third- or fourth-seat major-suit opening bid, opener continues in the following manner:

2 ◇ shows a full opening bid. This is completely artificial.

2 of the same major shows a subminimum opening bid.

See page *51* for a complete description.

REVERSE FLINT. *See* FLINT.

REVISED LANDY. A modification of the LANDY convention. After an enemy opening bid of 1 NT, minor-suit overcalls are used as follows:

2 ♣ shows both minors.

2 ◇ shows both majors.

[Defense to]

See page *27* for our recommended defense.

RIPSTRA. A defense to an enemy opening bid of 1 NT, as invented by J.G. Ripstra of Wichita, Kan. Overcalls in either minor suit are major-suit takeouts, but with this distinction:

2 ♣ shows both majors, with clubs equal to or longer than diamonds.

2 ◇ shows both majors, with diamonds longer than clubs.

[Defense to]

See page *27* for our recommended defense.

ROMAN. An ITALIAN TEAM SYSTEM developed by Walter Avarelli and Giorgio Belladonna. Principal features include ONE CLUB FORCING (but not necessarily strong), super-strong 1 NT opening (17 to 20 points), CANAPE style, and a variety of ASKING BIDS. Other features and offspring are listed separately below.

ROMAN BLACKWOOD. A variation in responding to BLACKWOOD that will sometimes determine which ace is missing (when the partnership holds three aces). The responses are:

5 ♣ shows 0 or 3 aces.

5 ◇ shows 1 or 4 aces.

5 ♡ shows 2 aces of the same color or adjacent in rank.

5 ♠ shows 2 unlike aces (clubs/hearts or diamonds/spades).

See ROMAN KEY-CARD BLACKWOOD for a more popular method.

ROMAN GERBER. An adaptation of the responses to GERBER to correspond to those of ROMAN BLACKWOOD.

ROMAN JUMP OVERCALLS. The use of a jump overcall, after an enemy opening bid of one of a suit, to show a two-suited hand containing the suit bid plus the next higher suit. The strength is typically that of a minimum opening bid. For example, over an enemy

1 ◇ opening:

2 ♡ shows hearts and spades.

2 ♠ shows spades and clubs.

3 ♣ shows clubs and diamonds.

Most practitioners of Roman jump over-calls also use a jump overcall of 2 NT to show a strong, undisclosed two-suiter.

[Defense to]

See page 83 for our recommended defense.

ROMAN KEY-CARD BLACKWOOD. A combination of the advantages of KEY-CARD BLACKWOOD and ROMAN BLACKWOOD. The king of the agreed trump suit is counted as an ace, making a total of five "key cards." Several variations are played, but the following responses are the most popular:

5 ♣ shows 0 or 3 key cards.

5 ◇ shows 1 or 4 key cards.

5 ♡ shows 2 or 5 key cards, without the trump queen.

5 ♠ shows 2 or 5 key cards, with the trump queen.

ROMAN KEY-CARD GERBER. An adaptation of the responses to GERBER to correspond to those of ROMAN KEY-CARD BLACKWOOD.

ROMAN TWO CLUBS. An opening bid of 2 ♣ to show a three-suited hand of 12 to 16 high-card points. The responses are similar to those to the more popular ROMAN TWO DIAMONDS.

[Defense to]

See page 175 for our recommended defense.

ROMAN TWO DIAMONDS. An opening bid of 2 ◇ to show a three-suited hand of 17 to 20 high-card points. A response of 2 NT is constructive and demands that opener bid his short suit, thus pinpointing his three suits. Minimum suit responses are natural and not forcing, but opener must make the cheapest available rebid if responder has bid his short suit.

[Defense to]

See page 175 for our recommended defense.

ROSENKRANZ REDOUBLE. A method devised by Dr. George Rosenkranz of Mexico City to indicate an honor (ace, king, or queen) in partner's suit, after the enemy has made a NEGATIVE DOUBLE of his overcall. For example:

Opp.	Partner	Opp.	You
1 ◇	1 ♠	DBL*	RDBL

♠ K 7 2
♡ 8 4
◇ 9 5 3 2
♣ Q 9 7 4

*Negative.

Your redouble shows a high spade honor. In contrast, any other action would deny same.

Some players also employ a "Rosenkranz double," in which a double of a bid by right-hand opponent shows an honor in partner's suit.

ROTH-STONE. A highly successful bidding system developed by Alvin Roth and Tobias Stone of New York City. Principal features include SOUND OPENING BIDS, STRONG NO-TRUMPS with ROTH TWO DIAMONDS, FIVE-CARD MAJORS with ONE NOTRUMP FORCING, CONSTRUCTIVE MAJOR RAISES, WEAK JUMP-SHIFT RESPONSES, STRONG ARTIFICIAL TWO-CLUB OPENING with positive 2 ◇ response, and WEAK TWO-BIDS. Many of the system's ideas have been adopted by STANDARD bidders over the years.

ROTH-STONE ASTRO. A variation of the ASTRO convention, as used in the ROTH-STONE system. After an enemy opening bid of 1 NT, the following agreements apply:

Double shows hearts and spades.

2 ♣ shows clubs and spades.

2 ◇ shows diamonds and spades.

2 ♡ or 2 ♠ shows that suit.

2 NT shows clubs and diamonds.

3 ♣ shows clubs and hearts.

3 ◇ shows diamonds and hearts.

[Defense to]

See page 27 for our recommended defense.

ROTH TWO DIAMONDS. A variation of DOUBLE-BARRELLED STAYMAN, as devised by Alvin Roth of New York City. A response of 2 ◇ to partner's opening bid of 1 NT is not only game-forcing Stayman, but also indicates slam interest.

SAN FRANCISCO. A variation of BLACK-WOOD which enables the showing of aces and kings with one bid. A point value is assigned (ace=2, king=1), and the responses are:

5 ♣ shows 0 to 2 points.
5 ◇ shows 3 points.
5 ♡ shows 4 points.
5 ♠ shows 5 points.
5 NT shows 6 points, etc.

By inspecting his own hand, the 4 NT bidder can usually tell what the response represents in aces and kings.

SCHENKEN. A bidding system developed by the late Howard Schenken and commonly known as the "Big Club." Principal features include ONE CLUB FORCING (17+ high-card points), STRONG NOTRUMPS, FOUR-CARD MAJORS, LIMIT RAISES, and WEAK TWO-BIDS in the majors only. *See also* SCHENKEN TWO DIAMONDS and the UNUSUAL TWO-NOTRUMP OPENING.

SCHENKEN TWO DIAMONDS. An opening bid of 2 ◇ to ask for specific aces, as used in the SCHENKEN system. The responses are:

2 ♡ shows no aces.
2 ♠, 3 ♣, or 3 ◇ shows that ace.
2 NT shows the ace of hearts.
3 ♡, 3 ♠, 4 ♣, or 4 ◇ shows that ace plus the next lower suit ace.
3 NT shows two non-touching aces.

After any of the above responses, the cheapest step rebid by opener asks for kings in a similar manner. Any further cheapest step rebid asks for queens.

SECOND NEGATIVE. An artificial weakness-showing rebid by responder, after having made the TWO-DIAMOND RESPONSE TO STRONG ARTIFICIAL TWO-CLUB OPENING, in order to respect opener's forcing rebid. Many players employ a bid of 2 NT for this purpose. For example:

Partner	You		
		♠	5 4
		♡	10 8 6 4
2 ♣	2 ◇	◇	9 8 4 2
2 ♠	2 NT	♣	7 5 3

Your 2 NT rebid is a "nothing" bid, since you cannot pass 2 ♠.

An improved method is to use the "cheaper minor" suit (3 ♣ in the above auction) as the second negative. *See page 96 for a complete description.*

SHORT CLUB. A bidding philosophy in which an opening bid of 1 ♣, although not forcing, may be made on as little as a doubleton if opener's hand contains no other "biddable" suit. This treatment allows an opening bid of 1 ◇ to promise at least four cards. A more popular strategy is CONVENIENT MINORS.

[Defense to]

It is probably best to treat this as you would any other natural 1 ♣ opening bid. Even though it might be short, most of the time it isn't.

SHORT-SUIT GAME TRY. A unique form of TRIAL BID, in which opener's shortest suit (typically a singleton) is bid to invite game. For example:

		You	Partner
♠	A K 6 5 4		
♡	K J 7		
◇	3	1 ♠	2 ♠
♣	K J 7 4	3 ◇	

Your 3 ◇ rebid is a game try, indicating that diamonds is your shortest suit.

The short-suit game try allows very accurate evaluation, but the drawback is the information disclosed to the enemy (who are also listening). We recommend the LONG-SUIT GAME TRY.

SLAM-TRY STAYMAN. *See* ROTH TWO DIAMONDS.

SMITH. A defense to preemptive opening bids of two and three of a suit, invented by Curtis Smith of Conroe, Tex. The cheapest club bid (3 ♣ or 4 ♣) is equivalent to a TAKEOUT DOUBLE of opener's suit. A double is thus reserved for penalty. Compare with FISHBEIN and CHEAPER MINOR FOR TAKEOUT.

SMOLEN TRANSFER BIDS. An adjunct to STAYMAN and JACOBY TRANSFER BIDS originated by Mike Smolen of Los Angeles. After a 2 ◇ reply to Stayman, responder, holding five-four or six-four in the majors, jumps to three of his four-card major. This allows the 1 NT bidder to become declarer in responder's long major. For example:

Partner	You		
		♠	K J 8 7 5
		♡	A J 9 6
1 NT	2 ♣	◇	7
2 ◇	3 ♡	♣	J 10 2

You show five spades and four hearts! With five hearts and four spades, you would bid 3 ♠.

After this bid, opener may raise responder's long major with three trumps, or return to 3 NT with a doubleton. In the latter case, responder, with six cards in his long major, may bid four of the suit immediately below his real suit as a further transfer bid.

SOLID-MINOR PREEMPTS. The use of opening bids of 3 ♣ and 3 ♢ to show a solid suit (headed by the A-K-Q), typically of seven cards, with little or no outside strength. The purpose is to invite partner to bid 3 NT if he can provide the necessary stoppers. Some players loosen the requirements to include suits headed by the A-K-J or even A-Q-J.

SOLOWAY JUMP SHIFTS. An effective method of more narrowly defining the strong jump-shift response, as devised by Paul Soloway of Seattle. After partner's opening bid of one of a suit, a jump shift shows 17 or 18 points, and is made on three types of hands: (1) One-suiters, (2) semi-balanced hands, and (3) hands containing good support for opener's suit. At his second turn, responder clarifies his jump shift as follows:

> Rebid of same suit shows type (1).
> Rebid in notrump shows type (2).
> Raise of opener's suit shows type (3) with no singleton or void.
> New suit shows type (3) with a singleton or void in the unbid suit.

Responder, of course, may have more than 18 points, but in that event he must take the initiative to drive the bidding beyond game.

S-O-S REDOUBLE. The use of a redouble of an enemy penalty double (or a penalty pass of a TAKEOUT DOUBLE) as a demand for partner to rescue. *See page 159* for a complete description.

SOUND OPENING BIDS. A bidding philosophy, most notably associated with the ROTH-STONE system, that raises the requirements for first- and second-seat opening bids of one of a suit. This usually involves increasing the STANDARD AMERICAN requirements by about one point. Compare with LIGHT OPENING BIDS.

SOUND PREEMPTS. The philosophy of adhering to the traditional "rule of two and three" for preemptive opening bids. In other words, preemptor is expected to be within two tricks of his bid if vulnerable, or three tricks if not vulnerable. Compare with LIGHT PREEMPTS.

SOUTH AFRICAN TEXAS. A variation of the TEXAS TRANSFER BID that utilizes a bid of 4 ♣ as the transfer to 4 ♡, and 4 ♢ as the transfer to 4 ♠, after partner's opening bid of 1 NT. Other than being easier to remember, this method is clearly inferior to regular Texas, as it prevents responder from using GERBER.

SPLINTER BID. The very popular use of an unusual jump bid to show a singleton or void in the suit bid and excellent trump support for partner's last bid suit. This is forcing to game and shows slam interest. For complete coverage, see pages *31* and *199*. *See also* FRAGMENT BID, MINI-SPLINTER BID, and VOID-SHOWING BIDS.

SPLINTER RESPONSES TO ONE NO-TRUMP. The use of three-level jump responses to partner's opening bid of 1 NT to show a singleton or void in the suit bid, and a three-suited hand with slam interest. This is customarily played in conjunction with JACOBY TRANSFER BIDS and MINOR-SUIT TRANSFER BIDS. *See page 24* for our recommended method.

SPUTNIK. *See* NEGATIVE DOUBLES.

STANDARD. Common name for STANDARD AMERICAN.

STANDARD AMERICAN. The bidding system that is considered standard in the U.S. Although closely associated with the GOREN system, there has been a steady drift away in several aspects. For example, the STRONG TWO-BID, as advocated in Goren, is slowly being replaced by the STRONG ARTIFICIAL TWO-CLUB OPENING and WEAK TWO-BIDS. Also, FIVE-CARD MAJORS and LIMIT RAISES are becoming more and more popular. *See also* BRIDGE WORLD STANDARD.

STAYMAN. The ever-popular response of 2 ♣ to partner's opening bid of 1 NT to ask for a four-card major suit, as developed by Samuel Stayman of New York City. The two common variations are "forcing" Stayman and "nonforcing" Stayman. Forcing Stayman dictates that responder's rebid of two in a major suit is forcing on opener. Nonforcing Stayman dictates otherwise. We recommend "nonforcing" Stayman, which is covered in detail on page 2. *See also* TWO-WAY STAYMAN, CUE-BID STAYMAN, and CHECKBACK STAYMAN.

STAYMAN [System]. A bidding system invented by Samuel Stayman. Principal features include STRONG NOTRUMPS with STAYMAN TWO DIAMONDS, CONVENIENT MINORS with CANAPE tendencies, FIVE-CARD MAJORS, STRONG ARTIFICIAL TWO-CLUB OPENING (at least eight playing tricks), and a super-strong 2 ◇ opening.

STAYMAN TWO DIAMONDS. A variation of TWO-WAY STAYMAN as used by Samuel Stayman. The 2 ◇ response to partner's opening bid of 1 NT shows a game-forcing unbalanced hand containing minor-suit length. Opener must rebid in a suit of concentrated honor strength, or bid 2 NT to show scattered strength.

STEP RESPONSES. Any of a variety of methods to show point count or "controls" over partner's forcing opening bid, by a series of graded steps. Below is one popular method of showing controls (ace = 2, king = 1) over a STRONG ARTIFICIAL TWO-CLUB OPENING:

2 ◇ shows 0 or 1 control.
2 ♡ shows 2 controls.
2 ♠ shows 3 controls (an ace and a king).
2 NT shows 3 controls (three kings).
3 ♣ shows 4 controls.
3 ◇ shows 5 controls, etc.

After the response showing the number of controls held, all further bidding is natural. A similar method may be used over ONE CLUB FORCING.

STRONG ARTIFICIAL TWO-CLUB OPENING. The extremely popular use of an opening bid of 2 ♣ as the strong, artificial, forcing bid, as invented by the late David Bruce (formerly Burnstine). This is usually played in conjunction with WEAK TWO-BIDS. *See* page *93* for a complete description.

[Defense to]
See page *174* for our recommended defense.

STRONG CUE-BID. The use of a direct cue-bid of an enemy opening bid of one of a suit as a strong takeout device. As originally played, this showed the equivalent of a STRONG TWO-BID, and was forcing to game; however, many players relax these requirements. Even so, the strong cue-bid occurs so infrequently that it is far more practical to adopt the MICHAELS CUE-BID or one of its variations.

STRONG JUMP OVERCALLS. The use of a jump overcall in a suit to show a hand of about 15 to 17 high-card points with at least a good six-card suit. For example:

Opp.	*You*		
		♠	A 5
		♡	K Q J 10 7 5
1 ♣	2 ♡	◇	A Q 3
		♣	6 5

Compare with INTERMEDIATE JUMP OVERCALLS and WEAK JUMP OVERCALLS.

STRONG NOTRUMPS. A general description of all 1 NT opening bids in the range of 15 to 18 points. The GOREN system advocates 16 to 18, but there is a modern trend toward 15 to 17. Some players prefer a middle-of-the-road range, e.g., 15+ to 18−. Compare with WEAK NOTRUMPS.

STRONG TWO-BIDS. The use of an opening bid of two in any suit as a natural, strong, forcing bid. Although a basic part of the CULBERTSON and GOREN systems, this treatment has steadily lost ground to the STRONG ARTIFICIAL TWO-CLUB OPENING and WEAK TWO-BIDS.

STRUCTURED REVERSES. The specialized handling of the auctions following opener's reverse bid, so as to improve bidding accuracy. This is accomplished by adhering to a prearranged "structure." *See* page *45* for our recommended methods.

SUPER GERBER. A method of ace asking devised by Robert Goldman of Dallas, Tex., for use in two awkward situations: (1) when a minor-suit fit has been established, a jump to four of the cheapest unbid suit asks for aces; (2) when partner's last bid was 3 NT, a bid of four of the cheapest unbid suit asks for aces (but if all suits have been bid, then 5 ♣ asks for aces).

In all cases, the responses to the ace asking bid are similar to GERBER, i.e., in successive steps. Thus:

1 step shows 0 or 4 aces.
2 steps shows 1 ace.
3 steps shows 2 aces.
4 steps shows 3 aces.

To ask for kings, asker must repeat the suit used to ask for aces. For example, if 4 ♡ is used as ace asking, then 5 ♡ asks for kings.

SUPER PRECISION. A souped-up version of the PRECISION system, as developed by Benito Garozzo and Giorgio Belladonna, which includes many of the ideas of the ITALIAN TEAM SYSTEMS. The system is highlighted by a great variety of specialized asking bids.

SUPPORT DOUBLES. The use of a double of an enemy suit bid to show three-card support for partner's suit. This is an offshoot of the COMPETITIVE DOUBLE, and is typically used by the opening bidder after a major-suit response at the one-level. For example:

You	Opp.	Partner	Opp.
1 ◇	P	1 ♡	2 ♣
<u>DBL</u>			

♠ A Q 7
♡ K 10 3
◇ A 9 5 4 2
♣ 5 4

Your double shows exactly three hearts. Thus, a raise to 2 ♡ would promise four trumps.

SWISS. The use of responses of 4 ♣ and 4 ◇ to partner's opening bid of one of a major suit as artificial "FORCING RAISES." These bids typically show balanced hands, although different methods are used to distinguish between the two. One variation, known as "value Swiss," is used in the ACES SCIENTIFIC system. The meanings are:

4 ♣ shows 14 to 16 high-card points.
4 ◇ shows 12 to 14 high-card points.

Other variations distinguish trump quality or the number of controls held, and are known, respectively, as "trump Swiss" and "control Swiss." In all variations, a bid of 4 ♣ customarily shows a better hand than 4 ◇.

TAKEOUT DOUBLE. A double of an enemy suit bid that requests partner to "take it out" by bidding his longest suit. *See page 111* for complete coverage.

TEXAS TRANSFER BIDS. The use of four-level transfer bids after partner's opening bid of 1 NT, as originated by David Carter of St. Louis, Mo. A response of 4 ◇ is a transfer to 4 ♡, and 4 ♡ is a transfer to 4 ♠. *See page 13* for a complete description.

THREE CLUBS/DIAMONDS INVITATIONAL OVER ONE NOTRUMP. The use of a jump response of 3 ♣ or 3 ◇ to partner's opening bid of 1 NT as a game invitation. Typically, this shows a six-card suit and about 5 to 7 high-card points, assuming STRONG NOTRUMPS. Most players also impose certain minimum suit requirements.

THREE CLUBS/DIAMONDS PREEMPTIVE OVER ONE NOTRUMP. The use of a jump response of 3 ♣ or 3 ◇ to partner's opening bid of 1 NT as a weak sign-off bid. Typically, this shows a six-card suit in a "bust" hand. Practitioners of this bid usually play that a response of 2 ♣ (STAYMAN) followed by 3 ♣ or 3 ◇ shows a good hand and is forcing to game. *See page 3* for more information.

THREE-NOTRUMP BALANCED FORCING RAISE. The use of a 3 NT response to partner's major-suit opening bid as an artificial "FORCING RAISE" that contains no singleton or void suit, as invented by Monroe Ingberman of White Plains, N.Y. This is customarily played in conjunction with LIMIT MAJOR RAISES and SPLINTER BIDS. *See page 32* for a complete description.

THREE-NOTRUMP MINOR-SUIT PREEMPT. The use of an opening bid of 3 NT to show the equivalent of a normal 4 ♣ or 4 ◇ preempt. Partner usually responds 4 ♣ to allow opener to pass (with clubs) or correct to 4 ◇. This opening is often used by advocates of TRANSFER PREEMPTS, since their opening bids of 4 ♣ and 4 ◇ have artificial meanings.

[Defense to]
See page 177 for our recommended defense.

THREE-SUITED OPENING BIDS. Any of a variety of opening bids to show a three-suited hand. *See* ROMAN TWO DIAMONDS, MINI-ROMAN TWO DIAMONDS, PRECISION TWO DIAMONDS, and ROMAN TWO CLUBS.

[Defense to]
See page 175 for our recommended defense.

THREE-WAY TWO DIAMONDS. *See* MULTICOLORED TWO DIAMONDS.

TOP-AND-BOTTOM CUE-BID. A variation of the MICHAELS CUE-BID in which a direct cue-bid of an enemy opening bid of one of a suit is used to show the highest and lowest unbid suits. That is:

2 ♣ over 1 ♣ shows diamonds and spades.

2 ◇ over 1 ◇ shows clubs and spades.

2 ♡ over 1 ♡ shows clubs and spades.

2 ♠ over 1 ♠ shows clubs and hearts.

[Defense to]

See page *83* for our recommended defense.

TRANSFER BIDS. *See* JACOBY TRANSFER BIDS, TEXAS TRANSFER BIDS, MINOR-SUIT TRANSFER BIDS, SMOLEN TRANSFER BIDS, SOUTH AFRICAN TEXAS, and TRANSFER PRE-EMPTS.

TRANSFER PREEMPTS. The use of an artificial opening bid to show a "preemptive opening" in some other designated suit. The most common variety, known as NAMYATS, employs an opening bid of 4 ♣ to show hearts, and 4 ◇ to show spades. The purpose is to indicate a "good" preempt (8½ or more playing tricks), whereas an opening bid of 4 ♡ or 4 ♠ shows a weaker hand. Responder typically accepts the transfer by bidding four of opener's major, but may also bid the next higher suit as an artificial slam try. *See also* THREE-NOTRUMP MINOR-SUIT PREEMPT.

[Defense to]

See page *177* for our recommended defense.

TRIAL BID. Any of a variety of methods to invite game after a single major raise. *See* LONG-SUIT GAME TRY, SHORT-SUIT GAME TRY, WEAK-SUIT GAME TRY, HELP-SUIT GAME TRY, and TWO-WAY GAME TRIES.

TRUMP SWISS. *See* SWISS.

TRUSCOTT DEFENSE. *See* ONE CLUB FORCING, [Defense to].

TRUSCOTT TWO DIAMONDS. A variation of TWO-WAY STAYMAN invented by Alan Truscott of New York City. The 2 ◇ response to partner's opening bid of 1 NT is forcing to game and asks opener to define his exact distribution. This is accomplished through a series of specialized rebids, using "relay" bids by responder.

TRUSCOTT TWO NOTRUMP. The use of a 2 NT response, after an opponent's TAKE-OUT DOUBLE, to show a LIMIT RAISE of partner's opening bid of one of a suit, as devised by Alan Truscott of New York City. Consequently, WEAK JUMP RAISES may be used. This convention is also known as "Jordan." *See* page *73* for our recommended use.

A variation, known as "Reverse Truscott," reverses the above procedures. That is, 2 NT shows the preemptive raise, and the jump raise is a limit raise. Some players adopt this strategy in the minor suits to avoid declaring notrump from the "wrong" side when 3 NT is a lively possibility.

TWO-CLUB OPENINGS. *See* STRONG ARTIFICIAL TWO-CLUB OPENING, NATURAL TWO-CLUB OPENING, TWO CLUBS 19 TO 21, and ROMAN TWO CLUBS.

TWO CLUBS FOR TAKEOUT IN BALANCING POSITION. *See* BALANCING TWO CLUBS FOR TAKEOUT.

TWO CLUBS GENERAL TAKEOUT. A defense to an enemy opening bid of 1 NT that utilizes a bid of 2 ♣ as an artificial takeout device. The 2 ♣ bidder does not promise any particular suit or suits, but invariably has tolerance for the major suits.

[Defense to]

See page *27* for our recommended defense.

TWO CLUBS 19 TO 21. A weaker variation of the STRONG ARTIFICIAL TWO-CLUB OPENING, in which hands in the range of 19 to 21 points are opened with 2 ♣. Typically, this is played in conjunction with STRONG TWO-BIDS in the other suits. A response of 2 ◇ is the NEGATIVE RESPONSE, after which all minimum rebids by opener are not forcing. This bid has attracted a little following, but not in expert circles.

[Defense to]

See page *174* for our recommended defense.

TWO-DIAMOND OPENINGS. *See* FLANNERY, ROMAN TWO DIAMONDS, MINI-ROMAN TWO DIAMONDS, PRECISION TWO DIAMONDS, SCHENKEN TWO DIAMONDS, MULTICOLORED TWO DIAMONDS, and MEXICAN TWO DIAMONDS.

TWO-DIAMOND RESPONSE TO STRONG ARTIFICIAL TWO-CLUB OPENING. Any of a variety of methods of employing an artificial 2 ◇ response to the STRONG ARTIFICIAL TWO-CLUB OPENING. Below are the popular variations:

Negative. Responder shows 0 to 7 high-card points, or some other fixed range. This is the most popular treatment.

Negative or waiting. Responder usually has

a *negative* reply, but might have a stronger hand with no convenient bid. This is our recommendation. *See* page *95* for a complete description.

Automatic. Responder must bid 2 ◇ regardless of his hand.

Positive. Responder shows 8 or more high-card points, or some other fixed range. This method was devised by Alvin Roth of New York City.

Step response. *See* STEP RESPONSES.

See also SECOND NEGATIVE.

TWO-NOTRUMP NEGATIVE RESPONSE. The use of a bid of 2 NT as the artificial NEGATIVE RESPONSE to partner's forcing bid. This is the standard agreement for responding to STRONG TWO-BIDS and ACOL TWO-BIDS. *See also* SECOND NEGATIVE.

TWO-OVER-ONE GAME FORCE. An agreement that a two-level response in a new suit, after partner's major-suit opening bid, is forcing to game. Typically, this is played in conjunction with ONE NOTRUMP FORCING. The purpose is to eliminate the need for further jump bids. For example:

Partner	You		
		♠	K Q 7
		♡	A 6
1 ♠	2 ♣	◇	7 5 3
2 ♡	2 ♠	♣	A Q 10 9 6

There is no need to jump to 3 ♠. Your 2 ♠ bid is unlimited and forcing, and saves bidding room to explore for a possible slam.

Many players make an exception to the game force when responder immediately rebids his suit. For example, a 3 ♣ rebid in the above auction (instead of 2 ♠) may or may not be forcing according to partnership agreement.

TWO-WAY GAME TRIES. A method of incorporating both the LONG-SUIT GAME TRY and the SHORT-SUIT GAME TRY, as invented by Robert Ewen of Miami, Fla. After a single major raise, opener's cheapest step rebid (2 ♠ or 2 NT) is artificial and forces responder to make a "relay" bid (2 NT or 3 ♣), after which opener's next bid is a long-suit game try. Consequently, any immediate rebid (other than the cheapest) is a short-suit game try.

TWO-WAY STAYMAN. Any of a variety of methods of combining both 2 ♣ and 2 ◇ as

inquiries after partner's opening bid of 1 NT. The 2 ♣ response is generally used as "non-forcing" STAYMAN, but the 2 ◇ response has many variations. *See* DOUBLE-BARRELLED STAYMAN, ROTH TWO DIAMONDS, STAYMAN TWO DIAMONDS, AUGUST TWO DIAMONDS, MURRAY TWO DIAMONDS, and TRUSCOTT TWO DIAMONDS.

UNLIMITED TWO-NOTRUMP RESPONSE. The use of a 2 NT response to partner's opening bid of one of a suit to show 13 or more points, i.e., with no upper limit. This is typically used after major-suit openings, by players who employ an artificial 3 NT response, such as the THREE-NOTRUMP BALANCED FORCING RAISE. *See* page *33* for a complete description.

UNUSUAL NOTRUMP OVERCALL. The use of a notrump overcall as an artificial takeout bid, as invented by Alvin Roth of New York City. A direct jump overcall of 2 NT is the most common application; however, a variety of other situations arise where a notrump bid is obviously "unusual." Many players use this bid exclusively to show the minor suits, but a more practical agreement is a takeout for the "two lower unbid" suits. *See* page *136* for complete coverage.

[Defense to]

See page *83* for our recommended defense. *See also* UNUSUAL OVER UNUSUAL.

UNUSUAL OVER UNUSUAL. A method of defending against an opponent's UNUSUAL NOTRUMP OVERCALL. After a 2 NT overcall of partner's major-suit opening, responses of 3 ♣ and 3 ◇ are artificial, showing hearts and spades, respectively. For example, if partner has opened 1 ♠, these meanings apply:

3 ♣ shows a *heart* suit and enough strength to force.

3 ◇ shows a LIMIT RAISE (or better) in spades.

3 ♡ shows a heart suit, but is not forcing.

3 ♠ shows a spade fit, but less than a limit raise.

We recommend a more general defense, known as INVISIBLE CUE-BIDS, which is applicable to all kinds of two-suited overcalls.

UNUSUAL POSITIVE. An agreement used

by PRECISION system players to provide an alternative to the IMPOSSIBLE NEGATIVE. Holding a POSITIVE RESPONSE containing 4-4-4-1 shape, responder jumps in his singleton directly over the ONE CLUB FORCING opening. A variation is to jump in the suit immediately below the singleton, which allows opener to conveniently "cue-bid" responder's singleton as an ASKING BID.

UNUSUAL TWO-NOTRUMP OPENING.

An opening bid of 2 NT to show at least five cards in each minor suit, as advocated in the SCHENKEN system. The strength is generally that of a minimum opening bid, but this may vary according to partnership agreements.

[Defense to]

See page *176* for our recommended defense.

UPPER-SUITS CUE-BID. *See* HIGHER-SUITS CUE-BID.

VALUE SWISS. *See* SWISS.

VANDERBILT CLUB. One of the earliest bidding systems ever to advocate the use of ONE CLUB FORCING, as invented by the late Harold Vanderbilt (also the inventor of contract bridge). Although popular in its time, the system is rarely played in its entirety today. However, many of its ideas have been adopted by the more current 1 ♣ systems, such as SCHENKEN or BLUE TEAM CLUB.

VARIABLE NOTRUMPS. The practice of varying the point range of an opening bid of 1 NT, according to such factors as vulnerability or table position. One common method, as used in the ACOL system, is to play STRONG NOTRUMPS when vulnerable, and WEAK NOTRUMPS when not vulnerable.

VOID-SHOWING BIDS. The use of an unusual jump bid that can have no possible natural meaning to show a void suit and, by inference, a good trump fit with partner's last-bid suit. This treatment has lost in popularity to the SPLINTER BID.

VOID-SHOWING OVER BLACKWOOD.

Any of a variety of methods to show a void suit in response to BLACKWOOD. A void may never be counted as an ace. The simplest method, practiced by many players, is to make your normal response, except one level higher. That is:

6 ♣ shows 0 aces and a void.
6 ◇ shows 1 ace and a void.
6 ♡ shows 2 aces and a void.
6 ♠ shows 3 aces and a void.

Unfortunately, the above procedure lacks in efficiency. *See* page *190* for our recommended method.

VOLUNTARY BID OF FIVE IN A MAJOR SUIT. A slam invitation which is also a form of ASKING BID. The voluntary bid of five in a major suit asks partner to proceed to slam if he has control (first- or second-round) of the enemy suit or unbid suit. This bid may also be used to inquire about the trump suit. *See* page *194* for a complete description.

WALSH. A popular West Coast bidding system, developed primarily by Richard Walsh, and based on many of the ideas of ROTH-STONE. Principal features include STRONG NOTRUMPS with JACOBY TRANSFER BIDS, FIVE-CARD MAJORS with ONE NOTRUMP FORCING, LIMIT MAJOR RAISES (promising a singleton), INVERTED MINOR RAISES, TWO-OVER-ONE GAME FORCE, and the STRONG ARTIFICIAL TWO-CLUB OPENING. The system includes a number of modern bidding gadgets.

WEAK JUMP OVERCALLS. The use of a jump overcall in a suit to show a weak hand, usually with a good suit, as invented by Oswald Jacoby of Dallas, Tex. This popular treatment is now considered to be STANDARD. *See* page *132* for a complete description.

WEAK JUMP RAISES. The use of a jump raise (below game) in partner's suit to show a weak hand, i.e., a preemptive bid. Most commonly, this is used in conjunction with another convention to show stronger hands. *See* INVERTED MINOR RAISES, TRUSCOTT TWO NO-TRUMP, INVITATIONAL CUE-BID, CUE-BID LIMIT RAISE, and JUMP CUE-BID LIMIT RAISE.

WEAK JUMP-SHIFT RESPONSES. The use of a jump-shift response to partner's opening bid of one of a suit to show a weak hand, usually with a six-card or longer suit. *See* page *37* for a complete description.

WEAK NOTRUMPS. A general description of all 1 NT opening bids in the range of 12 to 15 points. The KAPLAN-SHEINWOLD system advocates 12 to 14 (occasionally 11) and the PRECISION system advocates 13 to 15. Practitioners of weak notrumps claim that the pre-

emptive value more than compensates for the extra risk involved.

[Defense to]

See pages *126* and *160* for our recommended defense.

WEAK-SUIT GAME TRY. A very slight variation of the LONG-SUIT GAME TRY, where opener makes his TRIAL BID in his weakest side suit that contains length (three or more cards).

WEAK TWO-BIDS. The very popular use of opening bids of 2 ◇, 2 ♡, and 2 ♠ to show a weak hand with a six-card suit, as originated by the late Howard Schenken. The strength is typically from 5 to 11 high-card points, and most partnerships specify certain minimum suit requirements. Some players use WEAK TWO-BIDS in the major suits only, preferring to use 2 ◇ for some other purpose, such as FLANNERY. *See* page *101* for complete coverage.

WEISS. A defense to preemptive opening bids of two and three of a suit, which utilizes the CHEAPER MINOR FOR TAKEOUT convention. A double, however, is used as an OPTIONAL DOUBLE rather than for penalty.

WESTERN CUE-BID. The use of a low-level cue-bid in the enemy suit, after partner has already bid, to ask for a stopper. Partner is requested to bid notrump if he can stop the enemy suit. Compare with ALL-PURPOSE CUE-BID, EASTERN CUE-BID, and DIRECTIONAL ASKING BID.

WOLFF SIGN-OFF. A method of stopping below game after opener has made a jump rebid of 2 NT, as devised by Robert Wolff of Dallas, Tex. Responder's 3 ♣ rebid forces opener to bid 3 ◇ (except to show three-card support for responder's major suit), after which responder may pass or sign off. For example:

Partner	You		
		♠	J 9 8 7 5
		♡	4 3
1 ◇	1 ♠	◇	K 5 4 3
2 NT	3 ♣	♣	8 2

Partner must bid 3 ◇ (or 3 ♠ with three trumps), which you will gladly pass.

WOODSON TWO-WAY NOTRUMPS. A unique opening bid of 1 NT to show either 10 to 12, or 16 to 18 points, as invented by William Woodson of Matthews, N.C. A response of 2 ♣ is used to clarify opener's strength, as well as to discover something about his shape. This bid has acquired little following.

[Defense to]

The uncertainty regarding opener's strength creates problems for the defense, just as it does for the opening side. It is probably best to defend as you would against WEAK NOTRUMPS, since opener will usually have the 10 to 12 point range. *See* pages *126* and *160* for our recommended defense.

ABOUT THE AUTHORS

William S. Root holds the rank of World Master. He has won many national championships (including three Spingolds, four Reisingers, and two Vanderbilts) and has represented the United States in both the Olympiad and the Bermuda Bowl. He is regarded as one of the world's outstanding bridge teachers and has authored several books including *Standard Bidding* (published by Crown), considered the bidding bible by his many fans and students.

Richard Pavlicek of Fort Lauderdale, Florida, is a leading bridge teacher, writer, and editor. As a player, he is held in the highest esteem by his expert peers and has won four national championships (one Grand National, two Reisingers, and one Vanderbilt) and many regional championships. He has amassed over 8,000 master points, many times more than the 300 required for the rank of Life Master.

Since the original publication of this book, Messrs. Root and Pavlicek as a partnership have won *three* national team championships using the conventions contained herein.

A NOTE ON THE TYPE

This book was set by computer in a face called Times Roman, designed by Stanley Morison for *The Times* (London) and first introduced by that newspaper in 1932.

Among typographers and designers of the twentieth century, Stanley Morison has been a strong forming influence.